AMERICA PERCEIVED:

A View from Abroad in the 18th Century

AMERICA PERCEIVED

AMERICA PERCEIVED:
A View from Abroad
in the 18th Century

Edited by
James Axtell

Pendulum Press, Inc.

West Haven, Connecticut   El Monte, California

Clothbound Edition   ISBN 0-88301-144-1   Complete Set
0-88301-146-8   This Volume

Paperback Edition   ISBN 0-88301-123-9   Complete Set
0-88301-125-5   This Volume

Library of Congress Catalog Card Number 73-94108

Published by
Pendulum Press, Inc.
An Academic Industries, Inc. Company
The Academic Building
Saw Mill Road
West Haven, Connecticut 06516

Printed in the United States of America

CONTENTS

ABOUT THE EDITOR

James Axtell, after receiving his B.A. from Yale University, went on to study at Oxford International Summer School, and later received his Ph.D. from Cambridge University. Mr. Axtell has taught at Yale University and currently is Associate Professor of history at Sarah Lawrence College. He has published many articles, reviews, and essays and has served as general editor of several educational publications. He is the author of the forthcoming book, *The School upon a Hill: Education and Society in Colonial New England.*

FOREWORD

> Oh wad some power the giftie gie us
> To see ourselves as others see us!
> It wad frae monie a blunder free us,
>   An' foolish notion.
> Robert Burns, "To a Louse" (1786)

AMERICA PERCEIVED was created as a companion to THE AMERICAN PEOPLE series and as an independent collection of primary sources for the study of American history. Like its companion, it is founded on the belief that the study of history in the schools and junior levels of college generally begins at the wrong end. That study usually begins with abstract and pre-digested *conclusions*—the conclusions of other historians as filtered through the pen of a textbook writer—and not with the primary sources of the past and unanswered *questions* —the starting place of the historian himself.

Since we all need, use, and think about the past in our daily lives, we are all historians. The question is whether we can be skillful, accurate, and useful historians. The only way to become such is to exercise our historical skills and interests until we gain competence. But we have to exercise them in the same ways the best historians do or we will be kidding ourselves that we are *doing* history when in fact we are only absorbing sponge-like the results of someone else's historical competence.

Historical competence must begin with one crucial skill—the ability to distinguish between past and present. Without a sharp sense of the past as a different time from our own, we will be unable to accord the people of the past the respect that we would like to receive from

7

the people of the future. And without according them that respect, we will be unable to recognize their integrity as individuals or to understand them as human beings like ourselves.

A good sense of the past depends primarily on a good sense of the present, on experience, and on the imaginative empathy to relate ourselves to human situations not our own. Since most students have had a relatively brief experience of life and have not yet given full expression to their imaginative sympathies, THE AMERICAN PEOPLE was designed to draw upon the one essential prerequisite for the study of history that all students possess—the lives they have lived from birth to young adulthood. It asked us to look at the American experience from the *inside*, through the eyes of the participants who lived through the American life cycles, with the understanding gained from living through our own. AMERICA PERCEIVED seeks to draw more upon our imaginative sympathy by asking us to look at America from the *outside*, through the eyes of visitors, travellers, and critics whose lives and values were very different from those of the Americans they saw.

One view (inside or outside) is not necessarily better—that is, more accurate, sensitive, objective, complete—than the other. Both views are necessary to take the full measure of the country in all its complexity. The value of the view ultimately depends upon the observer. The quality of a foreigner's observations depends less upon his initial attitude toward America than upon his personal qualities—his objectivity, breadth of vision, accuracy of perception, sensitivity to human character, and tolerance of cultural difference. For example, although a perceptive visitor may come to America expecting the worst, his observations may be of great value because he can accurately see some of the country's dark spots and contradictions that perhaps remain hidden to Americans or to other visitors who come expecting only the best. On the other hand, the observations of an insensitive visitor who comes expecting the best may be of small value because he is too accepting of what well-meaning Americans tell him or because he is unable to see the country's faults and contradictions as well as its more obvious strengths and consistencies.

Foreign observers possess one quality that gives special value to their views of America: their foreignness. They are the products of different cultures which do not share all the assumptions, values, and standards of Americans. They see the world differently than Americans because they have been taught by their culture to see the world differently. In any culture there are aspects of life—they may be good or bad—which for some reason its own members are either unable to see or take so much for granted that they are never mentioned. But few cultures develop exactly the same blind spots about the same aspects of life. Consequently, the visiting members of one culture may be able to see those unrecognized or unmentioned aspects of another culture simply because they are used to seeing them—or not seeing them as the case may be—in their own culture. It is this angle of vision that gives the perceptions of foreigners their primary historical value.

But foreigners' observations usually have one built-in limitation: they are static snapshots of America frozen in time. Because of their relatively short stay, travellers seldom capture a full view of the historical development of the country that made it what it is when they see it. They record only the end product of a long process. Of course curiosity, historical research, and a good interviewing technique can overcome some of this limitation, but they can seldom erase it completely. Consequently, to gain an idea of historical change—as well as stability—we must place these snapshots in chronological order and compare them. This is sometimes difficult because travellers may not focus upon comparable subjects in successive periods, but in general the same range of subjects will capture visitors' interest, especially in a period of moderate or slow change. Visitors are adept at avoiding fads.

Since the experience of each student is the only prerequisite for the study of primary sources at the first level, annotations and introductory material have been reduced to a minimum, simply enough to identify the sources, their authors, and the circumstances in which they were written.

But the remains of the past are mute by themselves. Many sources have survived that can tell us what happened in the past and why, but they have to be questioned properly to reveal their secrets. So by way of illustration, a number of questions have been asked in each chapter, but these should be supplemented by the students whose experiences and knowledge and interests are, after all, the flywheel of the educational process. Although the questions and sources are divided into chapters, they should be used freely in the other chapters;

the collection should be treated as a whole. And although most of the illustrative questions are confined to the sources at hand, questions that extend to the present should be asked to anchor the acquired knowledge of the past in the immediate experience of the present. Only then will learning be real and lasting and history brought to life.

INTRODUCTION

At the beginning of the 18th century, the American colonies were little more than tiny pockets of population huddled between the cold Atlantic and the imposing spine of the Appalachian Mountains. New England had grown to respectable size through immigration and a low death rate, but the total population of America was only about 250,000 souls—black and white—spread over some eleven colonies. Most of these people lived on widely scattered farms or in small towns. Boston was considered a large city with 6,700 inhabitants while Philadelphia in only seventeen years had become the largest metropolis in America with less than ten thousand persons. New York was only half that size.

But the new Americans, as promoters and travellers continually advertised, enjoyed a bountiful climate, fertile fields, and generally good health, which meant that they doubled their numbers about every 22-1/2 years. This was the factor that, perhaps more than anything else, spelled the ultimate victory of the English colonists over the native Indian populations and their less numerous but diplomatically adept French allies. Until French Canada fell to the British in 1760, the English were pinned to the Atlantic seaboard. When Montreal surrendered two years after Wolfe's dramatic seizure of Quebec, English colonists were at last free to spill over the Appalachians into the rich farming country of Ohio, Kentucky, and Tennessee, no longer fearful of the lightning attacks of French and Indian war parties. By 1775 the American colonies could boast a strapping population of 2-1/2 million, more than enough to wrestle from the British monarchy their independence.

It was to this growing, changing country that European visitors came in the 18th century. Most of them came for a short time—a few months, a year or two—on business that usually had little to do with idle sightseeing. Not unnaturally in a rough new country, most were men—scientists, ministers, and most frequently soldiers—and most stayed on the well-trodden roads between Charleston and Boston. Consequently they saw little of the fiercely independent Indian people except a few docile creatures who had been reduced to poverty, ill-health, and dependence by European disease, war, and alcohol. But they did see the burgeoning numbers of Negro slaves at work in southern plantations and northern towns, which they commented upon at great length. They also noticed two other American characteristics: the heterogeneous character of the colonies and their inhabitants and the begrudging but necessary toleration of the many religious denominations that had come to America with those colonists. In the 18th century, differences were perhaps the main thing that Americans had in common, and foreign observers were eager to catalog them.

But they were equally quick to characterize "The American" as a distinct genus and to compare him with their own or other national groups. To Europeans, America was a laboratory for a momentous social experiment, the outcome of which would reverberate through their tradition-bound societies in unpredictable ways. So they looked and listened with special interest in hopes of taking the full measure of "this new man, this American." In the pages that follow, a number of their conclusions are presented for our reconsideration, for no country is ever finished with the task of discovering what it has been in the past and deciding what it should be in the future.

I. THE CHARACTER OF THE COLONIES

The Carolinas

Most visitors in the 18th century did not visit the Carolinas, which were relatively new colonies. Those who did usually approached them from the south, from the West Indies or Latin America. Did this color their view of the Carolinas? What were the advantages of living there in the 18th century? Did the advantages outweigh the disadvantages? Why do you think Miss Schaw's account was less favorable than Miranda's? How was the Carolina character a direct reflection of Carolina society and economy? Did each sex have a different character? Could the Carolina character have been any different? Under what circumstances?

Certainly the most colorful visitor to 18th-century America was Francisco de Miranda, the hero of three revolutions, "the precursor of Spanish-American independence," world citizen, "walking encyclopedia," and lover extraordinaire. A hedonist in practice, an aristocrat in taste, and a democrat in principle, Miranda was born to the family of a linen merchant and planter in Caracas, Venezuela in 1750. In 1771 he sailed to Spain to finish his university education—which he never did—and instead bought a captaincy in the Spanish army. While serving in Cuba against England for the American-French effort, he was indicted by the Spanish king for suspected trade with England while he was arranging the release of Spanish prisoners in Jamaica. To avoid arrest, he slipped into the newly independent American colonies on a whaler with the hope of making his way to Spain to make a personal appeal to the king. But once in the republican air of America he denounced all Spanish control of Latin America and set out on a revolutionary career that saw him serve as a general in the French Revolution, declare Venezuelan independence in 1811 at the side of Simón Bolívar, and finally die in a Cadiz prison in 1816. His observations are taken from The New Democracy in America: Travels of Francisco de Miranda in the United States, 1783-84, *translated by Judson P. Wood and edited by John S. Ezall (Norman: University of Oklahoma Press, 1963), pp. 23-24, 33-35. Copyright 1963 by the University of Oklahoma Press.*

The inhabitants of the region [South Carolina] are generally rich and love the countryside and rural life, as a result of which one sees here very fine country houses. Hunting, dancing, and smoking tobacco in pipes are the favorite diversions. Society is not very animated in the city, despite the fact that there is no lack of educated and knowledgeable persons. The youth are generally vain and ignorant. The women are more agreeable although somewhat shy when one first meets them, and they dress with the greatest taste (except for the hairdress, which they do themselves with much carelessness). The number of this sex is very large compared to that of the men; there is no lack of those who make the computation of five to one, and the reason they give is the large number of Tories killed by the Whigs in the past war and of the latter which the Tories and British likewise destroyed. In District No. 96 alone (and I know this from good authority) there are twelve hundred widows. Whoever wants to choose a wife, therefore, should come to this land of abundance!

The whole region is infested with the ague and to such an extreme in the summer—when the effluvia of the stagnant waters increase and penetrate the atmosphere more—that, even though people of some ease are always able to go to the city or seaports to preserve themselves from the contagion by breathing the pure air of the breeze, almost all suffer more or less. The doctors have made a very singular observation, which is that if in this season one changes air (that is, those who live in the country go to the city, or vice versa), the fever attacks unfailingly. Similarly, it has been observed that the effects of this contagion upon the stranger, and especially upon the balsamic European blood, are much more violent and marked than upon the natives. The latter are so accustomed to the evil that if, in greeting them, one asks, "How are you?" they answer, their teeth chattering with the cold of the ague, "Pretty well, only the fever!"

In the year 1729 it happened that a brigantine proceeding from Madagascar stopped at Sullivan Island on its way to England and its captain offered a small sack of rice to the governor, from which source this plant propagated throughout the region. Oh, with how much reason did the introducer of this benefit deserve the remembrance and applause of these people! But see how difficult it is to destroy a habit and preconception: it was only after much time and great efforts on the part of the most prudent men that the cultivation became general and the people realized the incomparable advantage it offered them. To a similar chance the island of Jamaica owes the introduction of the valuable pasture called guinea grass.

In addition this region produces a great deal of corn, some wheat, very good fruit, pomegranates, nuts, cotton, mulberries, and grapes. Grapevines are found wild and in great abundance in virgin and remote forests, and as a result, several individuals make wine, but neither is the juice suitable nor does the climate permit the grape to acquire a good taste; several experiments confirm this opinion. The pine, called lightwood, abounds; it produces turpentine, pitch, and tar, which form a considerable branch of commerce. The inhabitants boil a small, round fruit which the bayberry shrub produces in bunches and extract therefrom bayberry tallow, with which they make very good candles. This tallow is green and exudes a certain delicate and fragrant odor when it burns, which makes it preferable to wax; yet its consistency appears to be harder than that of wax.

The commerce of the state commences with vigor, but as yet there are no exact figures; for this reason we give those compiled with most accuracy just before the general revolution:

Ships	Sailors	Imports from England	Exports
140	1,680	£365,000	£395,666

The population, including whites and persons of color (the latter comprise more than half), is believed to amount to 225,000. The city of Charleston has about 16,000 inhabitants, who have been in imminent danger on various occasions. In the year 1752, among others, a terrible hurricane blew in, with the result that the water rose ten feet above the highest tide, ships broke from their moorings and ran aground, sloops and schooners rendered themselves into pieces against the houses on Bay Street, and the inhabitants, despairing of their lives, took refuge on the roofs. Miraculously the wind veered to the west and the waters went down five feet in ten minutes. The wooden pesthouse on Sullivan Island was taken by the sea for some miles up the river Cooper with fifteen people inside, nine of whom drowned. While I was here, at the beginning of October, the same scene began to develop; luckily the wind changed to the north, and only the lower rooms of the houses on South Bay were inundated. Acquaintances meeting on the streets the next day congratulated each other as if they had survived a great danger. Bad jests for certain!

The government of the state is entirely democratic, as are those of the other United States; a governor, senate, and house of representatives are a weak supplement to the three bodies which organize the admirable equilibrium of the British constitution. The salaries of the magistrates and officials of the state are quite moderate and do not, I believe, amount to three thousand pounds sterling. All the public expenses of the state before the war, according to a very accurate calculation, did not amount to eight thousand pounds.

Beaufort, situated on Port Royal Island about fifteen miles farther up from the mouth of Great River, is a town of the same size, with little difference, as Georgetown and the only other that merits such a denomination in the entire state.

Janet Schaw, the author of the Journal of a Lady of Quality, *was justified in her title by being born into an old Scottish family in a fashionable suburb of Edinburgh. At once deeply religious—Lowland Presbyterian style—and receptive to the progressive strains of the Scottish Enlightenment, Miss Schaw never married but in 1774, at the age of thirty-five or forty, sailed from Scotland for North Carolina in charge of three young relatives, the children of John Rutherford, a Carolina planter. Her unabashed comments on Carolina society and agriculture on the eve of Revolution are found in* Journal of a Lady of Quality; Being the Narrative of a Journey from Scotland to the West Indies, North Carolina, and Portugal, in the years 1774 to 1776, *ed. Evangeline Walker Andrews and Charles McLean Andrews (New Haven: Yale University Press, 1921), pp. 151-155, 163-164. Copyright © 1921, 1934, 1939 by Yale University Press.*

I think I have read all the descriptions that have been published of America, yet meet every moment with something I never read or heard of. I must particularly observe that the trees every where are covered over with a black veil of a most uncommon substance, which I am however at a loss to describe. It is more like sea weed than any vegetable I ever saw, but is quite black and is a continued web from top to bottom of the tallest trees and would be down to the ground, were it not eat up by the cattle. But as it is full of juice and very sweet, they exert their whole strength to obtain it, in which they receive no assistance from their Masters, tho' they own it is excellent feeding, but they are too indolent to take any trouble, and the cattle must provide for themselves or starve. The women however gather it at a certain season, lay it in pits as we do our green lint, till the husk rot. It is made up of small tubes, within each of which is a substance, which exactly resembles that of the baken hair with which we stuff chairs, matrasses, etc, etc. and which answers pretty well with a very little trouble and no cost.

The trees that keep clear from this black moss (as it is called) are crowned with the Mistletoe in much higher perfection than ever you saw it, and as it is just now in berry looks beautiful. Indeed all the trees do so at this Season. The wild fruits are in blossom and have a fine effect amongst the forest-trees. Amongst the various trees that grow here, none seems so fit for the Cabinet maker's use as the red Mulberry. Its colour is infinitely more beautiful than the mahogany and it is so hard and close as to resist vermine, and grows large enough to afford planks of any size, yet it is only used to burn or for the most common purposes. It grows spontaneously every where, and the White Mulberry is also found in every place, which points out that the making of silk in this part of the country could be done with great ease. But tho' I may say of this place what I formerly did of the West India Islands, that nature holds out to them every thing that can contribute to conveniency, or tempt to luxury, yet the inhabitants resist both, and if they can raise as much corn and pork, as to subsist them in the most slovenly manner, they ask no more; and as a very small proportion of their time serves for that purpose, the rest is spent in sauntering thro' the woods with a gun or sitting under a rustick shade, drinking New England rum made into grog, the most shocking liquor you can imagine. By this manner of living, their blood is spoil'd and rendered thin beyond all proportion, so that it is constantly on the fret like bad small beer, and hence the constant slow fevers that wear down their constitutions, relax their nerves and infeeble the whole frame. Their appearance is in every respect the reverse of that which gives the idea of strength and vigor, and for which the British peasantry are so remarkable. They are tall and lean, with short waists and long limbs, sallow complexions and languid eyes, when not inflamed by spirits. Their feet are flat, their joints loose and their walk uneven. These I speak of are only the peasantry of this country, as hitherto I have seen nothing else, but I make no doubt when I come to see the better sort, they will be far from this description. For tho' there is a most disgusting equality, yet I hope to find an American Gentleman a very different creature from an American clown. Heaven forefend else.

I am sorry to say, however, that I have met with few of the men who are natives of the country, who rise much above my former description, and as their natural ferocity is now inflamed by the fury of an ignorant zeal, they are of that sort of figure, that I cannot look at them without connecting the idea of tar and feather. Tho' they have fine women and such as might inspire any man with sentiments that do honour to humanity, yet they know no such nice distinctions, and in this at least are real patriots. As the population of the country is all the view they have in what they call love, and tho' they often honour their black wenches with their attention, I sincerely believe they are excited to that crime by no other desire or motive but that of adding to the number of their slaves.

The difference between the men and the women surprised me, but a sensible man, who has long resided here, in some degrees accounted for it. In the infancy of this province, said he, many families from Britain came over, and of these the wives and daughters were people of education. The mothers took the care of the girls, they were train'd up under them, and not only instructed in the family duties necessary to the sex, but in those accomplishments and genteel manners that are still so visible amongst them, and this descended from Mother to daughter. As the father found the labours of his boys necessary to him, he led them therefore to the woods, and taught the sturdy lad to glory in the stroke he could give with his Ax, in the trees he felled, and the deer he shot; to conjure the wolfe, the bear and the Alligator; and to guard his habitation from Indian inroads was most justly his pride, and he had reason to boast of it. But a few generations this way lost every art or science, which their fathers might have brought out, and tho' necessity no longer prescribed these severe occupations, custom has established it as still necessary for the men to spend their time abroad in the fields; and to be a good marksman is the highest ambition of the youth, while to those enervated by age or infirmity drinking grog remained a last consolation.

On our arrival here the stalks of last year's crop still remained on the ground. At this I was greatly surprised, as the season was now so far advanced, I expected to have found the fields completely ploughed at least, if not sown and harrowed; but how much was my amazement increased to find that every instrument of husbandry was unknown here; not only all the various ploughs, but all the machinery used with such success at home, and that the only instrument used is a hoe, with which they at once till and plant the corn. To accomplish this a number of Negroes follow each other's tail the day long, and have a task assigned them, and it will take twenty at least to do as much work as two horses with a man and a boy would perform. Here the wheel-plough would answer finely, as the ground is quite flat, the soil light and not a stone to be met with in a thousand acres. A drill too might easily be constructed for sowing the seed, and a light harrow would close it in with surprising expedition. It is easy to observe however from whence this ridiculous method of theirs took its first necessary rise. When the new Settlers were obliged to sow corn for their immediate maintenance, before they were able to root out the trees, it is plain no other instrument but the hoe could be used amongst the roots of the trees, where it was to be planted, and they were obliged to do it all by hand labour. But thro' this indolence some of them have their plantations still pretty much incumbered in that way, yet to do justice to the better sort, that is not generally the case. Tho' it is all one as to the manner of dressing their fields, the same absurd method continuing every where. If horses were hard to come at or unfit for labour, that might be some excuse, but far is it otherwise. They have them in plenty, and strong animals they are and fit for the hardest labour.

Virginia

Virginia, the oldest colony, was the terminus of most 18th-century tours of America. Why were towns so few? What effects did this have on southern society? on women? on the economy? on the arts and sciences? What were the advantages of living on a plantation? the disadvantages? What contribution did the fertility of the land make to the character of Virginia? Was it a society of opportunity for poor and middling as well as the rich? Was Virginia a one-product economy? What effect might this have had on her relations with England? What was the nature of master-slave relations? Would it have been easy to free all the slaves in the 18th century? Were there any difficulties involved? Why do you think so many Revolutionary leaders came from Virginia? Did the Virginia character lend itself readily to Revolution?

Francis Louis Michel was the eldest son of the Lord of Ralligen, a member of the Great Council of Berne, and prefect of Gottstatt in Switzerland. After receiving a military education in the French army, Michel travelled to America in 1701 to settle a Swiss colony in Virginia. His attempt was unsuccessful, but it ultimately led to the settlement of New Berne in North Carolina by Baron Christopher von Graffenried in 1710. The "Report of the Journey of Francis Louis Michel from Berne, Switzerland, to Virginia, October 2, 1701-December 1, 1702" was translated and edited by William J. Hinke in The Virginia Magazine of History and Biography, *vol. 24 (1916), pp. 1-43, 113-141, 275-303. The following excerpts are found on pp. 30-43, 114-115, 124-125.*

Regarding the fruitfulness of the country it may be said that almost everything grows that is put into the ground. Especially tobacco is the principal article there, with which trade is carried on. It passes for money, because gold and silver are seldom seen there, especially among the common people. All purchases or payments are made in tobacco. It is planted in such quantities that this year 150 ships, large and small, but not more than twenty small ones among them, left the country laden with tobacco. Merchants pass up and down through the country. They have their store houses or magazines filled with all kinds of goods which are needed there. When the inhabitants need something, they go to the nearest merchant, who gives them what they want. It is recorded according to agreement. When the tobacco is ripe, the merchant arrives to take what is coming to him. A hundred [pounds] are usually reckoned at twenty shillings. When the rainy season comes, the tobacco is packed solidly, one leaf above the other, into a barrel which holds or weighs from 700 to 1000 pounds. It is a laborious job, demanding much care. Tobacco is planted after the soil has been prepared. Then with a broad hoe the soil is loosened on top and made into round little heaps, six feet apart. It is planted in rainy weather. When it is fully grown it spreads so much that all the plants touch each other. It grows best in new soil, but the land must be very good if it is to bear tobacco for twenty years. However, it is not done. Hence the inhabitants do not live close together and the country is not settled in villages, because every twenty or thirty years new ground must be broken. A settler who has a piece of land, divides it into three parts, the first for tobacco and corn, the second and third parts as meadows for his cattle and as forest, if he needs wood. When the tobacco field does not want to bear any more, he sows corn in its place. After six or eight years it does not yield corn any more. Then he lets it lie fallow and takes up the second part and so forth. A workman may plant yearly from 15 to 2000 pounds of tobacco, besides six or eight barrels of corn.

As to corn, the ''Wirden'' or Turkish corn is grown in most cases. It is so productive that it yields fifty to a hundred fold. It makes pretty good bread. It is also pounded and cooked, called humin [hominy]. Its flour is taken and cooked thick in water. Then it is put into milk. It is mostly the food of servants. The flour is also frequently taken and a thick dough is made out of it with water. Then, by means of a hot fire and many coals, it is baked in a little while. When the corn is planted, a small hole is made and three or four grains are put into it. Then they are covered with ground. Like the tobacco they are always planted six feet apart. This grain is raised in great quantities and is used for people and cattle. The stalks grow over ten and even fourteen feet high and are very thick. They bear usually from two to four ears, while there are three or four stalks to a hole. Throughout the summer the weeds must be removed from time to time, as in the case of the tobacco. The ordinary price of this corn is two shillings a bushel, or about two measures as used here [in Switzerland].

The other kind is wheat, which is planted by every family for its use, in such places where the cattle have been penned in at night. After they have been in a field for three or four weeks, they are moved to another field. In this way the soil is fertilized, for no other manure is used. This grain bears twenty-five fold. It is planted as in our country and it costs in ordinary years three or four shillings per bushel.

Barley and oats are also planted and they turn out well usually. The inhabitants pay little attention to garden plants, except lettuce, although most everything grows here. But fresh seeds must be imported every year from Europe, for, if the seed of this country is planted, it turns into the wild kind again.

The custom of the country, when the harvest is to be gathered in, is to prepare a dinner, to which the neighbors are invited, and for which two men have sufficient work to do. There are often from thirty to fifty persons cutting grain, so that frequently they have work for only two hours.

This is one of the principal festivals or times of rejoicing. When I was unable to travel at one time, because of the rain, I stayed at a house, where they intended to cut wheat that day. When everything was ready to receive the guests at noon, it looked in the morning as if the weather was going to be favorable. Ten persons had already arrived, when the weather changed and turned into a violent rain, so that the hope to harvest in a few days came to nothing. Fresh meat cannot be kept in summer longer than twenty-four hours, hence the good people were compelled, if they did not want to let the sheep and chicken, which they had prepared, spoil, to entertain us, which lasted for a day and a half.

Fruit trees are growing in great abundance. I shall describe them according to their several kinds. The apple trees are very numerous, most of them not very large nor high, like pear trees. But they are exceedingly fruitful. I was at many places this year, where I could not estimate the large quantities which were rotting. They are the nicest apples that can be seen. There is a kind somewhat earlier than the others, they are called Cattalines. They are pointed and of a sour taste. The summer cider is made of them. A later kind is valued more highly and, like the first, cider is made of them, which keeps longer than the other. The gallon or four quarts cost one bit or four Batzen, according to our coin. It is drunk mostly during the winter. As the common man does not have good cellars, this drink cannot be kept during the summer, but it turns sour. There are also pears of all kinds, but they are not as common as the apples. There are several kinds of peaches, and in such quantities that people cannot eat the fourth part of them. The rest is fed to the pigs. It should be noted that this fruit ripens in a few days. Cherries, especially the cultivated cherries, are found in great abundance, where they are planted. Good wine is made of them.

All kinds of berries grow in the wilderness and also on the plantations, in such abundance that it cannot be estimated. There are also many different kinds, namely of black and white color. The best are brown, long and large. This berry is largely eaten by pigs and birds. Whoever has a desire for berries, does not need to buy them or ask for them, for the abundance is so great that no one pays any attention to them, nor are they used very much, because people do not want to take the trouble to pick them, as they have enough other food.

There are also plums, but they are not common. Also many other kinds of fruit, but they are not known to me. There is, especially among the garden plants, a certain kind of beans, not unlike the Turkish, which is planted with the Indian corn. It grows up along the stalks and is very productive. It is nourishing food. There is another kind which creeps on the ground. There are also different kinds of peas, planted in the gardens, but growing also outside of them. Besides, there are potatoes in great quantities and many kinds of melons. Some are cooked, others, like the water melons, are eaten raw, since this fruit is very refreshing in the hot summer because of its cool, sweet juice. They are grown in great quantities and one can get as many as he desires.

The water is no less prolific, because an indescribably large number of big and little fish are found in the many creeks, as well as in the large rivers. The abundance is so great and they are so easily caught that I was much surprised. Many fish are dried, especially those that are fat. Those who have a line can catch as many as they please. Most of them are caught with the hook or the spear, as I know from personal experience, for when I went out several times with the line, I was surprised that I could pull out one fish after another, and, through the clear water I could see a large number of all kinds, whose names are unknown to me. They cannot be compared with our fish, except the herring, which is caught and dried in large numbers. Thus the so-called catfish is not unlike the large turbot. A very good fish and one easily caught is the eel, also like those here [in Switzerland]. There is also a kind like the pike. They have a long and pointed mouth, with which they like to bite into the hook. They are not wild, but it happens rarely that one can keep them on the line, for they cut it in two with their sharp teeth. We always had our harpoons and guns with us when we went out fishing, and when the fish came near we shot at them or harpooned them. A good fish, which is common and found in large numbers, is the porpoise. They are so large that by their unusual leaps, especially when the weather changes, they make a great noise and often cause anxiety for the small boats or canoes. Especially do they endanger those that bathe. Once I cooled and amused myself in the water with swimming, not knowing that there was any danger, but my host informed me that there was. This is only a small part of what could be told about the fish there, but I could not learn everything in the short time I was there. The [larger] waters and especially the tributaries are filled with turtles. They show themselves in large numbers when it is warm. Then they come to the land or climb up on pieces of wood or trees lying in the water. When one travels in a ship, their heads can be seen everywhere coming out of the water. The abundance of oysters is incredible. There are whole banks of them so that the ships must avoid them. A sloop, which was to land us at Kingscreek, struck an oyster bed, where we had to wait about two hours for the tide. They surpass those in England by far in size, indeed they are four times as large. I often cut them in two, before I could put them into my mouth. The inhabitants usually catch them on Saturday. It is not troublesome. A pair of wooden tongs is needed. Below they are wide, tipped with iron. At the time of the ebb they row to the beds and with the long tongs they reach down to the bottom. They pinch them together tightly and then pull or tear up that which has been seized. They usually pull from six to ten times. In summer they are not very good, but unhealthy and can cause fever.

There are frogs in the water, which at night all together make a wonderful noise. Indeed, if one is not acquainted with it, it sounds as if the noise or sound was made by people. In the large waters of the wilderness there is a very large kind. When they call, their voice can be compared to the bellowing of an ox. It is not the same but as deep and audible as far. I saw one on the other side of the water at Manigkinton, which was a foot long, with an awful head or mouth. When he jumped into the water there was a splash as if one had thrown a pretty large stone into the water. There are also water snakes and all kinds of costly animals, which live in the water, such as beavers, otters and muskrats, which smell very agreeably. I left two in England. The Indians shoot many of these animals. By means of rum or other more insignificant things one can get them from them. They can afterwards be sold advantageously in London, especially the beavers, of which castors [beaver hats] are made in part.

Now I shall again turn to the land and report what animals are found there, first of all the tame animals. The horses, like the English breed, are very lightfooted. They never ride them in a walk, but always in a gallop, as if a deer was running. They are very common. It must be a poor man who cannot afford one. Not many people can be seen traveling on foot, even if it is only an hour's distance. They are seldom used to draw wagons or the plow, because the nature of the country does not demand it. They cost from three to eight pounds of sterling.

Horned cattle are found in large numbers, so that in summer time much milk is used. Butter is also made, as much as is needed. But most of the people know nothing of cheese. There were a few who undertook to make it. It was good but could not be compared to ours. The common farmer has usually from ten to forty heads of cattle. The gentlemen have about a hundred. There is little trouble taken with cattle, because they are left the whole year on the meadows. Not even a stable is built for them, but they are driven into pens, as stated above, in order to fertilize the ground, where wheat is to be planted. No hay is stored, for the winter is not like ours, and even if it snows a little or is cold, it passes away in a few days. It is true the poor cattle are at times half frozen and starved, as I have seen in spring by their bodies. But when the weather is severe, they are given corn. The north wind is said to blow very cold. But such weather does not last long, as soon as the south wind comes it is warm again.

Pigs are found there in such numbers that I was astonished. They are not large, but increase so rapidly that their number becomes large in a short time. Their meat or pork is considered by everybody as the best and most delicate. Many are taken every year alive to England. As they are fed with nuts, acorns, berries, apples and corn, they cannot be less then the best. They must be better than those which are fed with poorer food. This is shown by the Carolina ham, which smells after fish, because the pigs there are fed with fish. The pigs cause no care, as they are always left in the woods near the house or not far away. They find their food throughout the whole year. They often do not come home in eight weeks. But many are lost when they run off into the wilderness. On the frontiers the bears do some damage. Each farmer has his mark, with which he marks their ears.

Sheep are raised in constantly increasing numbers. They thrive well. But, as the necessary workmen are wanting to use the wool, they are kept only for their meat.

Turkeys, geese, ducks and chickens are very common. As to the game, this land is a real zoological garden, filled to overflowing with all kinds of animals. They might justly be called half wild, because they do not fight shy of man.

In the first place, stags are very plentiful, deer also. Bears are found in large numbers. They are not vicious, hence they are shot without fear. Then there are wild boars and wild horses; also raccoons, fierce animals like wild cats but larger; and the "monac" [woodchuck], an animal, unknown in this country [Switzerland] and not much larger than a cat, but of a different kind. We had one on our ship, on the return journey, but it died. Foxes and hares are much smaller than in this country, fox-squirrels are also numerous, but are more than four times larger than here and not of the color found here, but grey; also another kind of squirrel, like those above, but smaller. Furthermore, ground-squirrels, but they are very small and of brown color, more like mice. The fourth and last kind are bats, very small and pretty, of brown color, but with white belly. They fly only in the evening or at night. Instead of wings they have skin over their toes which they spread when they fly.

The feathered game is very common and tame. The first is properly the eagle. Then comes the turkey, whose number is very great. It is a large bird, which weighs from twenty to forty pounds. Many of them are shot because of the fine meat. The first two which I met in the woods, I thought I could overtake with running without shooting them. But when I came near them, they ran so fast that I could not catch up with them. Finally they flew away. Wild geese and ducks, together with all kinds of snipes and waterfowl, are very numerous during the winter season. They are unlike those here [in Switzerland] in size and color. They are not wild. No hunter will shoot at one or two of them, but they are hunted in uncounted numbers. Patridges are also numerous and tame. It is not an uncommon sight to see them eating with the chickens. They are smaller, but excel them in the fineness of their meat. I was surprized to see them sitting on trees and hear them sing. I have shot many of them for their good meat and because they are found everywhere, but never only one of them. Regarding the others I must confess that I do not know their names, because they are not like the European birds. One species is as large as a finch, of scarlet color, another is blue, others green and others have variegated colors, wonderfully mixed. Then there is a little bird, somewhat larger than a hornet, which always hovers over flowers [hummingbird]. When one looks at its wonderful colors, one cannot help being surprized. Another kind is also worthy of observation, because it has aurora color mixed with red. The noxious birds are like a species of blackbird, which do not a little damage when the corn is sown and cut. They come in incredibly large numbers. At such times the fields must be guarded. But that does not help much. When they are chased from one field they fly to another. They fear people hardly at all. Hence it happens that fields must often be sown three times. They even pick it out of the ground after it has sprouted. The most valuable species, because of their song, are the "mocketbort" [mocking bird], which are sold in England for two guineas and more. They can be compared to the nightingale, because, they change their sweet song in many different ways. They are not unlike a shrike. The "noisemaker" comes to the houses in spring. He screams at night with such a loud voice and so continuously that, if one is not accustomed to it, one can hardly sleep. I could catch a sight of many other species and still others I have forgotten.

Poisonous animals did not become known to me, except the so-called rattle snakes, a species which is large and much feared. They stay most generally at swampy places. When angry they rattle with their tail as if it were a bell. When they bite anybody he has to die. There is no help for him. Only the Indians know the secret, but they don't want to make it known. If one can come to them in time, they can cure him at once. At one occasion I traveled with some others from Manigkinton on a wet, rainy day. Seven miles from that place we came across such a snake in the forest, lying on the road. We had not seen any thus far. As we were looking at it, it rattled with the tail as with a bell, and, since we had heard that such were of the dangerous kind, we went back and intended to avoid it. Then it rose partly on its tail and we thought that it would attack us every moment. One man who was with me ran off. I had my gun ready to fire, but, as there was only one bullet in it, I was afraid to miss. Hence I turned slowly away. There is another large snake, but it is not poisonous like the one just mentioned. It is so delicate that one needs only to strike it gently on the head with a stick to kill it instantly.

In the hottest part of summer it is troublesome to travel because of vermin. Hence no one can lie or sleep on the ground, because so many vermin have crawled over the same, since the creation, that it is poisoned so to speak, for experience shows that those who work with bare feet in new soil are often poisoned all over.

In summer the mosquitoes are very annoying. Rains are usually warm and the sun has such power that, when something is planted, it grows in a short time. It is astonishing to see a thing, half grown or half ripe one day, reaching ripeness in a few days. The fruits are all ripe much earlier than in this country [Switzerland]. But this year everything has been very late compared with other years. The trees began to blossom in April. Half of June, July and August were very hot, so that one thought the air was on fire in some places and people were parched with thirst. But the cool springs are very refreshing at that time. Their water is not inferior to ours. If one desires a drink at that time, half a vessel of cold water is taken, sugar is put in with some vinegar and nutmeg, together with some good glasses full of rum. At times they mix in some lemon. It is a good drink. One could easily get drunk from it. It is called Pons [punch]. A tankard or half quart costs from four to six "Batzen."

They have also severe thunderstorms, such as we saw this year in June at Yorktown, when a ship, lying there at anchor, was covered with waves, which broke over the deck. The carpenter was in the sailor's cabin, the door was locked. There were two loopholes in the wall. Against one he placed his shoulder, which became black and burnt by the heat. At the other hole lay his axe, whose head was melted by the heat, which many people came to see.

Terrible winds, called hurricanes frequently come with such violence and force that people often fear that houses and trees will have to give way. But they are soon over. One can see and hear them come. Corn and other grain is often blown off the fields. The winter is not long nor cold. Not much snow falls. The cattle, as stated before, can stay outside, on the meadows, all the time, because they do not make hay. The north wind is said to be very cold in winter, but it does not last long. As soon as the south wind blows it is warm again. One can see trees split and bent through the cold. But it does not stay so long. During that time they make huge fires in the big fire places. There is as much wood as one desires at the door.

Regarding wild [forest] trees, it may be said justly that none can be found which are superior to them. I rightly regard as first the cedar tree, which is very common. The governor of late fenced in a garden. The trees were all cedars, whose wood is very durable. There is, furthermore, a kind of wood or spice, of saffran color, whose name I have forgotten. This wood is cut into chips. They are cooked afterwards and drunk. Every year much of it is exported to England. The tall, wild nut trees [walnuts] are very useful for building purposes, if fine work is desired. It is of brown color. This tree bears a fruit like our beech trees, but larger. It cannot be opened without a nail. The pigs usually eat them. There are chestnuts at some places, but they are small. The most numerous and the largest trees are the oaks. There are also very tall and straight red pines. White pines I have not seen, and also only one beech tree. The little boats, called canoes, are usually a trunk of a tree hollowed out. From six to ten persons can ride in them comfortably. Besides the trees mentioned there are many other species unknown to me by name. They blossom beautifully. Some of them are not like the trees here either in wood or in foliage, nor are they difficult to cut. The branches do not start way down the trunk, but far up. On one occasion a sloop or canoe came from Carolina. It was made of one piece, its size was astonishing. It had two sails and carried forty barrels of pork. The forests are very convenient to ride or hunt in. The trees are far apart, with no undergrowth on the ground, so that one can ride anywhere on horseback. The game is easily discovered, because of the openness of the forest. The hunting of the Indians helps not a little to clear the forests and pastures. It takes place in October, in the following manner: From twenty to forty persons and often more gather and make a circle, assigning to each a certain section in the circle. Afterwards each sets fire to the foliage and underbrush, which through the heat is dried up. The flames devour everything before them, until finally the area is much narrowed and the game, fleeing before the fire and the smoke, is driven together to a small space, around which the hunters stand, shooting down everything. Then they take only the skins and as much of the meat as they need. The rest they leave to decay. This is their great hunt. They are good shots. They do not hold the rifle as we do. Their left hand takes hold of the barrel as far forward as possible. Thus they direct it mostly with the left hand. I shall soon report more about them.

The wild horses are hunted in April and May, at the time of the year when, being famished after the winter, they fill themselves with the fresh grass to such an extent that they become lazy and are unable to run. The English place their best horses for four or five weeks into the stable, feed them with oats. Then they mount and ride their horses in companies while they hunt them. They are soon found, because they run about in large numbers. As soon as they are sighted, they are chased. They can stand the running for some time, but are finally overtaken by the horses that have been fed with oats. They are then caught, kept for a time with the tame horses and broken in. They develop great endurance. They are grey, but not quite as tall as the others. Their meat is good to eat. They are also caught in pits. When it is known which way they go to the water, a deep pit is dug, which is covered slightly. When the horse passes over it, it falls down and can't get out again, until it is bound with ropes and pulled out. There are people who make their living by this practice.

Turtles of different kinds are found in the woods. They are gathered and eaten by the negroes or slaves. The largest which I have seen was like a small hat in circumference. They are of various colors and very beautiful. There is especially a small species, which is found in large numbers on roads, mostly of a yellow color. They are most beautifully decorated. I took one of them with me and used it on board of ship as a drinking cup.

This is the small amount of information which I can give about things in general. There are many other facts regarding them unknown to me.

Before I continue my journey I find it necessary to report a good habit or custom which prevails there with regard to strangers and travelers. Namely, it is possible to travel through the whole country without money, except when ferrying across a river, which costs not less than 1 bitt or 4 Batzen. In the first place, there is little money in the country, the little that is found there consists mostly of Spanish coins, namely dollars. Tobacco is the money with which payments are made. There are also few ordinaries or inns. Moreover, it is not a country in which much traveling is done, though the inhabitants visit one another. Even if one is willing to pay, they do not accept anything, but they are rather angry, asking, whether one did not know the custom of the country. At first we were too modest to go into the houses to ask for food and lodging, which the people often recognized, and they admonished us not to be bashful, as this was the custom of rich and poor. We soon became accustomed to it. Thus we continued our journey.

About 400 dollars are necessary in order to set up a man properly, namely to enable him to buy two slaves, with whom in two years a beautiful farm can be cleared, because the trees are far apart. Afterwards the settler must be provided with cattle, a horse, costing at the usual price 4 lbs., a cow with calf 50 shillings, a mare [?] 10 shillings. Furniture and clothes, together with tools and provisions for a year, must also be on hand. It is indeed possible to begin with less and succeed, but then three or four years pass by before one gets into a good condition. The one who is not used to work in great heat, becomes sick and must suffer much, before he can make progress by his work alone. By the above method a man is put into such a condition the first year, that he can be happy and enjoy life. It is indeed said truthfully that there is no other country, where it is possible with so few means and so easily to make an honest living and be in easy circumstances. For two servants can raise a bigger crop than one needs; the cattle increase incredibly fast without trouble; fruit grows in abundance. When a tree or something else is planted one must be surprized to see it grow up so soon and bear fruit. Besides, in the gardens grows whatever one desires. The cows are pasturing round about the house during the whole year. They yield enough butter, cheese and milk. In addition there is no lack of game and fish. Besides it is a quiet land devoted to our religion, and he who wants to enjoy honest exercise finds opportunities enough for it, especially the one who loves field work or hunting. It is, therefore, possible to live an honest life, quietly and contentedly. Much evil is absent there, because there is no opportunity for it.

Poor people, such namely as ask for alms, are not seen. If one is disabled in means and strength, the county keeps him.

If one wants to hire out, as there are some who do so, he can get annually from 4 to 6 pounds from merchants; the wealthiest gentlemen do not pay more than 10 pounds. In short, provisions are there in abundance. It is a land for people, who desire with small means to reach a comfortable living and do not care for society and luxury.

After an elite English education at Westminster School and Queens' College, Cambridge, the Rev. Andrew Burnaby (1734?-1812) spent many of his early adult years travelling in America, Italy, and Corsica. When he settled down as vicar of Greenwich in 1769, he finally had time to arrange his journals and diaries for publication. Travels through the Middle Settlements in North-America. In the Years 1759 and 1760 *was published in London in 1775, just as the breach between the colonies and the mother country was becoming irreparable. The passages below are taken from pp. 19-22, 31-39 of the second London edition of 1775.*

Viewed and considered as a settlement, Virginia is far from being arrived at that degree of perfection which it is capable of. Not a tenth of the land is yet cultivated: and that which is cultivated, is far from being so in the most advantageous manner. It produces, however, considerable quantities of grain and cattle, and fruit of many kinds. The Virginian pork is said to be superior in flavour to any in the world; but the sheep and horned cattle being small and lean, the meat of them is inferior to that of Great Britain, or indeed, of most parts of Europe. The horses are fleet and beautiful; and the gentlemen of Virginia, who are exceedingly fond of horseracing, have spared no expence or trouble to improve the breed of them by importing great numbers from England.

The fruits introduced here from Europe succeed extremely well; particularly peaches, which have a very fine flavour, and grow in such plenty as to serve to feed the hogs in the autumn of the year. Their blossoms in the spring make a beautiful appearance throughout the country.

Virginia is divided into fifty-two counties, and seventy-seven parishes, and by act of assembly there ought to be forty-four towns; but one half of these have not more than five houses; and the other half are little better than inconsiderable villages. This is owing to the cheapness of land, and the commodiousness of navigation: for every person may with ease procure a small plantation, can ship his tobacco at his own door, and live independent. When the colony shall come to be more thickly seated, and land grow dear, people will be obliged to follow trades and manufactures, which will necessarily make towns and large cities; but this seems remote, and not likely to happen for some centuries.

The inhabitants are supposed to be in number between two and three hundred thousand. There are a hundred and five thousand tytheables, under which denomination are included all white males from sixteen to sixty; and all negroes whatsoever within the same age. The former are obliged to serve in the militia, and amount to forty thousand.

The trade of this colony is large and extensive. Tobacco is the principal article of it. Of this they export annually between fifty and sixty thousand hogsheads, each hogshead weighing eight hundred or a thousand weight: some years they export much more. They ship also for the Madeiras, the Streights, and the West-Indies, several articles, such as grain, pork, lumber, and cyder: to Great Britain, bar-iron, indigo, and a small quantity of ginseng, tho' of an inferior quality; and they clear out one year with another about [45,179] ton of shipping.

Their manufactures are very inconsiderable. They make a kind of cotton-cloth, which they clothe themselves with in common, and call after the name of their country; and some inconsiderable quantities of linen, hose, and other trifling articles: but nothing to deserve attention.

From what has been said of this colony, it will not be difficult to form an idea of the character of its inhabitants. The climate and external appearance of the country conspire to make them indolent, easy, and good-natured; extremely fond of society, and much given to convivial pleasures. In consequence of this, they seldom show any spirit of enterprize, or expose themselves willingly to fatigue. Their authority over their slaves renders them vain and imperious, and intire strangers to that elegance of sentiment, which is so peculiarly characteristic of refined and polished nations. Their ignorance of mankind and of learning, exposes them to many errors and prejudices, especially in regard to Indians and Negroes, whom they scarcely consider as of the human species; so that it is almost impossible, in cases of violence, or even murder, committed upon those unhappy people by any of the planters, to have the delinquents brought to justice: for either the grand jury refuse to find the bill, or the petit jury bring in their verdict, not guilty.

The display of a character thus constituted, will naturally be in acts of extravagance, ostentation, and a disregard of oeconomy; it is not extraordinary, therefore, that the Virginians out-run their incomes; and that having involved themselves in difficulties, they are frequently tempted to raise money by bills of exchange, which they know will be returned protested, with 10 per cent interest.

The public or political character of the Virginians, corresponds with their private one: they are haughty and jealous of their liberties, impatient of restraint, and can scarcely bear the thought of being controuled by any superior power. Many of them consider the colonies as independent states, not connected with Great Britain, otherwise than by having the same common king, and being bound to her with natural affection. There are but few of them that have a turn for business, and even those are by no means adroit at it. I have known them, upon a very urgent occasion, vote the relief of a garrison, without once considering whether the thing was practicable, when it was most evidently and demonstrably otherwise. In matters of commerce they are ignorant of the necessary principles that must prevail between a colony and the mother country; they think it a hardship not to have an unlimited trade to every part of the world. They consider the duties upon their staple as injurious only to themselves; and it is utterly impossible to persuade them that they affect the consumer also. Upon the whole, however, to do them justice, the same spirit of generosity prevails here which does in their private character; they never refuse any necessary supplies for the support of government when called upon, and are a generous and loyal people.

The women are, upon the whole, rather handsome, though not to be compared with our fair countrywomen in England. They have but few advantages, and consequently are seldom accomplished; this makes them reserved, and unequal to any interesting or refined conversation. They are immoderately fond of dancing, and indeed it is almost the only amusement they partake of: but even in this they discover great want of taste and elegance, and seldom appear with that gracefulness and ease, which these movements are so calculated to display. Towards the close of an evening, when the company are pretty well tired with country dances, it is usual to dance jiggs; a practice originally borrowed, I am informed, from the Negroes. These dances are without any method or regularity: a gentleman and lady stand up, and dance about the room, one of them retiring, the other pursuing, then perhaps meeting, in an irregular fantastical manner. After some time, another lady gets up, and then the first lady must sit down, she being, as they term it, cut out: the second lady acts the same part which the first did, till somebody cuts her out. The gentlemen perform in the same manner. The Virginian ladies, excepting these amusements, and now and then a party of pleasure into the woods to partake of a barbacue, chiefly spend their time in sewing and taking care of their families: they seldom read, or endeavour to improve their minds; however, they are in general good housewives; and though they have not, I think, quite so much tenderness and sensibility as the English ladies, yet they make as good wives, and as good mothers, as any in the world.

It is hard to determine, whether this colony can be called flourishing, or not: because though it produces great quantities of tobacco and grain, yet there seem to be very few improvements carrying on in it. Great part of Virginia is a wilderness, and as many of the gentlemen are in possession of immense tracts of land, it is likely to continue so. A spirit of enterprize is by no means the turn of the colony, and therefore few attempts have been made to force a trade; which I think might easily be done, both to the West Indies and the Ohio. They have every thing necessary for such an undertaking; viz. lumber, provisions, grain, and every other commodity, which the other colonies, that subsist and grow rich by these means, make use of for exports; but, instead of this, they have only a trifling communication with the West Indies; and as to the Ohio, they have suffered themselves, notwithstanding the superior advantages they might enjoy from having a water carriage almost to the Yoghiogheny, to neglect this valuable branch of commerce; while the industrious Pensylvanians seize every opportunity, and struggle with innumerable difficulties, to secure it to themselves. The Virginians are content if they can but live from day to day; they confine themselves almost intirely to the cultivation of tobacco; and if they have but enough of this to pay their merchants in London, and to provide for their pleasures; they are satisfied, and desire nothing more. Some few, indeed, have been rather more enterprising, and have endeavoured to improve their estates by raising indigo, and other schemes: but whether it has been owing to the

climate, to their inexperience in these matters, or their want of perseverance, I am unable to determine, but their success has not
answered their expectations.

*The American Revolution brought many French aristocrats to North
America as officers in the allied French forces. François-Jean de
Beauvoir, the Marquis of Chastellux, was one of the most illustrious.
As one of the three major-generals under Rochambeau, the commander of the French Expeditionary Forces in America, Chastellux
employed his free time between campaigns to travel throughout the
colonies. He transformed into letters the daily notes he took on these
journeys for his friends at home, and it was in this form that they
were published in 1786. Born in 1734 to a noble family, Chastellux
entered the army at thirteen, as his father had, and advanced to the
rank of colonel by the age of twenty-one. Although the military was
his career, his calling was the arts and letters. In camps throughout
Europe he wrote poetry and essays on music and economics. In 1772
his reputation as an enlightened philosophe was assured with the publication of a two-volume work on* Public Happiness. *Three years later
he received literary canonization by his admission to the exclusive
(40) French Academy. With these impressive credentials he came to
America in 1780, was present at Cornwallis's surrender at Yorktown
in 1781, and sailed back to France in 1783. The following passages
are taken from* Travels in North America in the Years 1780, 1781
and 1782 *by the Marquis De Chastellux, translated and edited by
Howard C. Rice, Jr. (Chapel Hill: University of North Carolina Press
for the Institute of Early American History and Culture, 1963), pp.
434-444.*

The Virginians differ essentially from the inhabitants to the north
and eastward of the Bay [Chesapeake], not only in the nature of their
climate, soil, and agriculture, but also in that indelible character which
every nation acquires at the moment of its origin, and which by per-
petuating itself from generation to generation, justifies this great principle, that *every thing which is partakes of that which has been.* The
discovery of Virginia dates from the end of the sixteenth century, and
the settlement of the colony took place at the commencement of the
seventeenth. These events took place in the reigns of Elizabeth and

James I. At that time the republican and democratic spirit was not common in England; that of commerce and navigation was only in its infancy; and the long wars with France and Spain had perpetuated, under another form, the same military spirit given to the nation by William the Conqueror, Richard *Coeur de Lion,* Edward III, and the Black Prince. There were no longer any knights, as in the time of the Crusades, but in their place arose a number of adventurers who served indiscriminately their own country or foreign powers, and gentlemen who disdained agriculture and commerce and had no other profession than arms; for at that period the military spirit maintained the prejudices favorable to the nobility, from which it was long inseparable; furthermore, nobility through elevation to the peerage being then less common in England than it is now, hereditary rank had kept more glamour and consideration. The first colonists of Virginia were composed, for the most part, of such soldiers and such gentlemen, some of whom went in search of fortune and others of adventures. And indeed, if the establishment of a colony requires all the industry of the merchant and the husbandman, the discovery and conquest of new lands seems more peculiarly suited to warlike and romantic ideas. Accordingly the first company which obtained the exclusive property of Virginia was principally composed of men most distinguished by rank or birth; and although all of these illustrious stockholders did not themselves become colonists, several of them were not afraid to cross the seas; and a Lord Delaware was among the first governors of Virginia. It was natural therefore that these new colonists, imbued with military principles and the prejudices of nobility, should carry them into the very midst of the savages whose lands they were coming to usurp; and of all our European ideas these were the most readily understood by these rude nations. I know that there now remain but a small number of these old families, but they have retained great standing, and the first impulse once given, it is not in the power of any legislator, or of time itself, to destroy its effect. The government may become democratic, as it is at the present moment; but the national character, the very spirit of the government, will always be aristocratic. Nor can this be doubted when one considers that another cause is still operating to produce the same result. I am referring to slavery, not because it is a mark of distinction or special privilege to possess Negroes, but because the sway held over them nourishes vanity and sloth, two vices which accord wonderfully with established prejudices. It will doubtless be asked how these prejudices have been reconciled with the present revolution, founded on such different principles. I shall answer that they have perhaps contributed to it; that while New England revolted through reason and calculation, Virginia revolted through pride. I shall add, as I have hinted at above, that in theory the very indolence of this people may have been useful to them, as it obliged them to rely upon a small number of virtuous and enlightened citizens, who led them further than they would have gone had they proceeded with no guide and consulted only their own dispositions. For it must be admitted that Virginia, at the beginning of the disturbances, stepped forth willingly; that she was the first to offer assistance to the Bostonians, and the first also to set on foot a considerable body of troops. But it may likewise be observed that as soon as the new legislature was established, and when, instead of leaders, she had a government in which the citizens had a share, then the national character prevailed, and everything went from bad to worse. Thus, States, like individuals, are born with a temperament of their own, the bad effects of which may be corrected by the régime of government and by habits, but which can never be entirely changed. Thus, legislators, like doctors, ought never presume to believe that they can bestow, at will, a particular temperament on bodies politic, but should attempt to understand the temper they already have, while striving to combat the disadvantages and increase the advantages resulting from it. A general glance at the different states of America will serve to substantiate this opinion.

The peoples of New England had no other motive for settling in the New World than to escape from the arbitrary power of their monarchs, who were both the sovereigns of the State and the heads of the Church, and who were at that time exercising the double tyranny of despotism and intolerance. They were not adventurers, they were men who wished to live in peace, and who labored to live. Their doctrine taught equality and enjoined work and industry. The soil, naturally barren, affording but scanty resources, they resorted to fishing and navigation; and at this hour, they are still friends to equality and industry; they are fishermen and navigators.

The states of New York and the Jerseys were settled by necessitous Dutchmen who lacked land in their own country, and who concerned themselves much more with domestic economy than with public government. These people have kept this same spirit: their interests and their efforts are, so to speak, individual; their views are centered on their families, and it is only from necessity that these families form a state. Accordingly, when General Burgoyne marched on Albany, it was the New Englanders who contributed most to stop his progress; and, if the inhabitants of the state of New York and of the Jerseys have often taken up arms and displayed courage, this is because the former were animated by an inveterate hatred against the Indians, whom the English always sent ahead of their own armies, and because the latter were impelled to take personal vengeance for the excesses committed by the troops of the enemy, when they overran their country.

If you go farther to the south, and cross the Delaware, you will find that the government of Pennsylvania, in its origin, was founded on two very opposite principles; it was a government of property, in itself a feudal, or if you will, a patriarchal government, but whose spirit was characterized by the greatest tolerance and the most complete liberty. Penn's family at first formed the vain idea of establishing a sort of Utopia, a perfect government, and then of deriving the greatest possible advantage from their immense property by attracting foreigners from all parts. As a result of this the people of Pennsylvania has no identity of its own, it is mixed and confused, and more attached to individual than to public liberty, more inclined to anarchy than to democracy.

Maryland, subjected at first to proprietary government, and considered only as a private domain, long remained in a state of the most absolute dependence. Now for the first time it deserves being regarded as a state; but this state seems to be taking shape under good auspices. It may become important after the present revolution, because it was nothing before.

There remain the two Carolinas and Georgia, but I am not sufficiently acquainted with these three states to subject them to my observations, which may not be as correct as they appear to me, but which are in any case delicate and require more than a superficial examination. I know only that North Carolina, peopled for the most part by Scotsmen, brought thither by poverty rather than by industry, is a prey to brigandage and to internal dissensions; and that South Carolina, whose only commerce is the export trade, owes its existence to its seaports, especially to the city of Charleston, which rapidly increased and became a commercial town, where foreigners have abounded, as at Marseilles and Amsterdam, so that the manners there are polished and easy, that the inhabitants love pleasure, the arts, and society—and that this country is in general more European than the rest of America.

Now if there be any accuracy in this sketch, let my readers compare the spirit of the states of America with their present government. I ask them to make the comparison at the present moment, twenty years hence, fifty years hence, and I am persuaded that although these governments resemble each other in that they are all democratic, there will always be found the traces of their former character, of that spirit which has presided over the formation of peoples and the establishment of nations.

Virginia will retain its distinctive character longer than the other states; either because prejudices are the more durable, the more absurd and frivolous they are, or because those which injure only a part of the human race are more noticeable than those which affect all mankind. In the present revolution the old families have with pain seen new men occupying distinguished situations in the army and in the magistracy. The Tories have even taken advantage of this circumstance to cool the ardor of the less zealous of the Whigs. But the popular party has maintained its ground, and one can only regret that it is not displaying as much activity in fighting the English as it does in quarreling over questions of precedence. It is to be feared, however, that when circumstances become less favorable to it, with the coming of peace, the popular party may be obliged either to give way entirely, or to maintain itself in power through factions, which would necessarily disturb the order of society. But if Reason must blush at beholding such prejudices so strongly established among new peoples, Humanity has still more to suffer from the state of poverty in which a great number of white people live in Virginia. It is in this state, for the first time since I crossed the sea, that I have seen poor people. For, among these rich plantations where the Negro alone is wretched, one often finds miserable huts inhabited by whites, whose wane looks and ragged garments bespeak poverty. At first I found it hard to understand how, in a country where there is still so much land to clear, men who do not refuse to work could remain in misery; but I have since learned that all these useless lands and those immense estates, with which Virginia is still covered, have their proprietors. Nothing is more common than to see some of them possessing five or six thousand acres of land, but exploiting only as much of it as their Negroes can cultivate. Yet they will not give away, or even sell the smallest portion of it, because they are attached to their possessions and always hope to increase eventually the number of their Negroes. These whites, without means and often too without ambition, are thus restrained on all sides and are reduced to the small number of acres they have been able to acquire. As land is not generally good in America, especially in Virginia, it takes a good deal of it to make cultivation profitable, as well as cattle to assist in gaining a livelihood. In the eastern states one sees many cleared farms, but the tracts of land which can be easily and very cheaply purchased there are always of at least two hundred acres. Besides, in the South, the climate is less healthy, and the new settlers, without sharing the wealth of Virginia, share all the disadvantages of the climate and even the indolence it inspires.

Beneath this class of inhabitants we must place the Negroes, whose situation would be even more lamentable than theirs, did not natural insensibility extenuate in some degree the sufferings attached to slavery. On seeing them ill lodged, ill clothed, and often overwhelmed with work, I concluded that their treatment was as rigorous as everywhere else. I was assured, however, that it was extremely mild in comparison to what they experience in the sugar colonies. You do not, indeed, generally hear, as in Santo Domingo and in Jamaica, the sound of whips and the cries of the unhappy wretches whose bodies are being lashed. This is because the people of Virginia are in general milder than the inhabitants of the sugar islands, who consist wholly of avid men, eager to make their fortune and return to Europe. Another reason is that the yield of agriculture in Virginia not being of so great a value, labor is not urged on the Negroes with so much severity. In fairness to all it should be added that the Negroes in Virginia for their part are not so much addicted to cheating and stealing as in the islands, because, since the propagation of the black species is very rapid and very considerable here, most of the Negroes are born in this country, and it is a known fact that they are generally less depraved than those imported directly from Africa. I must likewise do the Virginians the justice to declare that many of them treat their Negroes with great humanity. I must further add a still more honorable testimonial in their favor, that in general they seem grieved at having slaves, and are constantly talking of abolishing slavery and of seeking other means of exploiting their lands. It is true that this opinion, which is almost universally accepted, is inspired by different motives. The philosophers, and the young men who are for the most part educated in the principles of sound philosophy, consider only justice and the rights of humanity. The fathers of families, and those who are principally concerned with their interests, complain that the maintenance of their Negroes is very expensive, that their labor is neither so productive nor so cheap as that of day laborers or white servants, and, lastly, that epidemical disorders, which are very common, render both their property and their income extremely precarious. However this may be, it is fortunate that different motives concur in disgusting men with that tyranny which they exercise over those who may at least be described as of their own species, even though they cannot be called, in the strict sense of the term, their likes; for the more we observe the Negroes, the more must we be persuaded that the difference distinguishing them from us does not consist in color alone. Moreover, one cannot conceal the fact that the aboliton of slavery in America is an extremely delicate question. The Negroes in Virginia amount to two hundred thousand. They at least equal, if they do not exceed, the number of white men. Necessarily united by a common interest deriving from their situation, and brought together by the distinguishing badge of their color, they would doubtless form a distinct people, from whom neither succor, virtue, nor labor could be expected. Sufficient attention has not been paid to the difference between slavery, such as we have kept it in our colonies, and slavery as it was generally established among the ancients. A white slave, in ancient times, had no other cause of humiliation than his present lot; if he was freed, he could mix straightway with free men and become their equal. Hence that emulation among the slaves to obtain their liberty, either as a favor or to purchase it with the fruit of their labor. Two advantages resulted from this: the possibility of enfranchising them without danger, and that ambition generally prevalent among them, which turned to the advantage of morals and of industry. But in the present case, it is not only the slave who is beneath his master; it is the Negro who is beneath the white man. No act of enfranchisement can efface this unfortunate distinction; accordingly the Negroes do not seem very anxious to obtain their freedom, nor much pleased when they have obtained it. The free Negroes continue to live with the Negro slaves, and never with the white men, so that only when they have some special work or trade, and want to turn it to their profit, does their interest make them wish to leave the state of bondage. It appears, therefore, that there is no other method of abolishing slavery than by getting rid of the Negroes, and such a measure can only be carried out gradually. The best means would be to export a great number of males, and then to encourage the marriage of white men with the Negresses. For this purpose it would be necessary to abrogate the law according to which slavery is transmitted through the mothers; or at least to decree that any slave would become free by marrying a free man. Out of respect to property, it might perhaps be just to require of the latter a compensation to be fixed by law, to be paid either in labor or in money, as an indemnity to the owner of the Negresses thus freed; but it is certain, at all events, that such a law, aided by the less licit but already well-established commerce between the white men and Negresses, would give rise to a race of mulattoes, which would in turn produce a race of quadroons, and so on, until the color would be totally changed. . . .

We have seen the ill effects in Virginia of slavery and of too extensive estates: let us now examine the few good effects resulting from them. The Virginians have the reputation, and rightly so, of living nobly in their homes and of being hospitable; they receive strangers both willingly and well. This is because, on the one hand, having no large towns where they can gather, they know society only through the visits they make to each other; and, on the other hand, because their lands and their Negroes supplying them with the products and labor they need, this renowned hospitality is no burden to them. Their houses are spacious and well ornamented, but living quarters are not conveniently arranged; they think little of putting three or four persons in the same room; nor do people have any objection to finding themselves thus crowded in, because they experience no need to read and write, and all they want in a house is a bed, a dining room, and a drawing room for company. The chief magnificence of the Virginians consists in furniture, linen, and silver plate; in which they resemble our own forefathers who had no private apartments in their castles, but only a well-stored wine cellar and handsome sideboards. If they sometimes dissipate their fortunes, this is through gaming, hunting, and horse races; but the latter are of some utility, inasmuch as they encourage the training of horses, which are really of a very fine breed in Virginia. It will be seen that women have little share in the amusements of the men; beauty here serves only to find husbands; for the wealthiest among them give but a trifling dowry to their daughters and it is in general the young ladies' faces that determine their fortunes. The consequence of this is that they are often coquettish and prudish before marriage, and dull and tiresome afterwards. The convenience of being served by slaves still further increases their natural indolence; they always have a great number of slaves at hand to wait on them and on their children; they themselves suckle their infants, but that is all. The women, as well as their husbands, pay attention to the children as long as they are little, but neglect them when they are older. We may in general say of the Americans, as of the English, that they are very fond of their *little ones,* and care much less for their *children.* It would perhaps be untactful to inquire whether this sentiment is not really the natural one, and whether our efforts in France to counteract it are not the result of self-esteem or ambition. But we can always confidently affirm that the care we take of our children is a means of attaching ourselves to them and them to us—the nobility and utility of which cannot be denied.

I wanted to speak of the virtues peculiar to the Virginians, but in spite of my wishes, I have found only magnificence and hospitality to mention. I have been unable to add generosity to these; for they are strongly attached to their interests, and their great wealth, joined to their pretensions, further distorts this vice.

I should have begun these remarks by considering the subject of religion; but there is nothing noteworthy about it in this country, save for the way they manage to dispense with it. The predominant one before the Revolution was the Anglican religion, which, as is well known, requires episcopacy and that every priest must be ordained by a bishop. Before the war people went to England to study and to be ordained. It is therefore impossible, under the present circumstances, to fill the pastorates that have become vacant. What has been the consequence of this? The churches have remained shut; people have done without a minister, and have not even thought of any future arrangements for establishing an Anglican church independent of England. The most complete tolerance has been established; nor have the other communions made any gains from the losses of the former; each sect has remained as it was, and this sort of religious interregnum has caused no disorder. The clergy, furthermore, have received a severe setback in the new constitution, which forbids them any share in the government, even the right of voting at elections. It is true that the judges and lawyers have been subjected to the same exclusion, but this was from another motive, that of keeping public affairs free from competition with private affairs. The legislator feared the effects of such a conflict of interests; an attempt was made, in short, to form within the state a sort of separate body known as the judiciary. These views are perhaps good in themselves; but they have become a doubtful blessing in the present circumstances; for the lawyers, who are certainly the most enlightened part of the community, are removed from the civil councils, and the administration is entrusted either to the ignorant, or at least to the unskilled. This is the principal objection made here to the present form of government, which, I should add, appears to me good in many respects. The Virginia constitution is readily available in print, and anyone can easily obtain it for himself. However if an outline is here desired, I can say in a few words that the government is composed of: 1st. The Assembly of Deputies, named by the towns and counties, a body corresponding to the House of Commons. 2nd. A Senate, the members of which are elected by several counties grouped together, with the number of members varying according to the population of the counties—which corresponds to the House of Peers. 3d. An Executive Council, presided over by the Governor, and the members of which are chosen by the two Chambers, which takes the place of the executive power exercised by the King in England.

It is not mere chance that has led me to postpone to the end of these notes matters respecting the progress of the arts and sciences in Virginia. I have done so expressly because the mind, after bestowing its attention on the variety of human institutions, lingers with pleasure over those which tend to the perfection of understanding and to the progress of knowledge; and above all, because, since I have found myself under the necessity of speaking less advantageously of this state than I should have liked, I wish to conclude with a subject which is wholly to its credit. I shall therefore state that the College of William and Mary—the name alone denotes its founders—is a magnificent establishment which adorns Williamsburg and does honor to Virginia. The beauty of the building is surpassed by the richness of the library, and the worth of this library by several of the distinguished professors, such as Doctors [Rev. James] Madison, [George] Wythe,

[Carlo] Bellini, etc., etc., who may be looked upon as living books, in which both precepts and examples are to be found. I must likewise add that the zeal of these professors has already been crowned with very marked success, and that they have already formed many distinguished characters, now ready to serve their country in different capacities. Among these, I am pleased to mention Mr. [William] Short, with whom I was particularly well acquainted. And now, having done justice to the labors of the University at Williamsburg (for the College of William and Mary is in fact a university), I might add, if miracles need be cited to enhance her fame, that she has made *me* a Doctor of Law!

Williamsburg, May 1, 1782

Like many 18th-century visitors, Johann David Schoepf came to America with the European allies of the American revolutionaries. He served as chief surgeon to the Ansbach German troops from 1777 to 1784. A graduate of the University of Erlangen in medicine and natural science, he had done further work in forestry at Berlin and travelled widely in Europe before 1776. His long experience in the colonies gave rise to several professional papers on American subjects and to his Travels in the Confederation [1783- 84] *The passages below are taken from the translation of Alfred J. Morrison (Philadelphia: William J. Campbell, 1911), pp. 30-34, 38-40, 59-61, 91-95.*

Leesburg is the first Virginia town on this road, a place of few and insignificant wooden houses. From its high, pleasant, and healthful situation the proposal has been made to establish a Latin school here, and on the door of the tavern there was a special notice recommending the institution to the public which should certainly give it support, there being everywhere in America, outside the chief cities, a lack of suitable schools and educational establishments. It is not always the custom to hang shields before taverns, but they are easily to be identified by the great number of miscellaneous papers and advertisements with which the walls and doors of these publick houses are plaistered; generally, the more of such bills are to be seen on a house, the better it will be found to be. In this way the traveller is afforded a many-sided entertainment, and can inform himself as to where the taxes are heavy, where wives have run away, horses been stolen, or the new Doctor has settled.

Along this road it was matter of no little astonishment to see so much waste or new-cleared land, having just come from the very well settled and cultivated regions of Pensylvania and Maryland. The reason does not lie in any worse quality of the land, which is scarcely inferior to that beyond the Potowmack, but in the fact that individuals own great and extensive tracts of land, of which they will sell none, so as to leave their families the more. All of them are very much disposed to let land in parcels, they retaining possession and seeing their land as much as possible worked and settled by tenants; but tenants are not easily to be had, so long as it is anywhere possible to buy land. This policy, which will certainly be advantageous to the posterity of such rich and important families, has in the neighborhood of New York and elsewhere stood much in the way of cultivation and settlement, whereas the back parts of Pensylvania, Maryland, and even a portion of Virginia, have been more rapidly settled, poor families being able to get title to small tracts of land. The smallest possession has for every man more charm than the most imposing leasehold. In addition, the Virginians of the lower country are very easy and negligent husbandmen. Much and very good land, which would yield an abundant support to an industrious family, remains unused when once a little exhausted, no thought being given so far to dunging and other improvements. New land is taken up, the best to be had, tobacco is grown on it 3-4 years, and then Indian corn, so long as any will come. And in the end, if the soil is thoroughly impoverished, they begin again with a new piece and go through the rotation. Meantime wood grows again on the old land, and on the new is at pains to be cleared off; and all this to avoid dunging and all the trouble involved in a more careful handling of their cattle, if dung is to be had.

Although we had not yet come far into Virginia, there was to be observed already a considerable difference in the arrangements of the plantations and the character of the people on this side the Potowmack. A plantation in Virginia, and also in the lower parts of Maryland, has often more the appearance of a small village, by reason of the many separate small buildings, which taken all together would at times hardly go to make a single roomy and commodious house. Here are living-rooms, bed-chambers, guest-chambers, storerooms, kitchens, quarters for the slaves, and who knows what else, commonly so many small, separate, badly kept cabins of wood, without glass in the windows, of the structure and solidity of a house of cards. This plan is not so much the consequence of any particular taste, as of necessity. In the settlement of a new plantation there is concern for only the most indispensable buildings, and a hastily built block-house is all that is needed at first; but by degrees, the family increasing and more land brought into cultivation, greater convenience becomes an item. And thus are built gradually a good many small houses and cabins, commonly without the assistance of carpenters, patched together by the people themselves and their negroes. This being an easier method than to put together a large house all at once, one often sees such little houses growing up where there is neither material nor capital for bringing them together in one solid house. In such cabins then, about which all the evidences of negligence are to be remarked, it is nothing extraordinary to see the lady of the house, and women generally, clothed and adorned with great fastidiousness; for the fair sex in America cannot resist the propensity to make themselves fine, even when remotely situated they must forego the pleasure of being admired except by the casual traveller. We had gone many miles through the woods, had seen only a few wretched cabins, and arrived finally at a house that had been indicated to us, which appeared not greatly different from the rest, not a whole pane in the windows, neither rum, nor whiskey, nor bread to be had, a draughty, empty place; but in return we had the altogether unexpected pleasure of making our devoirs to several ladies dressed tastefully in silk and decked with plumes. But it must be observed that in the love of display the fair of the southern provinces go far beyond those of the northern, and that similar phenomena in similar circumstances are not to be looked-for in Pensylvania; as also, that the carelessness of the men in their dress is quite as striking as the vanity of the women.

We spent a night at a plantation where, according to the custom here, travellers are lodged for a price, under the style of 'Private Entertainment,' but no tavern is kept. In the item of public houses Virginia and the other southern provinces are worse off than the northern. The distinction between Private and Public Entertainment is to the advantage of the people who keep the so-called *Private houses*, they avoiding in this way the tax for permission to dispense rum and other drinks and not being plagued with noisy drinking-parties. Other public houses lacking, travellers are compelled to seek out these and glad to find them. Here, one eats with the family both thick and thin homany (a preparation of Indian corn), drinks water at pleasure, is not free to demand and has no right to expect what he wants, but pays quite as much as elsewhere, in houses where he lives as he pleases, is better served, and not obliged on coming and going to be very grateful for the reception. On the other hand, it must be said for these 'private houses' that in them one has to submit to a general interrogation but once, on the part of the family, whereas in the taverns every person coming in. Into the road again people directed us through impassable woods and swamps, where we should have stuck had not a good old man met us at the right time, and taken the trouble to show us the way. There was no tavern anywhere far and wide in the region, and he indicated to us the plantation of a Captain B. H., whose house, as he said, stands open to every traveller, and the man himself is obliged to strangers if they will call upon him. After a day of tedious and idle wandering-about we finally reached this belauded house, which stood on a very pleasant hill, with much open land about it. The customary negro cabins and other farm-buildings formed together a little village in which the finer and larger house of the Captain stood out well by contrast. We described our adventures to the Captain and the necessity we were under of asking for refreshments and a night's lodging, which he was willing for, but at the same time remarking that his house was no tavern. A reminder which we scarcely expected in a hospitable house (as later he boasted his was known to be throughout the country), and one not sustained by the hay, maize-bread, water, and fish (of which they take 2000 at a catch) we and our horses were entertained with.

Of the 4000 acres which the Captain owns, only a very small part has been made tillable for he himself, through his negroes, finds it impossible to work the whole or put it to use. He has a few Lease-holders, and wished there were more of them, because with them one may grow rich without work. He would prefer Germans for tenants, but so long as land is to be bought in the interior of America these will be wise enough not to spend their sweat on any land that is not their own, even if they must be content with very little. For other reasons as well, the German and Irish servants brought over in such numbers have been long unwilling to apprentice themselves in Virginia or Carolina, nor have they cared to settle there if not possessed of considerable property and able to buy slaves themselves. They are too proud to work with and among the negroes who in Virginia and Carolina are almost the only working people. For the Virginians as such are an indolent, haughty people whose thoughts and designs are directed solely towards paying the lord, owning great tracts of land and numerous troops of slaves. Any man whatever, if he can afford so much as 2-3 negroes, becomes ashamed of work and goes about in idleness, supported by his slaves. Thus the introduction of the negroes has been injurious to the moral principles of the inhabitants of these provinces, has made them sluggish and arrogant; and at times cruel, because of the despotic power they have over their slaves. Besides, the cultivation of the land merely by negroes is not the most profitable, which the people themselves see plainly enough and would like to get rid of them, but what is to be done with them and where are other working hands to be found?

The entire commerce of Virginia has for long been almost altogether in the hands of European houses who have maintained their warehouses and factors here. Among the Virginians few have concerned themselves in trade beyond the keeping of little shops here and there, and throughout the whole province there are still hardly any houses who would be disposed, or in a position, to undertake large affairs. And in all Virginia there is no commercial town which in the extent of its business may be compared with Philadelphia, New York, Boston, Baltimore, or Charleston; the natural situation and activities of those provinces bring together in their chief towns almost the whole trade of the interior, whereas in Virginia this is greatly distributed, owing to the numerous navigable streams penetrating the country; and thus in many small Virginia towns together there is hardly as much business done as in a single one of the large places mentioned, albeit the total value of Virginia exports exceeds in amount that of any of the other provinces. So far the raw products of Virginia are exported almost entirely through European ships and seamen, these also bringing in European manufactures and other articles of trade. For Virginia itself, beyond little coasting-vessels and a few West India trading-boats, likewise small, has no large shipping of its own and few sailors. The tobacco-trade alone formerly occupied several hundreds of English vessels, and some thousands of English seamen, and if only in that respect, was an object of the greatest consequence to Great Britain, which must now share the profits with other nations. To be sure, many merchant vessels are built in Virginia, but mainly for sale, and these are known and well-regarded as good, fast-sailing ships. Of the European merchants established here before the outbreak of the disturbances, and as British subjects compelled to leave during the war, divers came in the spring and summer with cargoes for Virginia, hoping to trade as before with their old friends and acquaintances. The government of Virginia, still full of bitter spleen, forbade them to land and obliged them to go elsewhere with their goods and seek other markets, which they soon found and not far off. Virginia then began to suffer for lack of European wares, and had to fetch, at a loss, from Philadelphia and Baltimore the very same it had at first prohibited. Besides, the ships of other European nations, against which there was no exception taken, if they came into the Bay were unwilling to be at the trouble of seeking purchasers for their cargoes among the few merchants scattered here and there, but preferred rather to go straight to one of the fore-mentioned places, where they could reckon upon a quicker sale. The Virginians moreover thought to deal on long credit, which they and all their neighbors have long been accustomed to at the hands of British merchants; but neither French nor Dutch were so agreeable as that, when the question was one of borrowing, and if they were, had oftentimes cause to rue their complaisance. Virginia needs and takes, (and has always), more foreign articles than it can pay for with its own produce, and so has been for a long time indebted to the British merchants, whose indulgence and confidence were almost without limit. And now since this unrestricted credit is not to be had from the merchants of other nations, the lack of hard money is felt at this time more than ever before, for equalizing the balance of the European trade which is against Virginia. The money spread about the country during the war is still a help; but as this becomes gradually exhausted, embarrassment will more and more increase, unless new channels open for getting gold and silver from the southern parts of America, or unless the produce of the land is augmented, as it may very well be, from the nature of the soil.

The want of hard money is felt not only in commercial affairs but also in the collection of the public revenues, and the government has been obliged to pass an act proclaiming that tobacco, hemp, flour, grain, and skins are to be accepted of the people in payment of their taxes. For this purpose special magazines have been established and inspectors appointed, whereby the state is subject to additional expense. And the government, having to set up as a merchant, and pay the costs of ware-houses, inspectors &c., must therefore exact more of the citizen who cannot pay cash money, or suffer loss itself.

At Smithfield we passed the evening in the agreeable society of some gentlemen of the neighborhood. The talk most of the time was of the great advantages which the Virginia state has over all other states in all the world, and the nation of Virginia over all other nations. It was insisted that the noble Virginians are the 'most polished nation' on God's earth, the gentlemen of France perhaps alone excepted. Sufficient proof was lacking for there was no one to contradict or interrupt the series of conclusions by which the affirmation was as naturally supported as that made by the little Frenchman: that he was the handsomest man under the moon. From the undeniable argument, that in fertility, size, navigable streams &c. Virginia is superior to the other American states, a number of propositions followed to substantiate the claim that in every respect Virginia is in advance of all other states, all other parts of the world. Who in America would dare count himself the equal of the noble Virginian? The poor New Englander who gains his bread in the sweat of his brow? or the Pensylvanian, who drudges like a negro and takes butter and cheese to market? or the North Carolina pitch-boiler? or the South Carolinian with his everlasting rice? Above all these stands the Gentleman of Virginia, for he alone has the finest horses, the finest dogs, the most negroes, the most land, speaks the best English, makes the most elegant bow, has the easy grace of a man of the world, and is a baron on his estates, which yield him everything and could yield still more! What country, what nation in Europe can boast of such advantages as those of Virginia?—Spain, perhaps, superstitious and slavish? or tyrannical Great Britain? or groaning Italy, under yoke and ban? or the soul-selling Germany? The remaining barbaric northern nations, with their frigid lands, (as little known as these) were all passed in review and reckoned out of the account. In evidence of an inborn higher morality it was brought out that during the last, seven years' war, when neither civil nor religious laws were adequately effective, no Virginian had been guilty of murder; for the shooting done by their army in the high grass or creeping about in the bush on their stomachs so as to surprise and kill British soldiers, alone, unarmed and off their guard, this they do not call murder. The great-mindedness of the Virginians was mentioned, but they did not speak of the cases, not rare, of mulattoes out of negresses by gentlemen, who then sell their own children to others as slaves. The hospitality of Virginia was boasted of, but it was admitted that for fear of the small-pox, or on the ground of other suspicions, their doors were oftentimes closed on strangers; and indeed their much-praised hospitality is by no means unrestricted, but is confined to acquaintances and those who are recommended. It seemed to be a contradiction when Mr. Whitefield, our host, (still defending the hospitality of his countrymen generally), confessed that travellers often had to go 20 miles and more to reach his house, after having knocked in vain at other doors. But it appeared still more contradictory when this self-exalting company began to describe the rude American Indians, giving as the plainest proof of their barbarick ideas that the proud Indians, belittling all other nations, compared the whites, with no exception of the noble Virginians, to white dogs' dung.

I have by no means put down all, and have added no word to what was really brought forward in this evening's conversation; but more would hardly have been needed to confirm the observation which has generally been made regarding the character of the Virginians. "The Virginians are a cheerful, hospitable, and on the whole a mannerly people; some of them have been taken to task for overmuch vanity and rodomontade, and this reproach is not altogether without reason," says Guthrie—and the same is to be found in Burnaby and other travellers, who all make use of the epithets, "careless," "loitering about," "sociable," "caroussing," "proud," "jealous," "boasting," "haughty," &c., when speaking of them. True it is, the gentlemen of property (and they are many) live on their estates careless and independent, if only they have paid their taxes and can balance outgo and income. If no impulse to political affairs rouses them from their inactivity, they spend their days in idleness or in such pleasures as a countrylife affords. For if they do perhaps comfortably oversee the sluggish work of their slaves, that cannot be called work or effort. They pass the greatest part of the summer on soft pallets, attended by one or several negroes to ward off the flies, light pipes, and proffer punch, sangry, toddy, or julap. But one should not blame them hastily but consider, that the majority of men everywhere, were there not other conditions and stimuli to prevent, would allow themselves the same indulgences, if tempted by a climate inviting to ease and offering an abundant support. Self-content, the Virginian avoids all efforts of mind and body involving anything beyond his pleasure. He reads, but he does not study so as to make a display of learning, possessing which, no title, rank, or lucrative office would compensate him for his midnight toils. A residence at lonesome country-seats is favorable to the muses, if these do indeed withdraw from the uproar of cities and distracting surroundings, if they luxuriate, philosophically calm, in the treasures of knowledge elsewhere assembled, and so bring about production. Such a life is unfavorable for kindling in young minds a love for science, enthusiasm, and the spirit of emulation. Thus the young people of Virginia follow after their fathers, relations, and neighbors, and grow up without much literary instruction, which they either have small occasion for or hold to be superfluous. A Virginia youth of 15 years is already such a man as he will be at twice that age. At 15, his father gives him a horse and a negro, with which he riots about the country, attends every fox-hunt, horse-race, and cock-fight, and does nothing else whatever; a wife is his next and only care. A gentleman of Petersburg told me that he would be sending his son to Edinburgh to make a doctor of him, since he now doubted whether he would ever marry and take over a plantation, his age being already 21 years. However, one would be very unreasonable if unwilling to admit that the Virginians on all occasions show clear and penetrating powers of mind; only it is a pity that a taste for the sciences is not yet so general among them as among their neighbors farther north. Also it must be granted that the Virginians have a rather superior look; they are for the most part well-built, slender, and of an active figure, their faces well-modelled, and one seldom sees among them crippled or deformed people, those excepted who have been maimed in the war or by accident.

Pennsylvania

Pennsylvania was in many ways the "All-American Colony" in the 18th century. What contribution did the Germans make to its success? What limitations did they have? Why was frontier life in Pennsylvania an apt symbol for the American experience? If you were advising immigrants, what stage of frontier development would you encourage them to join? Would you advise different groups differently?

Johann David Schoepf, Travels in the Confederation [1783-84], *translated by Alfred J. Morrison (Philadelphia, 1911), pp. 102-110.*

To be industrious and frugal, at least more so than the inhabitants of the provinces to the South, is the recognized and unmistakeable character of the Philadelphians and in great part of all those inhabiting Pensylvania. Without boasting, I daresay it is the fact that, in conjunction with the Quakers, the German-Pensylvania nation has had the largest share in the forming of this praiseworthy folk-character.

The German nation forms a considerable part, probably more than a third, of the state of Pensylvania. The Quakers, who at first gave the tone in political affairs, strove for that reason to win to their side the Germans, who were scattered about the country and commended themselves by their retired, industrious, and frugal manner of life. The Quakers have never gone very far from Philadelphia, individual members of the sect not liking to settle far from the rest, but preferring to draw together in little colonies. It was therefore a policy with them to be on good terms with the outlying inhabitants and they found it the easier to come by their ends through a good understanding with the Germans, since these together outnumbered any one of the other nationalities among the colonists, English, Scottish, Irish, and Swedish. The ancestors of these Germans came to America all in similar circumstances, as indeed many have come during and since the war. That is to say, they left the fatherland out of poverty or in the hope at least of finding better fortune, able to grow rich with less trouble. Many of them, indeed very many of them, have seen their desires fulfilled, although at first they were obliged to bind themselves out for a term of years so as to pay the cost of the voyage, if, as it often happened, they did not bring with them property in that amount. From very insignificant beginnings the most of them have come to good circumstances, and many have grown rich. For here the poor man who is industrious finds opportunities enough for gain, and there is no excuse for the slothful. Where a German settles, there commonly are seen industry and economy, more than with others, all things equal—his house is better-built and warmer, his land is better fenced, he has a better garden, and his stabling is especially superior; everything about his farm shows order and good management in all that concerns the care of the land. The Germans are known throughout America as an industrious people, but particularly those of them that come over from Europe, and in all the provinces it is desired that their numbers increase, they being everywhere valued as good citizens, and I daresay that Pensylvania is envied for the greater number of them settled there, since it is universally allowed that without them Pensylvania would not be what it is. The greater part of the German emigrants were originally of humble origin and meagre education, nor have they or their descendants greatly changed in their principles of action. On the whole they show little or no zeal to bring themselves up in any way except by small trade or handicrafts or farming. To use their gains for allowable pleasures, augmenting the agreeableness of life, this very few of them have learned to do, and others with a bad grace. The lucre is stuck away in old stockings or puncheon chests until opportunity offers to buy more land which is the chief object of their desires. In their houses, in the country expecially, they live thriftily, often badly. There is wanting among them the simple unaffected neatness of the English settlers, who make it a point, as far as they are able, to live seemly, in a well-furnished house, in every way as comports with the gentleman. The economy of the German farmer in Pensylvania is precisely the same as that customary in Germany—even when his next neighbor every day sets him a better example. A great four-cornered stove, a table in the corner with benches fastened to the wall, everything daubed with red, and above, a shelf with the universal German farmer's library: the Almanack, and Song-book, a small 'Garden of Paradise,' Habermann, and the Bible. It is in vain to look for other books, whereas in the cabins of the English there are not seldom seen, at the least, fragments of the *Spectator*, journals, magazines, or dictionaries. The highest delight of the German countryman in Pensylvania is—drink. He drives many miles to Philadelphia to market, sleeping in his wagon, living on the bread and cheese he takes along, but having made a good sale, he is certain to turn in at some grogshop on his way home—drinks in good spirits a glass of wine, drinks perhaps a second, and a third, recks no more and often leaves his entire wallet at the bung.

They give their children little education and have no fancy for seeing their sons parading in the pulpit or the Court-house. Not until this last war, (when several regiments were raised among the Pensylvania Germans), have any of them been seized with a passion to appear in a better light, by going about after posts of honor. Their conversation is neither interesting nor pleasing, and if so, it is because they have had a better bringing-up in Germany or, native-born, have become English quite, and thus they are no longer Germans and withdrawn by their own wish from intercourse with their people. In the towns there prevails an altogether different tone among the German families. They feel that no distinction of rank imposes any restraint on them, and behave as if farmers turned lords. I met at Philadelphia only one or two agreeable and intelligent women of German origin, but they spoke German very little and did not owe their breeding to their own people.

There is a striking contrast between the untaught class: German and English. In the same circumstances and with the same faculties the Englishman invariably shows more information; the German has the advantage in superstitions and prejudices and is less intelligent in political matters. However, the German country-people are extremely jealous of their liberties, and of their rights in the matter of sending members to the Assembly, although they find it difficult at times to get capable men. For it often happens that members chosen from among the German farmers and sent to the Assembly are not sufficiently equipped with the English language, and so make but dumb chair-fillers and never dare to give their opinions openly—and, when questions are to be decided, discreetly range themselves with the majority, sitting quietly by until they see which side has the numbers. Really they often know nothing of what the question is before the Assembly, because of the very slight tincture they have of the language. The story is that once an honorable German member heard that the business was whether to Move the House [vote], which he literally took to mean whether the house should be removed. He said nothing, but went out to the door and entirely around the large Assembly-house, then came back shaking his head and gave it as his opinion that it would be no easy matter. Just this year an old German countryman, no doubt an oracle among his tap-house friends, was elected to the Assembly from his district and sent to Philadelphia, where he was welcomed and congratulated. "Ey," said he, "I wish they had let me alone—what do I understand of all that chitter—I wish I was at home looking after my things." I have since seen members of that cut, in blue stockings and yellow-leather breeches, sleeping off boredom in the Assembly.

The lack as yet of numerous good schools and of capable teachers for the people; the further lack of educated and disinterested Germans who might by their example inspire imitation; the prevalent policy under the former regime of bestowing conspicuous office mainly on the English, European or American; and the extremely trifling advantages accruing to the merely educated German—such are the chief reasons, possibly, why the German nation in America has hitherto shown so little zeal in the item of self-advancement, preferring the gains from moderate labor and trade (certain and uncomplicated) to any difficult pestering with books.

The language which our German people make use of is a miserable, broken, fustian salmagundy of English and German, with respect both to the words and their syntax. Grown people come over from Germany forget their mother-tongue in part, while seeking in vain to learn the new speech, and those born in the country hardly ever learn their own language in an orderly way. The children of Germans, particularly in the towns, grow accustomed to English in the streets; their parents speak to them in one language and they answer in the other. The near kinship of the English and the German helps to make the confusion worse. If the necessary German word does not occur to the memory, the next best English one is at once substituted, and many English words are so currently used as to be taken for good German. In all legal and public business English is used solely. Thus English becomes indispensable to the Germans, and by contact and imitation grows so habitual that even among themselves they speak at times bad German, at times a worse English, for they have the advantage of people of other nationalities, in being masters of no one language. The only opportunity the Germans have of hearing a set discourse in their own language, (reading being out of the question) is at church. But even there, the minister preaching in German they talk among themselves their bastard jargon. There are a few isolated spots, for example in the mountains, where the people having less intercourse with the English understand nothing but German, but speak none the better. The purest German is heard in the Moravian colonies.—

And besides speaking scurvily, there is as bad writing and printing. Melchior Steiner's German establishment (formerly Christoph Sauer's)

prints a weekly German newspaper which contains numerous sorrow-
ful examples of the miserably deformed speech of our American
fellow-countrymen. This newspaper is chiefly made up of translations
from English sheets, but so stiffly done and so anglic as to be mawk-
ish. The two German ministers and Mr. Steiner himself oversee the
sheet. If I mistake not, Mr. Kunze alone receives 100 Pd. Pens. Current for his work. 'If we wrote in German,' say the compilers in
excuse, 'our American farmers would neither understand it nor read
it.'

It was hardly to be expected that the German language, even as
worst degenerated, could ever have gone to ruin and oblivion with
quite such rapidity—public worship, the Bible, and the estimable
almanack might, so it seems, transmit a language for many generations, even if fresh emigrants did not from time to time add new
strength. But probably the free and immediate intercourse now begun
between the mother-country and America will involve a betterment
of the language. Since America, in the item of German literature, is
30-40 years behind, it might possibly be a shrewd speculation to let
loose from their book-stall prisons all our unread and forgotten poets
and prosaists and transport them to America after the manner of the
English (at one time) and their jail-birds.

Jacques Brissot's life was a long tangle of passionate contention.
After a lower bourgeois upbringing and a disappointing attempt at
the law, he turned to the hazardous career of political journalism.
In 1784 he was unjustly imprisoned for two months, which radicalized
him into a revolutionary and a fanatical Americanist. The following
year, inspired by Crèvecoeur's Letters from an American Farmer *(see*
p. 00), he even thought of emigrating to America. Instead he turned
his pen to America's defense from the criticism—much of it inflated
by his zeal—of European observers. In 1786 he submitted the Marquis
de Chastellux's Travels *to a* Critical Examination *and two years later*
Filippo Mazzei's Historical and Political Researches on the United
States, *which had been written to clear up some of the misconceptions*
of America promoted by the romantic Crèvecoeur. An equally ardent
opponent of slavery, Brissot travelled to England in late 1787 to meet
abolitionist leaders and upon his return formed a Society of the
Friends of Blacks. In 1788 his dream was finally realized, and he

spent six months in America, commenting with his usual vigor and enthusiasm on everything he saw. The account of his travels was published in 1791, two years before he died on the guillotine for his revolutionary politics. The following passages on "Farming Life and the Settlement of the Frontier in Pennsylvania" are reprinted by permission of the publishers from New Travels in the United States of America, 1788, *by J. P.* Brissot de Warville, *translated by Mara Soceanu Vamos and Durand Echeverria, and edited by Durand Echeverria (Cambridge: Harvard University Press, 1964), pp. 264-273. Copyright 1964 by the President and Fellows of Harvard College.*

Until now, my friend, I have described to you only well-established farms and land in a state of full cultivation close to the cities. We now must go farther, plunge into the forests, and observe man in isolation, axe in hand, felling the revered and ancient oak of the Indians and replacing it with humble ears of wheat. We must follow this man, his progress, and his improvements; we must note how his cabin changes as it becomes the center for twenty other cabins which rise around it. An American farmer has communicated to me the principal elements of the following picture of rural life:

The first settler in the woods is generally a man who has outlived his credit or fortune in the cultivated parts of the state. His time for migrating is in the month of April. His first object is to build a small cabin of rough logs for himself and family. The floor of this cabin is of earth, the roof is of split logs; the light is received through the door and, in some instances, through a small window made of greased paper. A coarser building adjoining this cabin affords a shelter to a cow and pair of poor horses. The labor of erecting these buildings is succeeded by killing the trees on a few acres of ground near his cabin; since removing them entirely would require too great an effort, this is done by cutting a circle around the trees two or three feet from the ground. The ground around these trees is then plowed and Indian corn planted in it. The season for planting this grain is in May. It grows generally on new ground with but little cultivation, and yields in the month of October following from forty to fifty bushels per acre. After the first of September it affords a good deal of nourishment to his family, in its green or unripe state, in the form of what is called roasting ears. His family is fed during the winter by a small quantity of grain which he carries with him, and by fish and game. His cows and horses feed upon wild grass or the succulent twigs of the woods. For the first year he endures a great deal of distress from hunger, cold, and a variety of accidental causes, but he seldom complains or sinks under them. As he lives in the neighborhood of Indians, he soon acquires a strong tincture of their manners. His exertions, while they continue, are violent, but they are succeeded by long intervals of rest. His pleasures consist chiefly in fishing and hunting. He loves spiritous liquors, and he eats, drinks, and sleeps in dirt and rags in his little cabin.

In this situation he passes two or three years in idleness, independence, and an alternation of pleasure and labor. In proportion as population increases around him, he becomes uneasy and dissatisfied. Formerly his cattle ranged at large, but now his neighbors call upon him to confine them within fences to prevent their trespassing upon their fields of grain. Formerly he fed his family with wild animals, but these, which fly from the face of man, now cease to afford him an easy subsistence, and he is compelled to raise domestic animals for the support of his family. A growing society requires the establishment of government, taxes, and laws, and our settler revolts most against all these shackles. He cannot bear to surrender up a single natural right for all the benefits of government, and therefore he abandons his little settlement and seeks a retreat in the woods, where he again submits to all the toils which have been mentioned. Such is the attraction of independence that there are instances of many men who have broken ground on bare creation not less than four different times in this way, in different and more advanced parts of the state.

It has been remarked that the flight of this class of people is always increased by the preaching of the gospel. This will not surprise us when we consider how opposite its precepts are to their licentious manner of living. If our first settler was the owner of the spot of land which he began to cultivate, he sells it at a considerable profit to his successor; but if (as is oftener the case) he was a tenant to some rich landholder, he abandons it in debt; however, the small improvements he leaves behind him generally make it an object of immediate demand to a second species of settler.

This species of settler is generally a man of some property. He pays one third or one fourth part in cash for his plantation, which

consists of three or four hundred acres, and the rest in gales or install-
ments, as it is called here; that is, a certain sum yearly, without interest, till the whole is paid. The first object of this settler is to build
an addition to his cabin; this is done with hewed logs; and as sawmills
generally follow settlements, his floors are made of boards; his roof
is made of what are called clapboards, which are a kind of coarse
shingles split out of short oak logs. This house is divided by two
floors. His next object is to clear a little meadow ground and plant
an orchard of two or three hundred apple trees. His stable is likewise
enlarged, and, in the course of a year, he builds a large log barn,
the roof of which is commonly thatched with rye straw. He moreover
increases the quantity of his arable land, and instead of cultivating
Indian corn alone, he raises a quantity of wheat and rye. The latter
is cultivated chiefly for the purpose of being distilled into whiskey.
This species of settler by no means extracts all from the earth which
it is able and willing to give. His fields yield but a scanty increase,
owing to the ground not being sufficiently plowed and never being
manured. The hopes of the year are often blasted by his cattle breaking
through his half-made fences and destroying his grain. His horses perform but half the labor that might be expected from them if they were
better fed, and his cattle often die in the spring from the want of
provision and the delay of grass. His house as well as his farm bears
many marks of a weak tone of mind. His windows are unglazed, or,
if they have had glass in them, the ruins of it are supplied with old
hats or pillows. This species of settler is seldom a good member of
civil or religious society; with a large portion of an hereditary,
mechanical kind of religion, he neglects to contribute sufficiently
toward building a church or maintaining a regular administration of
the ordinances of the gospel. He is equally indisposed to support civil
government; with high ideas of liberty, he refuses to bear his proportion of the debt contracted by its establishment in this country. He
delights chiefly in company—sometimes drinks spirituous liquors to
excess—will spend a day or two in every week in attending political
meetings; and thus he contracts debts which compel him to sell his
plantation, generally in the course of a few years, to the third and
last species of settler.

This species of settler is commonly a man of property and good
character—sometimes he is the son of a wealthy farmer in one of
the interior and ancient counties of the state. His first object is to

convert every spot of ground over which he is able to draw water, into meadow. Where this cannot be done, he selects the most fertile spot on the farm and devotes it by manure to that purpose. His next object is to build a barn, which he prefers of stone. This building is in some instances 100 feet in front and 40 in depth. It is made very compact, so as to shut out the cold in winter; for these farmers find that their horses and cattle when kept warm do not require near as much food as when they are exposed to the cold. He uses economy, likewise, in the consumption of his wood. Hence he keeps himself warm in winter by means of stoves, which save an immense deal of labor to himself and his horses in cutting and hauling wood in cold and wet weather. His fences are everywhere repaired so as to secure his grain from his own and his neighbor's cattle. But further, he increases the number of the articles of his cultivation, and, instead of raising corn, wheat, and rye alone, he raises oats and buckwheat. Near his house he allots an acre or two of ground for a garden, in which he raises a large quantity of cabbage, potatoes, and turnips. Over the spring which supplies him with water he builds a milkhouse; he likewise adds to the number and improves the quality of his fruit trees. His sons work by his side all the year, and his wife and daughters forsake the spinning wheel to share with him in the toils of harvest. The last object of his industry is to build a dwelling house. This business is sometimes effected in the course of his life, but is oftener bequeathed to his son or the inheritor of his plantation; and hence there is a common saying among these farmers, "that a son should always begin where his father left off"; that is, he should begin his improvements by building a commodious dwelling house, suited to the improvements and value of the plantation. This dwelling house is generally built of stone—it is large, convenient, and filled with useful and substantial furniture. It sometimes adjoins the house of the second settler, but is frequently placed at a little distance from it. The horses and cattle of this species of settler bear marks in their strength, fat and fruitfulness of their being plentifully fed and carefully kept. His table abounds with a variety of the best provisions. His very kitchen flows with milk and honey—beer, cider, and wine are the usual drinks of his family. The greatest part of the clothing of his family is manufactured by his wife and daughters. In proportion as he increases in wealth, he values the protection of laws. Hence he punctually pays his taxes toward the support of government. Schools and churches likewise, as the means of promoting order and happiness in society, derive a due support from him.

Of this class of settlers are two thirds of the farmers of Pennsylvania. These are the men to whom Pennsylvania owes her ancient fame and consequence. If they possess less refinement than their southern neighbors who cultivate their lands with slaves, they possess more republican virtue. It was from the farms cultivated by these men that the American and French armies were chiefly fed with bread during the late revolution; and it was from the produce of these farms that those millions of dollars were obtained from Havana after the year 1780 which laid the foundation of the Bank of North America and which fed and clothed the American army till the peace of Paris.

This is a short account of the happiness of a Pennsylvania farmer. To this happiness this state invites men of every religion and country. It does not pretend to offer emigrants the pleasures of Arcadia or of the great cities of Europe. It is enough if affluence, independence, and happiness are ensured to patience, industry, and labor. The moderate price of land, the credit which arises from prudence, and the safety from the courts of law of every species of property render the blessings which I have described objects within the reach of every man.

From a review of the three different species of settlers, it appears that there are certain regular stages which mark the progress from the savage to civilized life. The first settler is nearly related to an Indian in his manners. In the second, the Indian manners are more diluted. It is in the third species of settlers only that we behold civilization completed. It is to the third species of settlers only that it is proper to apply the term of *farmers*.

While we record the vices of the first and second settlers, it is but just to mention their virtues likewise. Their mutual wants produce mutual dependence; hence they are kind and friendly to each other. Their solitary situation makes visitors agreeable to them; hence they are hospitable to strangers. Their want of money (for they raise but little more than is necessary to support their families) has made it necessary for them to associate for the purposes of building houses, cutting their grain, and the like; this they do in turns for each other, without any other pay than the pleasures which usually attend a country frolic. Perhaps what I have called virtues are rather *qualities*, arising from necessity and the peculiar state of society in which these people live. Virtue should in all cases be the offspring of principle.

I do not pretend to say that this mode of settling farms in Pennsylvania is universal. I have known some instances where the first settler has performed the improvements of the second and yielded to the third. I have known a few instances likewise of men of enterprising spirits who have settled in the wilderness and who, in the course of a single life, have advanced through all the intermediate stages of improvement that I have mentioned and produced all those conveniences which have been ascribed to the third species of settlers. There are instances likewise where the first settlement has been improved by the same family in hereditary succession till it has reached the third stage of cultivation. There are many spacious brick houses and highly cultivated farms in the neighboring counties of the city of Philadelphia which are possessed by the grandsons and great-grandsons of men who accompanied William Penn across the ocean.

I dare say this passion for migration which I have described will appear strange to you. To see men turn their backs upon the houses in which they drew their first breath—upon the church in which they were dedicated to God—upon the graves of their ancestors—upon the friends and companions of their youth—and upon all the pleasures of cultivated society, and exposing themselves to all the hardships and accidents of subduing the earth and thereby establishing settlements in a wilderness, must strike a European philosopher as a picture of human nature that runs counter to the usual habits and principles of action in man. But this passion, strange and new as it appears, is wisely calculated for the extension of population in America; and this it does, not only by promoting the increase of the human species in new settlements but in the old settlements likewise. There is a languor in population as soon as farmers multiply beyond the number of farms into which a township is divided. To remove this languor, which is kept up alike by the increase of the price and the division of farms, a migration of part of the community becomes absolutely necessary. And as this part of the community often consists of the idle and extravagant, who eat without working, their removal, by increasing the facility of subsistence to the frugal and industrious who remain behind, naturally increases the number of people, just as the cutting off the suckers of an apple tree increases the size of the tree and the quantity of fruit.

I have only to add upon this subject that the migrants from Pennsylvania always travel to the southward. The soil and climate of the western parts of Virginia, North and South Carolina, and Georgia afford a more easy support to lazy farmers than the stubborn but durable soil of Pennsylvania. Here, the ground requires deep and repeated plowing to render it fruitful; there, scratching the ground once or twice affords tolerable crops. In Pennsylvania the length and coldness of the winter make it necessary for the farmers to bestow a large share of their labor in providing for and feeding their cattle, but in the Southern states cattle find pasture during the greatest part of the winter in the fields or woods. For these reasons, the greatest part of the western counties of the states that have been mentioned are settled by original inhabitants of Pennsylvania. During the late war the militia of Orange county in North Carolina were enrolled, and their number amounted to 3,500, *every* man of whom had migrated from Pennsylvania. From this you will see that our state is the great outport of the United States for Europeans, and that, after performing the office of a sieve by detaining all those people who possess the stamina of industry and virtue, it allows a passage to the rest to those states which are accommodated to their habits of indolence and vice.

The unoccupied lands are sold by the state for about six guineas in certificates per hundred acres. But as most of the lands that are settled are procured from persons who had purchased them from the state, they are sold to the first settler for a much higher price. The quality of the soil—its vicinity to mills, courthouses, places of worship, and navigable water—the distance of land carriage to the seaports of Philadelphia or Baltimore—and the nature of the roads all influence the price of land to the first settler. The quantity of cleared land and the nature of the improvements, added to all the above circumstances, influence the price of farms to the second and third settlers. Hence the price of land to the first settler is from a quarter of a guinea to two guineas per acre; and the price of farms is from one guinea to ten guineas per acre to the second and third settlers, according as the land is varied by the before-mentioned circumstances. When the first settler is unable to purchase, he often takes a tract of land for seven years on a lease, and contracts, instead of paying a rent in cash, to clear fifty acres of land, to build a log cabin and a barn, and to plant an orchard on it. The tract, after the expiration of this lease, sells or rents for a considerable profit.

The third species of farmers I mentioned are generally Germans, who compose a large part of the population of Pennsylvania. The oldest German colony in the state is over one hundred years old. They are considered the most honest, the most industrious, and the most thrifty of farmers. They avoid contracting debts and of all Americans are the least given to the use of rum or spirits. As a result, they have large families, quite commonly of as many as twelve to fourteen children. Their only shortcoming is that they do not have the education of other Americans, an education which is necessary for participation in a democratic government. Nevertheless several men respected for their acquirements have arisen from among them—[David] Rittenhouse, [Adam] Kuhn, and [Frederick] Muhlenberg. There are proposals to bring the Germans into closer relationship with Americans and improve their education.

One of the reasons for emigrating to the back country of Pennsylvania is the hope of escaping land taxes, even though they are not very high, being less than a penny, or two *liards*, per pound of the appraised value, which is very low. Although this tax is modest, it still weighs heavily on large landowners and on the land jobbers. Rather than pay the accumulated taxes in arrears some allow their lands to be sold by the public treasury, and then repurchase them through a dummy at public auction for less than they would have had to pay in taxes.

You can well imagine that in a country where the government is so new and where men are so spread out and so intoxicated with liberty it is easy to evade taxes. Furthermore, there are many irregularities in the apportionment, so that you find landowners around Philadelphia who each year pay two per cent on the value of their land while others pay much less. The same is true of the poll tax, which is even more irregular because the regulations for its assessment are very vague. These faults can disappear only in time, but I did note with pleasure that bachelors pay higher taxes than married men.

Land in Pennsylvania varies in price, just as it varies in quality and in products. Around Lancaster there is some land which sells for four to twelve pounds an acre, but there is also a great deal which is stony and barren. Good virgin limestone land yields fifteen to twenty bushels of wheat an acre, and prime land, known as bottomlands, which has a thick layer of topsoil rich in vegetable matter, yields nine to ten quintals of hemp or forty to fifty bushels of corn per acre.

There is still much vacant land in the northern and western parts of the state, but I am told that there are very few good pieces that are not already taken. In remote woodlands you can see people searching for such land, which, if they find it, they take possession of by virtue of a warrant issued by the land office. This warrant orders the surveyor of the county where the land is located to survey it if it is vacant and to forward a copy of the survey so that the property may be registered. The buyer pays the state ten pounds in state debt certificates for 116 acres, which at the present rate of this paper amounts to two and a half pounds. Including the fee for the survey, the expense of the patent, etc., these lands cost approximately fifteen pence or sous an acre, and are then resold at a profit.

From this description of the different kinds of farming in this state, it is apparent that European families wishing to settle in America would not be well advised to attempt to clear land in the interior, or even to buy a farm that is only at the second stage of development.

1. A man who needs to think, to keep himself informed, and to exchange ideas with others would be unhappy isolated in a region where there are no means of communication and where all his neighbors are either far away or are lazy or ignorant.

2. It is almost impossible if you live so far inland to get articles from Europe, and if you do they are extremely expensive.

3. Above all it is impossible to accustom European women to such a way of life.

4. You are forced to build your own house and in the meantime you are uncomfortable waiting; you run risks, and your workers cheat you.

5. It is wrong to consider only the cost of the land without any buildings. Your calculations should be based rather on what it will cost after all building is finished. When you make the comparison you will see that you have much to gain in buying land with buildings.

Prudent Frenchmen who would like to become farmers in America ought to rent a farm in a settled region and spend a year there before they buy, getting to know their neighbors and learning how much income the land produces. Above all they must bring from Europe *families* of peasants used to farm work, for, I repeat, help is scarce here and very expensive. The usual price for indentured servants, whose time is bought for three years, is as follows: twelve to fifteen pounds for men over eighteen, and six to eight pounds for children between nine and twelve. I am not sure that the difference between the lower cost of an indentured servant and the higher wages paid to a free servant is not compensated by the better work done by the latter.

New York

In the 18th century most of New York was still in the possession of the Six Iroquois Nations. Consequently travellers saw very little of the colony save New York City and the frontier town of Albany huddled, like most of the white settlements, along the Hudson River. Of what value is Anne MacVicar Grant's recollection of frontier New York? What does it add to Burnaby's account? How could we test the accuracy of her account of the frontier character? According to Burnaby, what future did New York have?

In spite of its title, the Memoirs of an American Lady with Sketches of Manners and Scenes in America as They Existed Previous to the Revolution *was written by a foreign visitor. When Duncan MacVicar was sent to upstate New York with his Scottish regiment, his wife and three-year-old daughter Anne followed in 1758. After three years at Claverack, where precocious Anne was taught to read by her mother and to speak the Dutch language of her neighbors, and another at the frontier fort at Oswego on Lake Ontario, the MacVicars moved to Albany. There seven-year-old Anne became the boon companion of her sixty-one-year-old neighbor Madame Schuyler, the portly widow of the famous military leader Col. Philip Schuyler. From her "aunt's" generous conversation and her own observations, Anne gained her impressions of frontier New York that eventually found their way into her* Memoirs, *written some forty years after she and her family returned to Scotland in 1768. The excerpts which follow are taken from the second London edition of 1809, published anonymously, vol. I, pp. 34-37.*

The life of new settlers, in a situation like this, where the very foundations of society were to be laid, was a life of exigencies. Every individual took an interest in the general welfare, and contributed their respective shares of intelligence and sagacity to aid plans that embraced important objects relative to the common good. Every day called forth some new expedient, in which the *comfort* or *advantage* of the whole was implicated; for there were no degrees but those assigned to worth and intellect. This singular community seemed to have a common stock, not only of sufferings and enjoyments, but of information and ideas; some pre-eminence, in point of knowledge and abilities, there certainly was, yet those who possessed it seemed scarcely conscious of their superiority; the daily occasions which called forth the exertions of mind, sharpened sagacity, and strengthened character; avarice and vanity were there confined to very narrow limits; of money there was little; and dress was, though in some instances valuable, very plain, and not subject to the caprice of fashion. The wolves, the bears, and the enraged or intoxicated savages, that always hung threatening on their boundaries, made them more and more endeared to each other. In this calm infancy of society, the rigors of law slept, because the fury of turbulent passions had not awakened it. Fashion, that capricious tyrant over adult communities, had not erected her standard; that standard to which the looks, the language, the very opinions of her subjects must be adjusted. Yet no person appeared uncouth, or ill bred, because there was no accomplished standard of comparison. They viewed no superior with fear or envy; and treated no inferior with contempt or cruelty; servility and insolence were thus equally unknown; perhaps they were less solicitous either to please or to shine than the members of more polished societies; because, in the first place, they had no motive either to dazzle or deceive; and in the next, had they attempted it, they felt there was no assuming a character with success, where their native one was so well known. Their manners, if not elegant and polished, were at least easy and independent: the constant efforts necessary to extend their commercial and agricultural possessions, prevented indolence; and industry was the certain path to plenty. Surrounded on all sides by those whom the least instance of fraud, insolence, or grasping meanness, would have rendered irreconcileable enemies, they were at first obliged to "assume a virtue if they had it not;" and every circumstance that renders virtue habitual, may be accounted a happy one. I may be told that the virtues I describe were chiefly those of situation. I acknowledge it. It is no more to be expected that this equality, simplicity, and moderation, should continue in a more advanced state of society, than that the sublime tranquility, and dewy freshness, which adds a nameless charm to the face of nature, in the dawn of a summer morning, should continue all day. Before increased wealth and extended territory, these "wassel days" quickly receded; yet it is pleasing to indulge the remembrance of a spot, where peace and felicity, the result of a moral excellence, dwelt undisturbed, for, alas! hardly for, a century.

Rev. Andrew Burnaby, Travels through the Middle Settlements in North-America. In the Years 1759 and 1760 *(London, 1775), pp. 108-115.*

The province of New-York is situated between the 40th and 45th degree of north latitude, and about 75 degrees west longitude. It lies in a fine climate, and enjoys a very wholesome air. The soil of most parts of it is extremely good, particularly of Long Island: and it has the advantages of a fine harbour, and fine rivers. The bay has a communication with Newark bay, the Sound, Amboy river, and several others: it receives also Hudson's or North river, one of the largest in North-America, it being navigable for sloops as far as Albany, above 150 miles: whence, by the Mohock, and other rivers, running through the country of the Six [Iroquois] Nations, there is a communication, (excepting a few short carrying places,) with lake Ontario; and another with the river St. Laurence, through the lakes George, Champlain, and the river Sorel; so that this river seems to merit the greatest attention. These waters afford various kinds of fish, black-fish, seabass, sheeps-heads, rock-fish, lobsters, and several others, all excellent in their kind. The province in its cultivated state affords grain of all sorts, cattle, hogs, and great variety of English fruits, particularly the New-town pippin. It is divided into ten counties, and has some few towns, but none of any size, except Albany and Schenectady, the former of which is a very considerable place. The number of inhabitants amounts to near 100,000; 15 or 20,000 of which are supposed to be capable of bearing arms, and of serving in the militia; but I believe this number is exaggerated, as a considerable part of the 100,000 are Negroes, which are imported more frequently into this province than into Pensylvania. The people carry on an extensive trade, and there are said to be cleared out annually from New-

York, near [36,720] ton of shipping. They export chiefly grain, flour, pork, skins, furrs, pig-iron, lumber, and staves. Their manufactures, indeed, are not extensive, nor by any means to be compared with those of Pensylvania; they make a small quantity of cloth, some linen, hats, shoes, and other articles for wearing apparel. They make glass also, and wampum; refine sugars, which they import from the West Indies; and distil considerable quantities of rum. They also, as well as the Pensylvanians; till both were restrained by act of parliament, had erected several slitting mills, to make nails, &c. But this is now prohibited, and they are exceedingly dissatisfied at it. They have several other branches of manufactures, but, in general, so inconsiderable, that I shall not take notice of them: one thing it may be necessary to mention, I mean the article of ship-building, about which, in different parts of the province, they employ many hands.

The government of this colony is lodged in the hands of a governor appointed by the crown; a council consisting of twelve members, named by the same authority; and a house of twenty-seven representatives, elected by the people: four for the city and county of New York; two for the city and county of Albany; two for each of the other eight counties; one for the borough of West-Chester; one for the township of Schenectady; and one for each of the three manors of Renslaerwyck, Livingston, and Courtland. The legislative power is intirely lodged in their hands, each branch having a negative; except that, as in the other colonies, all laws must have the king's approbation, and not interfere with, or be repugnant to, the laws of Great Britain. . . .

The established religion is that of the church of England, there being six churches in this province with stipends (to the value of about 50 l. currency) annexed to each by law. The clergy are twelve in number, who, exclusive of what they acquire by the establishment abovementioned, or by contributions, receive, as missionaries from the Society for the Propagation of the Gospel, 50 l. sterling each. Besides the religion of the church of England, there is a variety of others: dissenters of all denominations, particularly presbyterians, abound in great numbers, and there are some few Roman Catholics.

Arts and sciences have made no greater progress here than in the other colonies; but as a subscription library has been lately opened, and every one seems zealous to promote learning, it may be hoped they will hereafter advance faster than they have done hitherto. The college is established upon the same plan as that in the Jerseys, except that this at New York professes the principles of the church of England. At present the state of it is far from being flourishing, or so good as might be wished. Its fund does not exceed 10,000 l. currency, and there is a great scarcity of professors. A commencement was held, nevertheless, this summer, and seven gentlemen took degrees. There are in it at this time about twenty-five students. The president, Dr. Johnson, is a very worthy and learned man, but rather too far advanced in life to have the direction of so young an institution. The late Dr. Bristow left to this college a fine library, of which they are in daily expectation.

The present state of this province is flourishing: it has an extensive trade to many parts of the world, particularly to the West Indies; and has acquired great riches by the commerce which it has carried on, under flags of truce, to Cape François, and Monte-Christo. The troops, by having made it the place of their general rendezvous, have also enriched it very much. However, it is burthened with taxes, and the present public debt amounts to more than 300,000 l. currency. The taxes are laid upon estates real and personal; and there are duties upon Negroes, and other importations. The provincial troops are about 2600 men. The difference of exchange between currency and bills, is from 70 to 80 per cent.

Rhode Island

From the moment of its founding, Rhode Island stood apart from its neighbors. What differences did travellers see there? Did they approve of them? Why would a contemporary want to live there? What kind of person would be likely to? Why was the *government* of Rhode Island said to influence its character when normally the *economy* or *climate* was said to be the dominant influence in other colonies? How objective do you think the Rev. Burnaby was in his description? What might explain his bias?

Rev. Andrew Burnaby, Travels through the Middle Settlements in North-America. In the Years 1759 and 1760 *(London, 1775), pp. 120-130.*

The province of Rhode Island is situated between the 41st and 42d degree of north latitude; and about 72 or 73 degrees west longitude; in the most healthy climate of North-America. The winters are severe, though not equally so with those of the other provinces; but the summers are delightful, especially in the island; the violent and excessive heats, which America is in general subject to, being allayed by the cool and temperate breezes that come from the sea. The soil is upon the whole tolerably good, though rather too stony; its natural produce is maize or Indian corn, with a variety of shrubs and trees. It produces in particular the button-tree; the spruce-pine, of the young twigs of which is made excellent beer; and the pseudo-acacia, or locust-tree; but none of those fine flowering trees, which are such an ornament to the woods in Carolina and Virginia. It enjoys many advantages, has several large rivers, and one of the finest harbours in the world. Fish are in the greatest plenty and perfection, particularly the tataag or blackfish, lobsters, and sea-bass. In its cultivated state, it produces very little, except sheep and horned cattle; the whole province being laid out into pasture or grazing ground. The horses are bony and strong, and the oxen much the largest in America; several of them weighing from 16 to 1800 weight. The butter and cheese are excellent.

The province of Rhode Island is divided into counties and townships; of the former there are four or five, but they are exceedingly small; of the latter between twenty and thirty; the towns themselves are inconsiderable villages: however, they send members to the assembly, in the whole about seventy. The number of inhabitants, with Negroes, and Indians, of which in this province there are several hundreds, amounts to about 35,000. As the province affords but few commodities for exportation; horses, provisions, and an inconsiderable quantity of grain, with spermaceti candles, being the chief articles; they are obliged to Connecticut, and the neighbouring colonies, for most of their traffic; and by their means carry on an extensive trade. Their mode of commerce is this; they trade to Great Britain, Holland, Africa, the West Indies, and the neighbouring colonies; from each of which places they import the following articles; from Great Britain, dry goods; from Holland, money; from Africa, slaves; from the West Indies, sugars, coffee, and molasses; and from the neighbouring colonies, lumber and provisions: and with what they purchase in one place they make their returns in another. Thus with the money they get in Holland, they pay their merchants in London; the sugars they procure in the West Indies, they carry to Holland; the slaves they fetch from Africa they send to the West Indies, together with lumber and provisions, which they get from the neighbouring colonies: the rum that they distil they export to Africa; and with the dry goods, which they purchase in London, they traffick in the neighbouring colonies. By this kind of circular commerce they subsist and grow rich. They have besides these some other inconsiderable branches of trade, but nothing worth mentioning. They have very few manufactures; they distil rum and make spermaceti candles; but in the article of dry goods, they are far behind the people of New York and Pensylvania.

The government of this province is intirely democratical; every officer, except the collector of the customs, being appointed, I believe, either immediately by the people, or by the general assembly. The people chuse annually a governor, lieutenant-governor, and ten assistants, which constitute an upper-house. The representatives, or lower-house, are elected every half year. These jointly have the appointment of all other public officers, (except the recorder, treasurer, and attorney-general, which are appointed likewise annually by the people,) both military and civil; are invested with the powers of legislation, of regulating the militia, and of performing all other acts of government. The governor has no negative, but votes with the assistants, and in case of an equality has a casting voice. The assembly, or two houses united, are obliged to sit immediately after each election; at Newport in the summer, and in the winter alternately at Providence and South-Kingston in Narraganset: they adjourn themselves, but may be called together, notwithstanding such adjournment, upon any urgent occasion by the governor. No assistant, or representative is allowed any salary or pay for his attendance or service.

There is no established form of religion here; but church of England men, independents, quakers, ana-baptists, Moravians, Jews, and all other sects whatsoever, have liberty to exercise their several professions. The Society for the Propagation of the Gospel sends only four missionaries.

Arts and sciences are almost unknown, except to some few individuals; and there are no public seminaries of learning; nor do the Rhode Islanders in general seem to regret the want of them. The institution of a library society, which has lately taken place, may possibly in time produce a change in these matters.

The character of the Rhode-Islanders is by no means engaging, or amiable: a circumstance principally owing to their form of government. Their men in power, from the highest to the lowest, are dependent upon the people, and frequently act without that strict regard to probity and honour, which ever ought invariably to influence and direct mankind. The private people are cunning, deceitful, and selfish: they live almost intirely by unfair and illicit trading. Their magistrates are partial and corrupt: and it is folly to expect justice in their courts of judicature; for he, who has the greatest influence, is generally found to have the fairest cause. Were the governor to interpose his authority, were he to refuse to grant flags of truce, or not to wink at abuses; he would at the expiration of the year be excluded from his office, the only thing perhaps which he has to subsist upon. Were the judges to act with impartiality, and to decide a cause to the prejudice or disadvantage of any great or popular leader, they would probably never be re-elected; indeed, they are incapable in general of determining the merits of a suit, for they are exceedingly illiterate, and, where they have nothing to make them partial, are managed almost intirely by the lawyers. In short, to give an idea of the wretched state of this colony, it has happened more than once, that a person has had sufficient influence to procure a fresh emission of paper-money, solely to defraud his creditors: for having perhaps borrowed a considerable sum of money, when the difference of exchange has been 1200 per cent. he has afterward, under sanction of the law, repaid only the same nominal sum in new currency, when the difference has amounted perhaps to 2500 per cent.—Such alas! is the situation and character of this colony. It is needless, after this, to observe that it is in a very declining state; for it is impossible that it should prosper under such abuses. Its West Indian trade has diminished; owing indeed, in some measure, to the other colonies having entered more largely into this lucrative branch of commerce: it has lost during the war, by the enemy, above 150 vessels: its own privateers, and it has generally had a great many, have had very ill success: having kept up a regiment of provincial troops, it has also been loaded with taxes, and many of the people have been oppressed by the mode of collecting them: for, the assembly having determined the quota of each township, the inhabitants have been assessed by the town-council, consisting of the assistants residing there, the justices of the town, and a few freeholders elected annually by the freemen; and these have been generally partial in their assessments, as must necessarily happen under a combination of such circumstances.—After having said so much to the disadvantage of this colony, I should be guilty of injustice and ingratitude, were I not to declare that there are many worthy gentlemen in it, who see the misfortunes of their country, and lament them; who are sensible that they arise from the wretched nature of the government, and wish to have it altered; who are courteous and polite; kind and hospitable to strangers; and capable of great acts of generosity and goodness, as I myself experienced during a very severe fit of illness which I lay under at this place.

Massachusetts

The land of the Puritans seldom drew favorable notice from 18th-century visitors. How had the Massachusetts character changed since the 17th century? What vestiges of the old Puritanism remained? Had anything taken the place of Puritanism as a driving force in the society? What effects did this have upon society and the economy?

Rev. Andrew Burnaby, Travels through the Middle Settlements in North-America. In the Years 1759 and 1760 *(London, 1775), pp. 135-144, 146-147.*

The situation of the province of Massachusets-Bay, including the district of Plymouth, is between the 41st and 43rd degree of north latitude, and about 72 degrees west longitude. The climate, soil, natural produce, and improved state of it, are much the same as of Rhode Island. It is divided into counties, and townships; and each township, if it contains forty freeholders, has a right to send a member to the assembly: the present number of representatives amounts to between 130 and 140; of which Boston sends four.

The number of souls in this province is supposed to amount to 200,000; and 40,000 of them to be capable of bearing arms. They carry on a considerable traffick, chiefly in the manner of the Rhode-Islanders; but have some material articles for exportation, which the Rhode-Islanders have not, except in a very trifling degree: these are salt fish, and vessels. Of the latter they build annually a great number, and send them, laden with cargoes of the former, to Great Britain, where they sell them. They clear out from Boston, Salem, Marblehead, and the different ports in this province, yearly, about [70,284] ton of shipping. Exclusive of these articles, their manufactures are not large; those of spirits, fish-oil, and iron, are, I believe, the most considerable. They fabricate beaver-hats, which they sell for a moidore a piece; and some years ago they erected a manufactory, with a design to encourage the Irish settlers to make linens; but at the breaking out of the war the price of labour was inhanced so much, that it was impossible to carry it on. Like the rest of the colonies they also endeavour to make woollens, but have not yet been able to bring them to any degree of perfection; indeed it is an article in which I think they will not easily succeed; for the American wool is not only coarse, but, in comparison of the English, exceedingly short. Upon the best inquiry I could make, I was not able to discover that any one had ever seen a staple of American wool longer than seven inches; whereas in the counties of Lincoln and Leicester, they are frequently twenty-two inches long. In the southern colonies, at least in those parts where I travelled, there is scarcely any herbage; and whether it is owing to this, or to the excessive heats, I am ignorant, the wool is short and hairy. The northern colonies have indeed greater plenty of herbage, but are for some months covered with snow; and without a degree of attention and care in housing the sheep, and guarding them against accidents, and wild beasts, which would not easily be compensated, it would be very difficult to increase their numbers to any great amount. The Americans seem conscious of this fact, and, notwithstanding a very severe prohibition, contrive to procure from England, every year, a considerable number of rams, in order to improve and multiply the breed. What the lands beyond the Alleghenny and upon the banks of the Ohio may be, I do not know; they are said to be very rich: but the climate I believe is not less severe; and I think, upon collating different accounts, that the severity of heat and cold is not much abated by cultivation. The air becomes dryer and more wholesome, in proportion as the woods are cut down, and the ground is cleared and cultivated; but the cold is not less piercing, nor the snow less frequent. I think therefore upon the whole, that America, though it may with particular care and attention, produce small quantities of tolerably good wool, will yet never be able to produce it in such plenty and of such a quality as to serve for the necessary consumption of its inhabitants.

The government of this province is lodged in the hands of a governor or lieutenant-governor, appointed by the king; a council of twenty-eight persons, chosen annually, with the governor's approbation, by the general assembly; and a house of representatives annually elected by the freeholders. The governor commissions all the militia, and other military officers; and, with consent of the council, also nominates and appoints all civil officers, except those that are concerned in the revenue. He calls and adjourns the assembly, and has in every respect a very extensive authority. His salary, with perquisites, amounts to about 1300 l. sterling per year. The governor and council together have the probate of wills, and the power of granting administrations and divorces. . . .

The established religion here, as in all the other provinces of New England, is that of the congregationalists; a religion, different in some trifling articles, though none very material, from the presbyterian. There are, besides these however, great numbers of people of different persuasions, particularly of the religion of the church of England; which seems to gain ground, and to become more fashionable every day. A church has been lately erected at Cambridge, within sight of the college; which has greatly alarmed the congregationalists, who consider it as the most fatal stroke, that could possibly have been levelled at their religion. The building is elegant, and the minister of it (the reverend Mr. Apthorpe,) is a very amiable young man, of shining parts, great learning, and pure and engaging manners.

Arts and Sciences seem to have made a greater progress here, than in any other part of America. Harvard college has been founded above a hundred years; and although it is not upon a perfect plan, yet it has produced a very good effect. The arts are undeniably forwarder in Massachusets-Bay, than either in Pennsylvania or New York. The public buildings are more elegant; and there is a more general turn for music, painting, and the belles lettres.

The character of the inhabitants of this province is much improved, in comparison of what it was: but puritanism and a spirit of persecution is not yet totally extinguished. The gentry of both sexes are hospitable, and good-natured; there is an air of civility in their behaviour, but it is constrained by formality and preciseness. Even the women, though easiness of carriage is peculiarly characteristic of their nature, appear here with more stiffness and reserve than in the other colonies. They are formed with symmetry, are handsome, and have fair and delicate complexions; but are said universally, and even proverbially, to have very indifferent teeth.

The lower class of the people are more in the extreme of this character; and, which is constantly mentioned as singularly peculiar to them, are impertinently curious and inquisitive. I was told of a gentleman of Philadelphia, who, in travelling through the provinces of New England, having met with many impertinencies, from this extraordinary turn of character, at length fell upon an expedient almost as extraordinary, to get rid of them. He had observed, when he went into an ordinary [inn], that every individual of the family had a question or two to propose to him, relative to his history; and that, till each was satisfied, and they had conferred and compared together their information, there was no possibility of procuring any refreshment. He, therefore, the moment he went into any of these places, inquired for the master, the mistress, the sons, the daughters, the men-servants and the maid-servants; and having assembled them all together, he began in this manner. "Worthy people, I am B. F. of Philadelphia, by trade a —, and a bachelor; I have some relations at Boston, to whom I am going to make a visit: my stay will be short, and I shall then return and follow my business, as a prudent man ought to do. This is all I know of myself, and all I can possibly inform you of; I beg therefore that you will have pity upon me and my horse, and give us both some refreshment."

The province of Massachusets-Bay has been for some years past, I believe, rather on the decline. Its inhabitants have lost several branches of trade, which they are not likely to recover again. They formerly supplied, not only Connecticut, but other parts of the continent, with dry goods, and received specie in return: but since the introduction of paper-currency they have been deprived of great part of this commerce. Their ship-trade is considerably decreased, owing to their not having been so careful in the construction of vessels as formerly: their fisheries too have not been equally successful: they have had also a considerable number of provincial troops in pay during the course of the present war, and have been burthened with heavy taxes. These have been laid upon estates, real and personal. Some merchants in Boston, I have been credibly informed, have paid near

400 1. sterling annually.—Assessments are made by particular officers, who, with the select men, constables, overseers, and several others, are elected annually by the freemen, for the direction and management of each particular township.

There is less paper-money in this colony, than in any other of America: the current coin is chiefly gold and silver: and Boston is the only place, I believe, where there is a mint to coin money.

I was told of a very impolitic law in force in this province, which forbids any master, or commander of a vessel to bring strangers into the colony, without giving security that they shall not become chargeable to it.

Upon the whole, however, notwithstanding what has been said, Massachusets-Bay is a rich, populous, and well-cultivated province.—

II. CITY LIFE

Charleston

In a southern society of plantations and few towns, why had
Charleston become one of America's great cities? What were its social
and economic advantages? its disadvantages and dangers? How did
the life of the city accommodate itself to the dominant plantation system outside? What role did religion play in forming the city's character?

The New Democracy in America: Travels of Francisco de Miranda
in the United States, 1783-84, *translated by Judson P. Wood and
edited by John S. Ezall (Norman, Oklahoma, 1963), pp. 25-26.
Copyright 1963 by the University of Oklahoma Press.*

The city is quite large and contains very good houses of brick and
wood, the number of which is calculated at fifteen hundred, although
a large section is in ruins as the result of a fire which occurred three
or four years ago. Among the burnt buildings is the House of Assembly, the ruins of which reveal that it was one of the best and most
spacious. It is incredible how many times history tells us the city has
suffered from this voracious element. The location is pleasant and very
advantageous for commerce, as it is exactly at the flowing together
of the rivers Ashley and Cooper, both of which are spacious and
navigable; the ocean breezes refresh it and make its habitation more
bearable in the summer, when the heat and diabolic multitude of mosquitoes exceed all exaggeration. The most remarkable buildings are

the House of Assembly, the New and Old churches, and the Exchange; their architecture is simple and passably well designed. The steeple of the New Church is quite high and can be seen at a considerable distance, not only from the sea but also from the interior, since the surrounding land is extremely low and flat. The streets are straight and spacious, with brick pavements on both sides for the comfort of those who go on foot; the most conspicuous of these are Meeting, Broad, and Church streets. Near the House of Assembly is the statue of [British Prime Minister William] Pitt, standing on a marble pedestal with an iron fence around it. The execution is of average merit, the size natural, and the costume Roman (a strange idea). It is in the attitude of orating, the right hand resting on a book on which one reads "Stamp Act," and this, one infers, was the motive for the erection of the monument in honor of this great man. He lacks, at the present time, part of his right arm, taken away by a cannon ball during the last siege.

There is no theater or spectacle whatsoever. The only place women are seen in large numbers is in church on Sundays, and so it happens that the congregation is always large and very brilliant. The interiors of the churches are plain and very clean, which makes them more pleasant and adds luster to the gathering. The hours of service are ten-thirty in the morning and four o'clock in the afternoon. There is no lack of congregation at the latter hour, as the object of youth is not only the zeal for religion but also other advantages which only the church provides here, there being no walks or public gathering places. Proof of this is that the old people and heads of families scarcely attend at all, and only accidentally is one of these seen in church!

Johann David Schoepf, Travels in the Confederation [1783-84], *translated by Alfred J. Morrison (Philadelpha, 1911), pp. 164-169.*

Charleston is one of the finest of American cities; Philadelphia excepted, it is inferior to none, and I know not whether, from its vastly more cheerful and pleasing plan, it may not deserve first place, even if it is not the equal of Philadelphia in size and population. The city contains a number of tasteful and elegant buildings, which however are mostly of timber. This circumstance is explained in part by the natural scarceness of stone in this region; but there seems no reason why bricks might not be used here for building quite as well as at Philadelphia and New York, since nowhere are better materials to be had, or in greater plenty. The number of the houses is estimated to be about 1500. In the plan of the houses especial regard is had to airy and cool rooms. Most of the houses have spacious yards and gardens, and the kitchen is always placed in a separate building, the custom throughout the southern provinces, to avoid the heat and the danger of fire. The chief streets are wide, straight, and cross at right angles; but they are not paved, and hence give rise to a double inconvenience, in rainy and in dusty weather. The greatest length of the city is little short of a mile.

Its situation is 32° 40'n. latitude, and 83° 40'w. longitude, on a point of land between the Cowper and the Ashley rivers, the spot where Captain Sayle landed the first planters in the year 1669, settling there with them because, for fear of the savages, they dared not strike farther inland. A plan for the building of a magnificent city was sketched and sent over by the Lords Proprietors, to whom King Charles the Second had assigned the province of Carolina, but so far this has not been fully carried out.

Both the rivers named are navigable, but for trading-vessels only the Cowper as much as 20 miles above the city. Merchant-men find commodious and safe anchorage between the city and a little island in the Cowper river. This part of the river is called the Bay, and along this side of the city the shore is furnished with excellent wharves of cabbage-trees. The entrance to the harbor is made more difficult by a bar which ships of more than 200 tons cannot pass without lightening cargo. The advantageous site of the city has not been neglected in its fortification; towards the land side as well as at the south-western point there have long been regular works of masonry, which during the war were considerably increased and improved both by the Americans and the English, but are now again fallen to decay. On the landside the city has but one approach, protected by a gate with several walled defences of oyster-shells and lime. Among the public buildings of the city the handsome State-house, the Main-guard opposite, the Bourse; and the two churches, St. Philipp and St. Michael, are conspicuous, all designed after good plans. Two lines of framed barracks, for the one-time English garrisons are not at present made use of. The tower of St. Michael's church is 190 feet high, and has long served as landmark for incoming ships. It was formerly painted white; the American Commodore Whipple hit upon the idea of painting it black on the side towards the sea whence it can be seen very far, so as to make it invisible to British ships, whose visits were dreaded. But the result so far from being that desired was directly the opposite, for in clear weather the black side is far more distinct, and on gloomy, cloudy days it is seen quite as far and appears, if anything, larger than before.

There is a German Lutheran congregation here, with its own church and minister, but it is not very numerous.

The name of the city, since the last peace, has been changed from Charlestown to Charleston, and at the same time its rank, that of a Town until then, made that of a City. By the English rule those towns only are called cities which have a Bishop and are incorporated, or those which exercise their own granted privileges under the presidency of a Mayor and other officers and use a special city-seal. A bishop Charleston has not, but the dignity of a Mayor, called Superintendent, has been given it under this elevation of rank conferred by the Provincial Assembly.

The number of the inhabitants was formerly reckoned at 10-12000, of which half or probably two thirds were blacks, but at present it is not possible to say exactly what the number is, since no precise baptismal or death lists are kept. The population, besides, has considerably diminished both by voluntary emigration and by the banishment of many of the most estimable citizens of the royalist party. But certainly the number of the white inhabitants is greatly less than that of the blacks, browns, and yellows to be seen here of all shades. In winter the city is less active than in summer. About Christmas most of the families retire to their country-seats, and spend there the greater part of what remains of the winter. One reason for this is that at that festival season the negroes are allowed somewhat more liberty, and fearing they might use it in a bad way, the proprietors deem it well to be present themselves and at the same time look after the progress of their plantation affairs. With the coming of the sweltry summer days all that can hasten back to town. The nearness of the sea and the cooler winds blowing thence make summer in the city pleasanter and wholesomer than farther inland among woods and swamps.

The manners of the inhabitants of Charleston are as different from those of the other North American cities as are the products of their soil. The profitable rice and indigo plantations are abundant sources of wealth for many considerable families, who therefore give themselves to the enjoyment of every pleasure and convenience to which their warmer climate and better circumstances invite them. Throughout, there prevails here a finer manner of life, and on the whole there are more evidences of courtesy than in the northern cities. I had already been told this at Philadelphia, and I found it to be the case; just as in general on the way hither, the farther I travelled from Pennsylvania towards the southern country, there were to be observed somewhat more pleasing manners among the people, at least there was absent the unbearable curiosity of the common sort, which in the more northern regions extends to shamelessness and exhausts all patience. There is courtesy here, without punctiliousness, stiffness, or formality. It has long been nothing extraordinary for the richer inhabitants to send their children of both sexes to Europe for their education. The effect of this on manners must be all the greater and more general since there were neither domestic circumstances to stand in the way nor particular religious principles, as among the Presbyterians of New England or the Quakers of Pensylvania, to check the enjoyment of good-living. So luxury in Carolina has made the greatest advance, and their manner of life, dress, equipages, furniture, everything denotes a higher degree of taste and love of show, and less frugality than in the northern provinces. They had their own playhouse, in which itinerant companies from time to time entertained the public, but it was burned some time ago. A like misfortune overtook an elegant dancinghall. A French dancing master was the promoter of this building; the necessary amount was advanced him by the first minister of the town who not only had no hesitation in a matter of furthering the pleasure of his parishioners, but afterwards when the property fell to him, the Frenchman being unable to return the loan, made no scruple of receiving the rent; whereas in the New England states the bare thought of such a thing would have disgraced any minister. Pleasures of every kind are known, loved, and enjoyed here. There are publick concerts, at this time mainly under the direction of German and English musicians left behind by the army, for as yet few of the natives care greatly for music or understand it. A liking for exclusive private societies, Clubs so-called, prevails here very generally. There are as many as 20 different Clubs, and most of the residents are members of more than one. These social unions give themselves strange names at times, as: Mount Sion Society, Hell-fire Club, Marine Anti-Britannic Society, Smoking Society, and the like. All the games usual in England are in vogue here. As regards dress, the English taste is closely followed; also the clergy and civil officers wear the garb customary in England. The ladies bestow much attention upon their dress, and spare no cost to obtain the newest modes from Europe. Milliners and hair-dressers do well here and grow rich.

Charleston, at sundry times and by opposite elements, has been threatened with complete destruction. A great part of the town has several times gone up in fire, and with a loss of considerable stores of merchants' wares. Again, violent and lasting hurricanes have seemed as if certain to destroy the place. The low situation of the town exposes it, if north-east storms hold somewhat long, to the danger of furious overflow, these winds checking the northwestern course of the gulf-stream flowing along the coast from the Mexican gulf, and driving it and other water of the ocean against the flat coast of Carolina. From the same causes also the two rivers flowing by the town are checked, and in a very brief space the water often rises to an incredible height.

Philadelphia

"The Cradle of Liberty" and "The City of Brotherly Love"—how was Philadelphia's dual character formed in the 18th century? Did it deserve both titles equally? Why did many travellers consider it the First City in America? What geographical, social, and cultural advantages did it enjoy? Was its economy prospering? for all classes? What were the signs of prosperity? Was it a healthy place to live? a safe place? a convenient place? Was it a town planned for the future as well as the present? What best accounts for its success as a city?

One of the most perceptive observers of 18th-century America was Pehr Kalm, a Swedish scientist, man of letters, and minister. Born in 1716, Kalm studied botany at Uppsala University under Carl von Linné, the famous Linnaeus, whom he accompanied to Russia for field work in 1744. The following year he was honored for his work with membership in the Swedish Academy of Sciences. In 1747 he was appointed to the first chair of Natural History and Economy (practical husbandry and agriculture) at Abo Academy in Finland (which then belonged to Sweden), but he requested leave almost immediately to tour the American colonies and Canada on behalf of the Swedish Academy. His assignment was to expand the number of useful plants and trees in Sweden by locating adaptable species in the comparable environment of North America. The literary result of his four-year expedition was published in three volumes as En Resa til Norra America *(Stockholm, 1753-61), followed by English, French, Dutch, and German translations in the 18th century. The following observations are taken from* The America of 1750. Peter Kalm's Travels in North America. The English Version of 1770, *revised and edited by Adolph B. Benson (New York: Wilson-Erickson, 1937), pp. 18-20, 25-34, 50-51, 94-95.*

Philadelphia, the capital of Pennsylvania, a province which forms a part of what formerly was called New Sweden, is one of the principal towns in North America and next to Boston the greatest. It is situated almost in the center of the English colonies and its latitude is thirty-nine degrees and fifty minutes, while its west longitude from London is near seventy-five degrees.

This town was built in the year 1683, or as others say in 1682, by the well-known Quaker William Penn, who got this whole province by a grant from Charles the Second, King of England, after Sweden had given up its claims to it. According to Penn's plan the town was to have been built upon a piece of land which is formed by the union of the rivers Delaware and Schuylkill, in a quadrangular form, two English miles long and one broad. The eastern side would therefore have been bounded by the Delaware, and the western by the Schuylkill. They had actually begun to build houses on both these rivers; for eight capital streets, each two English miles long, and sixteen lesser streets (or lanes) across them, each one mile in length, were marked out with a considerable width, and in straight lines. The place was at that time almost entirely a wilderness covered with thick forests, and belonged to three Swedish brothers called Svenssöner (Svensons, sons of Sven or Swen) who had settled on it. They reluctantly left the place, the location of which was very advantageous. But at last they were persuaded to leave it by Penn, who gave them, a few

English miles from there, twice the space of the land they inhabited. However, Penn himself and his descendants after him have, by repeated mensurations, considerably lessened the ground belonging to the Swedes, under pretence that they had taken more than they should.

But settlers could not be induced to come in sufficient numbers to fill a place of such size. The plan therefore about the river Schuylkill was laid aside till more favorable circumstances should occur, and the houses were built only along the Delaware. This river flows along the eastern side of the town, is of great advantage to its trade, and gives a fine prospect. The houses which had already been built upon the Schuylkill were moved hither by degrees. This town accordingly lies in a very pleasant country, from north to south along the river. It measures somewhat more than an English mile in length, and its breadth in some places is half a mile or more. The ground is flat and consists of sand mixed with a little clay. Experience has shown that the climate of this place is very healthy.

The streets are regular, pretty, and most of them fifty feet, English measure, broad. Arch Street measures sixty-six feet in breadth, and Market Street, the principal thoroughfare, where the market is kept, near a hundred. The streets which run longitudinally or from north to south are seven in number, exclusive of a small one which runs along the river to the south of the market and is called Water Street. The lanes which go across and were intended to reach from the Delaware to the Schuylkill, number eight. They do not run exactly from east to west, but deviate a little from that direction. All the streets, except two which are nearest to the river, run in a straight line and make right angles at the intersections. Some are paved, others are not, and it seems less necessary since the ground is sandy and therefore soon absorbs the wet. But in most of the streets is a pavement of flags, a fathom or more broad, laid before the houses, and four-foot posts put on the outside three or four fathoms apart. Those who walk on foot use the flat stones, but riders and teams use the middle of the street. The above-mentioned posts prevent horses and wagons from injuring the pedestrians inside the posts, and are there secure from careless teamsters and the dirt which is thrown up by horses and carts. Under the roofs are gutters which are carefully connected with pipes, and by this means, those who walk under them when it rains or when the snow melts need not fear being wetted by the water from the roofs.

The houses make a good appearance, are frequently several stories high and built either of bricks or of stone; but the former are more commonly used, since they are made near the town and are of good quality. The stone which has been employed in the building of houses is a mixture of a loose and quite small-grained limestone and of a black or grey glimmer, running in undulated veins which run scattered between the bendings of other veins and are of a gray color excepting here and there some single grains of sand of a paler hue. The glimmer forms the greatest part of the stone, but the mixture is sometimes of another kind, as I shall relate below under the date of the eleventh of October. This stone is now obtained in great quantities in the country, is easily cut, and has the good quality of not attracting moisture in a wet season. Very good lime is burnt everywhere hereabouts for masonry.

The houses are covered with shingles. The wood for this purpose is taken from the *Cupressus thyoides* L. or a tree which Swedes here call the "white juniper tree", and the English "the white cedar". Swamps and morasses formerly were full of them, but at present these trees are for the greatest part cut down and no attempt has as yet been made to plant new ones. The wood is very light, rots less than any other in this country, and for that reason is exceedingly good for roofs, for it is not too heavy for the walls and will last forty or fifty years. But many people already begin to fear that these roofs will in time be looked upon as having been very detrimental to the city. For being so very light, most people who have built their houses of stone or bricks have been led to make their walls extremely thin. At present this kind of wood is almost entirely gone. Whenever, therefore, in process of time these roofs decay, the people will be obliged to have recourse to the heavier materials of tiles or the like, which the walls will not be strong enough to bear. The roof will therefore require more support or the people be obliged to pull down the walls and build new ones, or to take other steps for securing them. Several people have already in late years begun to make roofs of tiles. . . .

I now proceed to mention the other public buildings in Philadelphia.

The *Town Hall,* or the place where the assemblies are held, is situated in the western part of the town. It is a fine, large building having a tower with a bell, and is the greatest ornament in the town. The deputies of each province commonly meet in it every October, or even more frequently if circumstances require it, in order to consider the welfare of the country and to hold their parliament or diets in miniature. There they revise the old laws and make new ones.

On one side of this building stands the *Library* which was first begun in the year 1742 on a public spirited plan formed and put into execution by the learned Mr. Franklin. For he persuaded first the most substantial people in town to pay forty shillings at the outset, and afterwards annually ten shillings, in Pennsylvania currency, towards purchasing all kinds of useful books. The subscribers are entitled to make use of them. Other people are likewise at liberty to borrow them for a certain time, but must leave a pledge and pay eight-pence a week for a folio volume, sixpence for a quarto, and fourpence for all of a smaller size. As soon as the time allowed a person for the perusal of a volume has elapsed, it must be returned or he is fined. The money arising in this manner is employed for the salary of the librarian and for purchasing new books. There is already a fine collection of excellent works, most of them English; many French and Latin, but few in any other language. The subscribers were kind enough to order the librarian, during my stay here, to lend me every book which I should want without any payment. The library is open every Saturday from four to eight o'clock in the afternoon. Besides the books, several mathematical and physical instruments and a large collection of natural curiosities are to be seen in it. Several little libraries were founded in the town on the same principle or nearly so.

The *Court House* stands in the middle of Market Street to the west of the market. It is a fine building with a small tower and a bell. Below and around this building the market is properly held every week.

The building of the *Academy* is in the western part of the city. It was formerly a meeting-house of the followers of [Rev. George] Whitefield, but they sold it in the year 1750, and it was destined to become the seat of higher learning, or to express myself in more exact terms, to be a college. It was therefore fitted up for this purpose. The young men here are taught only those things which they learn in our common schools and gymnasia; but in time such lectures are intended to be given as are usual in real universities.

At the close of the last war a *redoubt* was erected here, on the south side of the town near the river, to prevent the French and Spanish privateers from landing. But this was done after a very strong debate. For the Quakers opposed all fortifications as contrary to the tenets of their religion, which do not allow Christians to make war either offensive or defensive, but direct them to place their trust in the Almighty alone. Several papers were then handed around for and against the opinion. But the enemy's privateers having taken several vessels belonging to the town in the river, many of the Quakers, if not all of them, found it reasonable to further the building of the fortification as much as possible, at least by a supply of money.

Of all the natural advantages of the town, its temperate climate is the most considerable, the winter not being over severe, and its duration but short and the summer not too hot; the country round about bringing forth those fruits in the greatest plenty which are raised by husbandry. Their September and October are like the beginning of the Swedish August. And the first days in their February are frequently as pleasant as the end of April and the beginning of May in Sweden. Even their coldest days in some winters have been no severer than the days at the end of spring are in the middlemost parts of Sweden and the southern ones of Finland.

The good and clear water in Philadelphia is likewise one of its advantages. For though there are no fountains in the town, there is a well in every house and several in the streets, all of which furnish excellent water for boiling, drinking, washing and other uses. The water is commonly found at the depth of forty feet. The water of the River Delaware is likewise good. But in making the wells a fault is frequently committed which in several places of the town spoils the water which is naturally good. . . .

Trade. The Delaware is exceedingly convenient for trade. It is one of the largest rivers: it is three English miles broad at its mouth, two miles at the town of Wilmington, and three quarters of a mile at Philadelphia. This city lies within ninety or a hundred English miles from the sea, or from the place where the river Delaware discharges itself into the bay of that name. Yet its depth is hardly ever less than five or six fathoms. The largest ships therefore can sail right up to the town and anchor in good ground in five fathoms of water on the side of the bridge. The water here has no longer a saltish taste, and therefore all destructive worms which have fastened themselves to the ships in the sea and have pierced holes into them either die or drop off, after the ship has been here for a while.

The only disadvantage which commerce has here is the freezing of the river almost every winter for a month or more. For during that time navigation is entirely stopped. This does not happen at Boston, New York and other towns which are nearer the sea.

The tide comes up to Philadelphia and even goes thirty miles higher to Trenton. The difference between high and low water is eight feet at Philadelphia.

The cataracts of the Delaware near Trenton and of the Schuylkill at some distance from Philadelphia make these rivers useless further up the country in regard to the conveyance of goods either from or to Philadelphia. They must therefore be carried on wagons or carts. It has therefore already been thought of making these two rivers navigable [for greater distances and] for larger vessels.

Several ships are built annually of American oak, in the docks which are found in several parts of and near the town, yet they can by no means be compared with those built of European oak in point of goodness and durability.

The town carries on a great trade both with the inhabitants of the country and with other parts of the world, especially the West Indies, South America and the Antilles, England, Ireland, Portugal and the various English colonies in North America. Yet none but English ships are allowed to come into this port.

Philadelphia reaps the greatest profits from its trade with the West Indies. For thither the inhabitants ship almost every day a quantity of flour, butter, meat and other victuals, timber, planks and the like. In return they receive either sugar, molasses, rum, indigo, mahogany and other goods or ready money. The true mahogany which grows in Jamaica is at present almost all cut down. Philadelphians send both West India goods and their own productions to England; the latter comprise all sorts of woods, especially black walnut and oak planks for ships, ships ready built, iron, hides and tar. Yet this latter is properly bought in New Jersey, the forests of which province are consequently more ruined than any others. Ready money is likewise sent over to England from whence in return they get all sorts of goods manufactured, viz. fine and coarse cloth, linen, iron ware and other wrought metals, and East India goods. For it is to be observed that England supplies Philadelphia with almost all stuffs and articles which are wanted here.

A great quantity of linseed goes annually to Ireland, together with many of the ships which are built here. Portugal gets wheat, corn, flour and grain which is not ground. Spain sometimes takes some grain. But all the money which is gotten in these several countries, must immediately be sent to England in payment for goods from thence, and yet those sums are not sufficient to pay all the debts.

But to show more exactly what the town and province have imported from England in different years I shall here insert an extract from the English customhouse books, which I obtained from the engineer, Lewis Evans, at Philadelphia and which will sufficiently answer the purpose. This gentleman had desired one of his friends in London to send him a complete account of all the goods shipped from England to Pennsylvania during a certain number of years. He got this account, and though the goods are not enumerated in it yet their value in money is calculated. Such extracts from the customhouse books have been made for every North American province, in order to convince the English parliament that those provinces have taken greater quantities of goods in that kingdom after they set up their own paper currency.

I have taken the copy from the original itself and it is to be observed that it begins with the Christmas of the year 1722, and ends about the same time of the year 1747. In the first column is the value of the foreign goods, the duty for which has already been paid in England. The second column shows the value of the goods manufactured in England and exported to Pennsylvania. And in the last column these two sums are added together, and at the bottom each column is added up. But this table does not include the goods which are annually shipped in great quantities to Pennsylvania from Scotland and Ireland, among which is a great quantity of linen.

The whole extent of the Philadelphia trade may be comprehended from the number of ships, which annually arrive at and sail from this town. I intend to insert here a table of a few years which I have taken from the gazettes of the town. The ships coming and going in one year are to be reckoned from the twenty-fifth of March of that year to the twenty-fifth of March of the next.

But it is much to be feared that the trade of Philadelphia and of all the English colonies will rather decrease than increase in case no provision is made to prevent it. I shall hereafter plainly show upon what foundation this decrease of trade is likely to take place. The town not only furnishes most of the inhabitants of Pennsylvania with the goods which they want, but several inhabitants of New Jersey come every day to trade.

THE VALUE OF THE GOODS ANNUALLY SHIPPED FROM ENGLAND TO PENNSYLVANIA

The year, from one Christmas to another	Foreign Goods for which the duty has already peen paid, & which therefore only req. receipts.			English manufactured Goods.			The Sums of these two preceding columns added together.		
	£	s.	d.	£	s.	d.	£	s.	d.
1723	5199	13	5	10793	5	1	15992	19	4
1724	9373	15	8	20951	0	5	30324	16	1
1725	10301	12	6	31508	1	8	42209	14	2
1726	9371	11	6	28263	6	2	37634	17	8
1727	10243	0	7	21736	10	0	31979	10	7
1728	14073	13	3	23405	6	2	37478	19	11
1729	12948	8	5	16851	2	5	29799	10	10
1730	15660	10	11	32931	16	6	48592	7	5
1731	11838	17	4	32421	18	9	44260	16	1
1732	15240	14	4	26457	19	3	41698	13	7
1733	13187	0	8	27378	7	5	40585	8	1
1734	19648	15	9	34743	12	1	54392	7	10
1735	18078	4	3	30726	7	1	48804	11	4
1736	23456	15	11	38057	2	5	61513	18	4
1737	14517	4	3	42173	2	4	56690	6	7
1738	20320	19	3	41129	5	0	61450	4	3
1739	9041	4	5	45411	7	6	54452	11	11
1740	10280	2	0	46471	12	9	56751	14	9
1741	12977	18	10	78032	13	1	91010	11	11
1742	14458	6	3	60836	17	1	75295	3	4
1743	19220	1	6	60120	4	10	79340	6	4
1744	14681	8	4	47595	18	2	62214	6	6
1745	13043	8	8	41237	2	3	54280	10	11
1746	18013	12	7	55595	19	7	73699	12	2
1747	8585	14	11	73819	2	8	82404	17	7
Total	343,789	16	0	969,049	1	6	1,312,838	17	6

The Year.	Ships arrived.	Ships sailed.
1735	199	212
1740	307	208
1741	292	309
1744	229	271
1745	280	301
1746	273	293

The town has two great fairs every year, one on May sixteenth and the other on November sixteenth. But besides these fairs there are every week two market days, *viz*. Wednesday and Saturday. On those days the country people in Pennsylvania and New Jersey bring to town a quantity of food and other products of the country, and this is a great advantage to the town. It is therefore to be wished that a similar regulation be made in our Swedish towns. You are sure to find on market days every produce of the season which the country affords. But on other days they are sought for in vain.

Provisions are always to be got fresh here, and for that reason most of the inhabitants never buy more at a time than what will be sufficient till the next market day. In summer there is a market almost every day, for the victuals do not keep well in the great heat. There are two places in town where these markets are kept, but that near the court-house is the principal one. It begins about four or five o'clock in the morning and ends about nine in the forenoon.

The town is not enclosed and has no other customhouse than the large one for the ships.

The governor of the whole province lives here and though he is nominated by the heirs of Penn he cannot take that office without being confirmed by the king of England.

The Quakers of almost all parts of North America have their great assembly here once a year.

In the year 1743 a society for the advancement of the sciences was started here. Its activity was to have embraced the curiosities of the three kingdoms of nature, mathematics, physics, chemistry, economics and manufactures. But the war, which ensued immediately, stopped all designs of this nature and since that time nothing has been done to revive it. . . .

There are three printers here and every week two English newspapers and one German are printed.

In the year 1732 on the fifth of September, old style, a little earthquake was felt here about noon and at the same time at Boston in New England and at Montreal in Canada, which places are above sixty Swedish miles apart.

In the month of November of the year 1737 the well known prince from Mount Lebanon, Sheich Sidi, came to Philadelphia on his travels through most of the English American colonies.—In the same year a second earthquake was felt about eleven o'clock at night, on the seventh of December. But it did not continue above half a minute and yet it was felt according to the accounts of the gazettes at the same hour in Newcastle, New York, New London, Boston and other towns of New England. It had, therefore, an areal influence of several miles. . . .

Population. I have not been able to find the exact number of inhabitants in Philadelphia. In the year 1746 they were reckoned to be above ten thousand, and since that time their number has incredibly increased. Neither can it be ascertained from the lists of mortality since they are not kept regularly in all the churches. I shall, however, mention some of those which appeared either in the gazettes or in printed lists separately.

Year.	Dead.	Year.	Dead.	Year.	Dead.
1730	227	1741	345	1745	420
1738	250	1742	409	1748	672
1739	350	1743	425	1749	758
1740	290	1744	410	1750	716

From these mortality lists it also appears that the diseases which are most fatal are consumption, fevers, convulsions, pleurisy, hemorrhages and dropsy.

The number of births cannot be determined since in many churches no order is observed with regard to this affair. The Quakers, who are the most numerous in this town, never baptize their children, though they keep a pretty exact account of all who are born among them. It is likewise impossible to guess at the number of inhabitants from the dead because the town gets such great supplies of immigrants annually from other countries. In the summer of the year 1749 nearly twelve thousand Germans came over to Philadelphia, many of whom stayed in that town. In the spring of the same year the houses in

Philadelphia were counted and found to be two thousand and seventy-six in number.

The town is now well filled with inhabitants of many nations, who in regard to their country, religion and trade are very different from each other. You meet with excellent masters in all trades and many things are made here fully as well as in Egland. Yet no manufactures, especially for making fine wool cloth, are established. Perhaps the reason is that it can be got with so little difficulty from England and that the breed of sheep which is brought over degenerates in process of time and affords but a coarse wool.

There is a great abundance of provisions here and their prices are very moderate. There are no examples of an extraordinary dearth.

Freedom. Everyone who acknowledges God to be the Creator, preserver and ruler of all things, and teaches or undertakes nothing against the state or against the common peace, is at liberty to settle, stay and carry on his trade here, be his religious principles ever so strange. No one is here molested because of misleading principles of doctrine which he may follow, if he does not exceed the above mentioned bounds. And he is so well secured by the laws, both as to person and property, and enjoys such liberties that a citizen here may, in a manner, be said to live in his house like a king. It would be difficult to find anyone who could wish for and obtain greater freedom.

Rapidity of Urban Growth. On careful consideration of what I have already said it will be easy to conceive why this city should rise so suddenly from nothing into such grandeur and perfection without any powerful monarch contributing to it, either by punishing the wicked or by giving great supplies of money. And yet its fine appearance, good regulations, agreeable location, natural advantages, trade, riches and power are by no means inferior to those of any, even of the most ancient, towns in Europe. It has not been necessary to force people to come and settle here; on the contrary foreigners of different languages have left their country, houses, property and relations and ventured over wide and stormy seas in order to come hither. Other countries, which have been peopled for a long space of time, complain of the small number of their inhabitants. But Pennsylvania which was no better than a wilderness in the year 1681, and contained hardly fifteen hundred people, now vies with several kingdoms in Europe in the number of inhabitants. It has received hosts of people which other countries, to their infinite loss, have either neglected, belittled or expelled.

Oldest Building. A wretched old wooden building on a hill near the river, located a little north of the Wicaco is preserved on purpose as a memorial to the poor condition of the place before the town was built on it. It belonged formerly to one of the Svensons, from whom, as before-mentioned, the ground was bought upon which to build Philadelphia. Its antiquity gives it a kind of superiority over all the other buildings in town, though in itself it is the worst of all. This hut was inhabited whilst yet stags, deer, elks and beavers at broad daylight lived in the future streets, church yards and marketplaces of Philadelphia. The noise of a spinning wheel was heard in this house before the manufactures now established were thought of or Philadelphia was built. But with all these advantages the house is ready to fall down, and after a few years it will be as difficult to find the place where it stood as it was unlikely at the time of its erection that one of the greatest towns in America should in a short time stand close to it.

A Custom. It was a custom in Philadelphia, upon meeting a woman on the street, to let her go on the side nearest the houses. To make her walk on the outside was considered boorish and unrefined. I have mentioned before that the streets here are like those of London, with pavements for pedestrians and wooden posts that prevent driving upon the people. Similarly, when walking with a lady, she must be allowed the side next to the houses. The same practice obtains when promenading with a gentleman of higher social station than oneself. I have seen men so vain in this effort to give honor to another that they have constantly shifted from the right to the left side of a person, depending upon the number of times they crossed a street together. The custom is supposed to have arisen from an attempt to protect the walking companion from the filth of the street, hence, the side next to it is held to be less honorable. . . .

Fuel. The best wood for fuel in everybody's opinion is hickory, or a species of walnut, for it heats well; but it is not good for fences since it cannot well withstand rotting after it is cut. The white and black oaks are next in goodness for fuel. The woods with which Philadelphia is surrounded would lead one to conclude that fuel must be cheap there. But it is far from being so, because the large and high forest near the town is the property of some people of quality and fortune who do not regard the money which they could make from it. They do not fell so much as they require for their own use and much less would they fell it for others. But they leave the trees for times to come, expecting that wood will become much more expensive. However, they fell it for joiners, coach-makers and other artisans, who pay exorbitantly for it. For a quantity of hickory, eight feet in length and four in depth, and the pieces being likewise four feet long, [i. e. a cord] they paid at present eighteen shillings of Pennsylvania currency. But the same quantity of oak only came to twelve shillings. The people who came at present to sell wood in the market were farmers who lived at a great distance from the town. Everybody complained that fuel in the space of a few years, had risen to a price many times as much as it had been formerly, and to account for this the following reasons were given: the town had increased to such a degree that it was four or six times bigger and more populous than some old people knew it to be when they were young. Many brick kilns had been made hereabouts which require a great quantity of wood. The country is likewise more cultivated than it used to be, and consequently large forests have been cut down for that purpose; and the farms built in those places also consume a quantity of wood. Lastly, people melt iron out of ore in several places about the town, and this work goes on without interruption. For these reasons it is concluded that in future times Philadelphia will be obliged to pay a high price for wood. . . .

Ship Building. Though the woods of Pennsylvania have many oaks, and more species of them than are found further north, people do not build so many ships in this province as they do in the northern part, and especially in New England. But experience has taught them that the same kind of tree is more durable the further north it grows, and that this advantage decreases the more it grows in warm climates. It is likewise plain that the trees in the south grow more every year, and form thicker ringlets than those in the north. The former have likewise much greater tubes for the circulation of the sap than the later. And for this reason they do not build so many ships in Pennsylvania, as they do in New England, though more than in Virginia and Maryland. Carolina builds very few, and its merchants get all their ships from New England. Those which are here made of the best oak are hardly serviceable above ten, or at the most twelve years; for then they are so rotten that nobody ventures to go to sea in them. Many captains of ships come over from England to North America in order to get ships built here. But most of them choose New England, that being the most northerly province; and even if they come over in ships which are bound for Philadelphia, they frequently on their arrival set out from Pennsylvania for New England. The Spaniards in the West Indies are said to build their ships of a peculiar sort of cedar, which holds out against decay and moisture, but it is not obtainable on the continent in the English provinces. Here are more than nine different sorts of oak, but with regard to quality not one of them is comparable to the single species we have in Sweden, and therefore a ship of European oak costs a great deal more than one made of the American variety.

Johann David Schoepf, Travels in the Confederation [1783-84], *translated by Alfred J. Morrison (Philadelphia, 1911), pp. 57-62, 97-102.*

Philadelphia lies under Latitude 39° 57' and Longitude west 75° 20', and so, nearly at the middle of the United States—the city, if not greatly beyond others in America in wealth and number of houses, far surpasses them all in learning, in the arts, and public spirit. The plain on which Philadelphia stands is elevated ground between the magnificent Delaware and the romantic Schuylkill. Granite is the underlying rock, which shows itself particularly along the banks of the Schuylkill. The distance apart of the rivers, in the neighborhood of the city, is not quite two miles; three miles below, they unite, and the tongue of land so formed, called the Neck, is for the most part lower and swampier than the site of the city. The plan of Philadelphia is fine and regular, but not wholly faultless. The larger and smaller cities of America have this advantage, that they have not grown from villages by chance but were planned from the beginning and have been enlarged by a plan. By the original chart Philadelphia is fixed within a rectangle from the bank of the Delaware to the Schuylkill and a little beyond. But at the present time not a third of the plan is filled in, and one must not be led into the error of thinking it complete, as represented in certain maps both of Philadelphia and of Pennsylvania. For notwithstanding the swift pushing-back of the city, centuries yet must go by before the ground plan is built up. The streets cross at right angles. Those along the Delaware run nearly

North and South and are parallel, as are those running East and West, or from the Delaware to the Schuylkill. Along the Delaware the line of houses, including the suburbs, extends for some two miles, and the breadth of the city, including the suburbs, is not quite a mile going from the river. Water-street, next to the Delaware, is narrow and considerably lower than the rest of the city. In this street are warehouses chiefly. Commodious wharves, for ships of as much as 500 tons, are built in behind the houses, and here a few feet of land, often made land, yield rich returns to the owners.

The remaining streets parallel with Water-street and the river, are called in their order First or Front-street, Second, Third, Fourth, Fifth, Sixth, Seventh; so many at present—the three last are still short. The cross streets running from east to west are the most elevated, and in their order from north to south are: Vine, Race, Arch, Market, Chesnut, Wallnut, Spruce, Union. From these a number of alleys traverse the chief quarters. Market-street is the best street and the only one 100 ft. in breadth; all the rest are only 50 ft. wide. Were all the streets as wide again the town would be by so much the finer and more convenient. It is easily seen that Quakers drew the plan, and dealt frugally with the space. Market-street is disfigured and the city is deprived of the view, otherwise splendid, towards the river and the Jersey side, by reason of the market-stalls, two long, open buildings set in the middle of the street and extending from First to Third-street. It is droll how the upper part of these buildings makes so extraordinary a distinction between East and West, rear and front. That is to say, the upper part of the Market-house is the Court-House, and built at either end are balconies, of which that at one end is the place where newly elected Governors are introduced to the people, and at the other end are the pillories for rogues.

It is a pity that when the town was laid off, there was such a total neglect to provide open squares, which lend an especial beauty to great towns, and grassed after the manner of the English, or set with shrubbery, are very pleasing to the eye. In Philadelphia there is nothing but streets all alike, the houses of brick, of the same height mostly, and built by a plan that seldom varies; some few are adorned outwardly by a particular pattern or are better furnished than the general within. Throughout the city the streets are well paved and well kept, highest down the middle, but next the houses there runs a footway sufficiently broad, and laid with flat stones; this side-way is often narrowed by the 'stoops' built up before the houses, or by the downsloping cellar and kitchen doors. There being a superfluity of space, it would have been easy, at the foundation of this new city, to avoid the inconveniences of old ones. At night the city is lit by lanterns placed on posts diagonally alternate at the side of the footway, but the lanterns are sparingly distributed and have no reflectors. The streets are kept clean and in good order by the householders themselves. Water and filth from the streets are carried off through conduits to the river. Appointed night-watchmen call out the hours and the state of the weather. Behind each house is a little court or garden, where usually are the necessaries, and so this often evil-smelling convenience of our European houses is missed here, but space and better arrangement are gained. The kitchen, stable, &c. are all placed in buildings at the side or behind, kitchens often underground. Vaults I do not remember seeing in any house. The attempt is made to avoid everything detrimental to the convenience or cleanliness of dwellinghouses. In the matter of interior decorations the English style is imitated here as throughout America. The furniture, tables, bureaux, bedsteads &c. are commonly of mahogany, at least in the best houses. Carpets, Scottish and Turkish, are much used, and indeed are necessities where the houses are so lightly built; stairs and rooms are laid with them. The houses are seldom without paper tapestries, the vestibule especially being so treated. The taste generally is for living in a cleanly and orderly manner, without the continual scrubbing of the Hollanders or the frippery and gilt of the French. The rooms are in general built with open fire-places but the German inhabitants, partly from preference and old custom, partly from economy, have introduced iron or tin-plate draught-stoves which are used more and more by English families (as a result of the increasing dearness of wood) both in living-rooms and in work-rooms. Here especially there are seen Franklins (named in honor of the inventor), a sort of iron affair, half stove, half fire-place. This is a longish, rectangular apparatus made of cast-iron plates and stands off from the wall, the front being open, in every respect a detached, movable fire-place. The comfortable sight of the open fire is thus enjoyed, and the good ventilation is healthful; moreover, the iron plates warm a room at less expense of fuel than is possible with the wall fire-place, from which most of the heat is lost.

In so warm a climate the inconveniences arising from the narrowness of the streets were felt at this time and must be whenever the weather is hot. During three days, June 23, 24, 25, Fahrenheit's thermometer stood constantly at 93-95 degrees. The city is so far inland that no wind from the sea brings coolness; round about is a dry, sandy soil; and in addition narrow streets, houses and footways of brick strongly reflecting the sun's rays—everything makes for a high degree of dead heat in the city. During these three days, not less than 30 sudden deaths were announced in the Philadelphia newspapers, martyrs to the heat by the coroners' returns, and also, very probably, victims of an indiscreet imbibition of cold drinks. But as everywhere else, not until after the event, were the people warned by public proclamation to keep clear of cold drinks.

The number of the inhabitants was placed at 20,000 as early as 1766, before the war at 30,000, and at present (counting strangers) is fixed at 30-40,000—with what certainty I am not prepared to say. On account of the many distinct religious sects, no exact register is so far kept of births and deaths, which if attempted might not be reliable. A strict enumeration of the inhabitants is difficult in America, (and merely political calculations are untrustworthy,) where people are continually moving about, leaving a place or coming in. . . .

The inhabitants of Philadelphia seemed to me to have retained something of that suspicious reserve which policy compelled them to adopt at the beginning of the war, and while it lasted, in their dealings with strangers—behavior due in the first instance partly to fear, partly to aversion for political dissentients. It has been said for a long time of Philadelphia that one might not gain a footing in houses there so easily as in the neighboring York, the explanation of which was chiefly that the Quakers excluded all but their own particular friends, and this behavior, imitated among the bulk of the inhabitants, has in some sort remained a characteristick. The war, however, which must be thanked in America for so many things, and the number of Europeans present in the country (especially the French) have worked already a positive revolution in America. Burnaby remarked with regret that people were not very courteous and hospitable to strangers; he would have less cause to say as much now. But I must acknowledge that those among the Philadelphians who have visited foreign countries are incomparably more engaging and polite than others who hold courtesy to be reserve; those who have travelled have learned by experience how obliging even the smallest attention is to a stranger, and they practice what elsewhere has pleased them. Not so, those entirely homebred. Two of my friends, Englishmen, came from York to see Philadelphia and found rooms in a house where strangers were customably taken in. It so happened that an American traveller, by the exchange of a room, made place for the two Englishmen. The lady of the house promised that the matter would be so arranged, but at the same time unreservedly remarked, 'you know,' (as if a thing of common knowledge in Philadelphia), 'you know that people do not like to inconvenience themselves to oblige a stranger.'

The behavior of the Philadelphians is for the rest only one among the consequences of the spirit of freedom, a British inheritance strengthened by removal to American soil and still more by the successful outcome of the war. From of old these were strong and active republicans. Freedom has been, since many years, the genius and the vow of Pensylvania and of all the North American states. Many and various as have been the reasons assigned for the outbreak of the war and the separation of the colonies from the mother-country, it has seemed to me that the true and only reason has been overlooked. There was a set purpose in America to make the land free and any pretext would serve. England might have removed one burden after another, might have given encouragement after encouragement, but fresh excuses would have been constantly sought and found so as to bring about a final breach. It is a matter of wonder to me, in this connection, that nobody mentions the prediction spoken of by Kalm who heard it as early as 1748 during his stay in America and gives it as a thing well-known. "I have often, he remarks, heard it said openly by Englishmen, and not only by those born in America but also by those recently come from Europe, that the English plantations in northern America would in 30-50 years form a separate kingdom, quite independent of England."

People think, act, and speak here precisely as it prompts them; the poorest day-laborer on the bank of the Delaware holds it his right to advance his opinion, in religious as well as political matters, with as much freedom as the gentleman or the scholar. And as yet there is to be found as little distinction of rank among the inhabitants of Philadelphia as in any city in the world. No one admits that the Governor has any particular superiority over the private citizen except in so far as he is the right hand of the law, and to the law, as occasion demands is respect paid, through the Governor; for the law equally regards and deals with all citizens. Riches make no positive material difference, because in this regard every man expects at one time or another to be on a footing with his rich neighbor, and in this expectation shows him no knavish reverence, but treats him with an open, but seemly, familiarity. Posts of honor confer upon the holder merely a conditional superiority, necessary in the eyes of every discreet man as a support of order and government. All rank and precedence is for the rest the acquirement of personal worth. Rank of birth is not recognized, is resisted with a total force.

Luxury, which is unavoidable in enlightened free nations, prevails here also, without, however, any dispossession of industry and thrift, being largely restricted to the luxury of the body; virtuosity, sensibility and other manifestations of soul-luxury are not yet become conspicuous here.

The taste in dress is chiefly English, extremely simple, neat, and elegant. The finest cloth and the finest linen are the greatest adornment. Only a few young gentlemen, especially those of the army, approximate to the French cut, but they by no means give themselves over to the ostentatious frippery by which, here also, certain Frenchmen are distinguished. The women, as everywhere, seeking to please allow themselves more variety of ornament. Every year dressed dolls are brought them from Europe, which, silent, give the law of the mode. However, distinction of rank among the feminine half, is not striking as a result of any distinct costume; in the item of dress each selects according to her taste, means, and circumstances.

The women of North America have long since been the subject of particular praise, regarding their virtue and good conduct, rendered them by both travellers and the homekeeping. It is not easy to find a woman, remarks one of their panegyrists, who makes a parade of unbelief, although they are not always members of any particular sect. Gallant adventure are little known and still less practiced in this last refuge of virtue pursued. Conjugal disloyalties, on either side, are punished by ineffaceable infamy, and the culprit, however protected by wealth, position, or other advantage, soon finds himself without honor, distrusted. This is no extravagant praise, and the *Abbé Robin* himself admits that his countrymen did not in America meet with their habitual good fortune in affairs of gallantry. The feminine part of America is none the less made for pleasure and partakes, and Rochefoucault would have likely assigned another reason for their virtue. Thus, a traditional practice of *bundling*, the vogue in certain parts of America, especially New England, might well give our European fair another idea of western restraint. That is to say, it is a custom there for young men to pay visits to their mistresses; and the young woman's good name is no ways impaired, so that the visit takes place by stealth, or after they are actually betrothed; on the contrary, the parents are advised, and these meetings happen when the pair is enamored and merely wish to know each other better. The swain and the maiden spend the evening and the night undisturbed by the hearth, or it may be go to bed together without scruple; in the latter case, with the condition that they do not take off their clothes; and if the anxious mother has any doubt of the strict virtue of her daughter, it is said she takes the precaution of placing both the daughter's feet in one large stocking, and in the morning looks to see if this guardian is still properly fixed, but the inquiry is commonly superfluous, the circumstance having rarely any other consequence than in regular betrothal, which is the object had in view in allowing the meeting. When it is said in praise of America that there are seldom other consequences due to the intimate association of the sexes, it must be remarked that people there generally marry with less forethought and earlier, and that in almost every house there are negresses, slaves, who count it an honor to bring a mulatto into the world.

Philadelphia boasted once of its especially good police, and knew nothing of tumultuary and mutinous gatherings of the people which were not seldom the case with their more northern neighbors. This advantageous character (due, like everything else good, to the peaceful principles of the Quakers), was lost during the war, when mobs often took possession of the city and particularly mishandled the Quakers in their quiet houses.

J. P. Brissot de Warville, New Travels in the United States 1788, *translated by Mara Soceanu Vamos and Durand Echeverria, edited by Durand Echeverria (Cambridge, 1964), pp. 253-263.*

When Voltaire considered the vices which corroded the Old World and the tender brotherly love which united the Quakers, he sometimes would cross the seas in his imagination and long to spend the rest of his life in the "city of brotherly love." What would he have said

had he been able for a few days to realize his dream and witness
the peace which reigns in Philadelphia?—No, I am wrong; Voltaire
would have hastened to return to Europe, for he was consumed with
pride and lived on adulation, and he would have got very little of
that here. The seriousness of the Quakers would have seemed to him
a kind of gloomy pedantry; he would have yawned at their meetings;
he would have been mortified to find that his epigrams went unap-
plauded; he would soon have been homesick for the glittering witti-
cisms of his polite Parisian roués.

Philadelphia may be considered the metropolis of the United States.
It is certainly the most beautiful and best-built city in the nation, and
also the wealthiest, though not the most ostentatious. Here you find
more well-educated men, more knowledge of politics and literature,
more political and learned societies than anywhere else in the United
States. Many other American cities are older but Philadelphia quickly
surpassed them all.

The Swedes were the first settlers on the land where the city is
today. Their church, the first to be built here more than a hundred
years ago, still stands on the banks of the Delaware. Penn, as I have
already mentioned, was reluctant to choose this angle of land formed
by the Schuylkill and Delaware Rivers. As the proprietor of an
immense grant of territory, he found it hard to have to build his city
on land which did not belong to him. But the arguments in favor
of this site persuaded him to buy it from the Swedes, and he gave
them in exchange some land in the interior of Pennsylvania. Several
Swedish families settled there, but their posterity have not prospered
and no longer are the owners of these grants. Today there are few
descendants left of the original Swedes, who numbered over one
thousand and made a number of other settlements. The Swedish
church still exists, however, and has been for many years in the care
of a Swedish minister, Dr. [Nicholas] Collins, a learned man of rare
merit. He writes very well in English and has produced several books
and pamphlets in that language, such as *The Foreign Spectator*, in
which he outlines the soundest republican principles. He is a fervent
apostle of liberty.

Penn introduced in his new colony a truly fraternal regime, a
familylike sort of government. Brothers who live together need for
their defense neither soldiers, nor forts, nor police, nor any of those
formidable constructions which give to most towns the appearance of

fortresses. Until recently Philadelphia had not felt the need of a public governing body or of a city hall; now, however, the necessity is beginning to be apparent because of the many foreigners and members of other sects who have established themselves here. For some time there have been complaints of disorders and of robberies committed at night on the outskirts of Philadelphia by thieves escaped from prison.

At ten o'clock in the evening all is quiet in the streets, and the profound silence is interrupted only by the cries of the few watchmen who form the only patrol. The streets are lighted at night by lamps placed at intervals, like those of London. On each street there are brick sidewalks and narrow gutters of brick or wood on both sides. Between the gutters and the street there are strong posts to prevent carriages from running up on the sidewalks, which are level with the street. These stout posts are made of a kind of cedar imported from the Carolinas. On all the streets one sees a surprisingly large number of public pumps.

At the door of each house there is a pair of benches where the family sits in the evening to enjoy the fresh air and watch the passers-by. This is certainly a bad habit, for the evening air is not always very healthy and its ill effects are not counteracted by exercise. People never take walks here; instead they have parties in the country.

There are few private coaches in Philadelphia, but one sees many attractive wagons which are used to convey families to the country; they are long, lightly built, and open, and can hold twelve persons. Also very common in the country are small chaises, open on all sides. One kind, known as the sulky, has a seat for only one person.

The horses which pull the carriages are in general neither handsome nor strong, but they travel well enough. I have not seen any of the fine horses mentioned by M. Crèvecoeur, which I thought would rival the enormous Belgian horses. I suspect Americans do not take good enough care of their horses and feed them badly; they are not bedded down with straw in the stable, and after a long and tiring trip they are allowed to graze.

Philadelphia is built on a regular plan of long, broad streets which cross each other at right angles and run from north to south and from east to west. This truly ornamental regularity is at first confusing to the stranger, for it is difficult to find one's way, especially since there are no street signs and no numbers on the doors. It is inconceivable that the Quakers, who are so fond of order, have not borrowed these two practices from the English, from whom they have adopted so many other things. This lack of signs and numbers is the bane of foreigners.

The shops which adorn the principal streets are remarkable for their cleanliness. You find here the same taste and the same quality as in London. The State House, in which the General Assembly meets, is, as I have already said, a fairly handsome building. Next to it a magnificent court of justice is now being constructed. M. Raynal's descriptions of the State House, the library, and other public buildings are exaggerated. He was deceived by the information he had been given. He speaks of streets 100 feet wide, of which there are none, except for Market Street; they generally have a breadth of 50 to 60 feet. He also speaks of 200-foot wharfs, of which there are none either; in fact they are in general rather small and unimpressive. He states that Penn's plan has been followed everywhere in the city. On the contrary, it was violated in the building of Water Street instead of the beautiful wharfs which Penn had planned. Raynal also speaks of slate-roofed houses and of marble monuments in churches and meeting halls. I have seen nothing of the sort.

Behind the State House there is a public garden, the only one in Philadelphia. It contains large squares of greenery intersected by pathways, and although it is not large, it is pleasant and one can breathe there.

All the space from Front Street on the Delaware to Front Street on the Schuylkill is already divided into streets and blocks for houses. Building is going on, but not as fast as in New York. The inhabitants of Philadelphia apparently wish to see the city grow. In this they are wrong, for it is already too big. When the population of a city becomes large, it is necessary to have almshouses, prisons, soldiers, police, and spies. Soon luxury begins to appear, that very luxury which Penn wished to avoid. Indeed, it has already begun to be apparent for some time, and you see carpets, and fine ones, in the houses. They are treasured by Americans; this is a taste they have inherited from their luxury-loving former masters, the English. A carpet in summer is an absurdity, yet it is kept on the floor out of vanity. The excuse is that it makes the house look better, which is to say that good sense and utility are less important than "show." Sensible people, however, are beginning to take up their carpets during the summer and leave the floors bare or covered with mats.

Quakers too have carpets, but the rigorously orthodox disapprove. I was told of a Quaker from Carolina who when he went to dine at the house of one of the wealthiest Quakers in Philadelphia was so offended at seeing the front hallway to the stairs covered with a carpet that he refused to enter the house. He said that he would not eat in a house of luxury, and that it was far better to clothe the poor than to clothe the floor.

If this Quaker justifiably criticized this ridiculous prodigality in carpets, how much more severely must he have censured the extravagance of the women of Philadelphia! I am not referring to the wives of the Quakers, of whom I shall speak later in a special chapter on the Society of Friends, but to the women of other sects, who wear hats and bonnets almost as varied as those seen in Paris. These women pay a great deal of attention to their dresses and hairdos and are too obviously affected to be pleasing. It is a great misfortune in a republic when women waste so much time on such foolishness and when men attach any importance to these things.

A very clever woman in this city is accused of having contributed more than any other to this taste for extravagant show. I am truly sorry to see her husband, who seems an agreeable, well-educated man, display in his house and furniture an ostentation which ought to have remained forever unknown in Philadelphia. And why does he do this? To attract a few European fops and empty-headed parasites. What does he gain by it? The jealousy and the censure of his fellow citizens and the criticism of foreigners. When a man of great wealth is intelligent, educated, wise, and benevolent, how easy it is for him to make himself loved and esteemed by devoting his fortune to useful public enterprises.

Despite the fatal consequences that might be expected from this luxury, we may say with assurance that there is no city in which morals are more respected than in Philadelphia. Adultery is unknown here, and there is no single instance of a wife of any sect failing in her duties.

This is perhaps due, as I was told by an American, to the civic status of women. They marry without doweries and bring only household goods to their new homes; only after the death of their parents can they expect to own any property. They are therefore entirely dependent on their husbands.

I was told, however, of a Mrs. Livingston, a daughter of Dr. Shippen, who lives separated from her husband. But this separation was arranged by an amicable agreement. The young woman married Mr. Livingston only in obedience to her father, a kind of obedience which is very rare in this country. The father promised to take his daughter back if she were not happy with her husband. She was not, she returned to her father's home, and she lives today the life of a virtuous and respected woman. . . .

There is no other city on this continent where as much printing is done as in Philadelphia. There are a great many printing presses, gazettes, and bookstores in the city, and likewise a large number of paper mills in the state. Pennsylvania is truly the general emporium of the United States. . . .

You can now easily see the reasons for the prosperity of Philadelphia. Its geographical position on a river navigable by large ships makes it a center for foreign trade, and at the same time it is the market place for the products of the fertile lands of Pennsylvania and the neighboring states. The vast rivers with their numerous branches that flow through Pennsylvania connect almost all points in the state, making easy the transportation of goods, which in turn raises the value of land and attracts settlers. One of these rivers can carry to the capital the produce of the remotest farms and even products of the forest trapped or hunted by the Indians. The climate, warmer than it is in the Northern states but cooler and more comfortable than in the Southern, also is a considerable attraction.

Yet I firmly believe that Pennsylvania does not owe its prosperity merely to these geographical advantages, but rather to the private morals of the inhabitants; to the universal toleration which has been practiced here since the very foundation of the colony; to the Quakers' simplicity and thrift; to their firm virtues; and to their industry, which, concentrated on two activities, farming and trade, has necessarily produced better and faster results than other sects have achieved. Many more children are born in the simple cabin of a hard-working farmer than in a gilded palace, and fewer of them die. Since population has always appeared to you to be the most exact index to the prosperity of a country, compare the following figures on the number of inhabitants paying the poll tax in Pennsylvania in four different years fairly close together:

1760	1770	1779	1786
31,667	39,765	54,683	66,925

You can see that the population has more than doubled in twenty-five years, in spite of the fearful depopulation caused by a seven-year war. Note also that these figures do not include the Negro population, which is about one third as large as the white. According to the calculations of the recent federal convention, the white population of the state was 360,000, which means that there were about three children per family.

Let us take another point of comparison: Albany was founded in 1614, Philadelphia in 1681. The latter now has 7,000 houses and over 50,000 inhabitants. Albany, on the other hand, has only seven hundred houses although it enjoys almost the same geographical advantages as Philadelphia. To what is this difference due? More to moral than to physical causes. The spirit of the Quaker religion keeps the people constantly and directly aware of the public good; while in Albany such a spirit is almost unknown, and everyone seeks his own enjoyment and cares little about others. This, I repeat, is the Dutch character, and the Dutch as founders of Albany form the base of the city's population.

The public spirit which the Quakers, more than any other sect, exhibit in all their activities has given birth to several useful institutions in Philadelphia. It is to this spirit that Philadelphia owes its Dispensary, which distributes free medicines to the sick who cannot afford to buy them. How easy, and often how inexpensive it is to do good! Let those blush who dissipate their fortunes on ostentation and idleness! Between December 12, 1786, and December 12, 1887, 1,647 patients were treated in this Dispensary, and the average treatment per person cost 5 shillings 9 pence. Thus with a little over 5,000 livres, 1, 647 people were made happy.

To this same public spirit, so ingenious in varying its good deeds, is owed the Benevolent Institution, whose purpose is to bring help to needy women in labor and to deliver them in their own homes. It is to this spirit also that is due the formation of another society, whose object it is to aid prisoners. The rules and regulations of this society were drawn up at a meeting held on May 8, 1787.

Philadelphians do not limit their charity to their brethren but extend it to strangers as well. They have formed a Hibernian Club for the assistance of immigrants from Ireland, like the similar group for Germans in New York. Members of these societies inquire about the nationality and plans of arriving immigrants and make efforts to find employment for them.

Philadelphia has formed a fire insurance company. The houses are built of brick and wood and therefore are especially inflammable. It is a society in which the insurers are the insured, an arrangement which makes impossible such abuses as those which occurred in your insurance company in Paris.

Among all these things which warm my heart and arouse my admiration, I nevertheless have found one injustice which grieves me, since it seems to tarnish all of Pennsylvania and particularly the city of Philadelphia, which exercises a great influence on the legislative body. Penn left to his family an immense property in America. During the last war his descendants sided with the English and withdrew to England. The government of Pennsylvania ordered the confiscation of their lands and revenues, with payment in compensation of £150,000 for all their property. This sum was to be paid in paper money, which was then greatly depreciated. Only the first payment was made. It cannot be denied that a very great injustice was done in the estimate of the property, in the form of payment, and in the delay. The state of Pennsylvania has too much respect for property and too much devotion to justice not to make eventual reparations for the wrongs done to the Penn family, which is now wholly dependent upon payments from the English government.

New York City

In the 18th century New York was well on its way to becoming the world's marketplace. What was the city's place in the famous "triangular trade"? Did New York's place in the British imperial system hinder the city's growth in any way? Why were the American colonies less effective in conducting war than French Canada? What potential for independence did the colonies have in 1750? What were the chief disadvantages of living in New York? the chief advantages? Why did many immigrants settle in Pennsylvania rather than New York? Was there a "New York character" in the 18th century?

The America of 1750. Peter Kalm's Travels in North America. The English Version of 1770, *edited by Adolph B. Benson (New York, 1937), pp. 134-143.*

New York probably carries on a more extensive commerce than any town in the English North American provinces, at least it may be said to equal them. Boston and Philadelphia however come very close to it. The trade of New York extends to many places, and it is said they send more ships from there to London than they do from Philadelphia. They export to that capital all the various sorts of skins which they buy of the Indians, sugar, logwood, and other dyeing woods, rum, mahogany and many other goods which are the produce of the West Indies, together with all the specie which they get in the course of trade. Every year several ships are built here, which are sent to London and there sold; and of late years a quantity of iron has been shipped to England. In return for all these, cloth is imported from London and so is every article of English growth or manufacture, together with all sorts of foreign goods. England, and especially London, profits immensely by its trade with the American colonies; for not only New York but likewise all the other English towns on the continent import so many articles from England that all their specie, together with the goods which they get in other countries must all go to Old England to pay their accounts there, for which they are, however, insufficient. Hence it appears how much a well regulated colony contributes to the increase and welfare of its mother country.

New York sends many ships to the West Indies with flour, grain, biscuit, timber, boards, meat and pork, butter, and other provisions, together with some of the few fruits that grow here. Many ships go to Boston in New England with grain and flour, and take in exchange, meat, butter, timber, different sorts of fish, and other articles, which they carry further to the West Indies. They now and then carry rum from Boston, which is distilled there in great quantities, and sell it here at a considerable advantage. Sometimes they send vessels with goods from New York to Philadelphia; and at other times they are sent from Philadelphia to New York, which is only done, as appears from the gazettes, because certain articles are cheaper at one place than at the other. They send ships to Ireland every year, laden with all kinds of West India goods, but especially with linseed, which is collected in this country. I have been assured that in some years no less than ten ships have been sent to Ireland, laden with nothing but linseed, because it is said the flax in Ireland does not give good seed. But probably the true reason is that the people of Ireland, in order to have the better flax, make use of the plant before the seed is ripe, and therefore are obliged to send for foreign seed. It becomes thus one of the chief articles of trade. At this time a bushel of linseed is sold for eight shillings of New York currency.

For the goods which are sold in the West Indies either ready money is accepted or West India goods, which are either first brought to New York or immediately sent to England or Holland. If a ship does not choose to take West India goods on its return to New York, or if nobody will freight it, it often goes to Newcastle in England to take on coal for ballast, which when brought home sells for a pretty good price. In many parts of the town coal is used both for kitchen fires and in other rooms, because it is considered cheaper than wood, which at present costs thirty shillings of New York currency per fathom, of which measure I have before made mention. New York has likewise some trade with South Carolina, to which it sends grain, flour, sugar, rum, and other goods, and takes rice in return, which is almost the only commodity exported from South Carolina.

The goods in which the province of New York trades are not numerous. It exports chiefly the skins of animals, which are bought of the Indians about Oswego; great quantities of boards, coming for the most part from Albany; timber and casks from that part of the country which lies about the Hudson River; and lastly wheat, flour, barley, .oats and other kinds of grain, which are brought from New Jersey and the cultivated parts of this province. I have seen vessels from New Brunswick, laden with wheat which lay loose on board, with flour packed up in barrels, and also with great quantities of linseed. New York also exports pork and other meat from its own province, but not in any great amount; nor is the quantity of peas which the people about Albany bring very large. Iron, however, may be had more plentifully, as it is found in several parts of this province and is of a considerable value; but all other products of this country are of little account.

Most of the wine which is drunk here and in the other colonies is brought from the Isle of Madeira and is very strong and fiery.

No manufactures of note have as yet been established here; at present they get all manufactured goods, such as woolen and linen cloth, etc., from England, and especially from London.

The Hudson River is very convenient for the commerce of this city, as it is navigable for nearly a hundred and fifty English miles into the country, and flows into the bay, a little west of the town. During eight months of the year this river is full of greater and lesser vessels, either going to New York or returning from there, laden either with native or foreign goods.

I cannot make a true estimate of the ships that annually come to this town or sail from it. But I have learned in the Pennsylvania gazettes that from the first of December in 1729 to the fifth of December of the following year 211 ships entered the port of New York and 222 cleared it; and since that time there has been a great increase of trade here.

The country people come to market in New York twice a week, much in the same manner as they do at Philadelphia, with this difference, that the markets are here kept in several places, and one has to go from one to another sometimes to get what one needs.

Government in New York. The *governor* of the province of New York resides here, and has a palace in the fort. Among those who have been entrusted with this post, William Burnet deserves a perpetual remembrance. He was one of the sons of Dr. Thomas Burnet (so celebrated on account of his learning) and seemed to have inherited the knowledge of his father. But his great assiduity in promoting the welfare of this province is what constitutes the principal merit of his character. The people of New York therefore still reckon him the best governor they ever had, and feel they cannot praise his services too much. The many astronomical observations which he made in these parts are inserted in several English works. In the year 1727, at the accession of king George the II. to the throne of Great Britain, he was appointed governor of New England. In consequence of this he left New York and went to Boston, where he died universally lamented on the seventh of September, 1729.

An *assembly of deputies* from all the different districts of the province is held at New York once or twice every year. It may be looked upon as a parliament or diet in miniature. Everything relating to the good of the province is here debated. The governor calls the assembly, and dissolves it at pleasure. This is a power which he ought only to make use of, either when no farther debates are necessary or when the members are not so unanimous in the service of their king and country as is their duty. It frequently happens, however, that led aside by caprice or by self-interested views, he exerts it to the prejudice of the province. The colony has sometimes had a governor, whose quarrels with the inhabitants have induced their representatives, or the members of the assembly, through malice to oppose indifferently everything he proposed, whether it was beneficial to the country or not. In such cases the governor has made use of his power, dissolving the assembly, and calling another soon after, which however he again dissolved upon the least mark of their ill humor. By this means he so tired them, by the many expenses which they were forced to bear in so short a time, that they were at last glad to unite with him in his endeavors for the good of the province. But there have likewise been governors who have called assemblies and dissolved them soon after, merely because the representatives did not act according to their whims or would not give their assent to proposals which were perhaps dangerous or hurtful to the common welfare.

The king appoints the governor according to his royal pleasure; but the inhabitants of the province make up his excellency's salary. Therefore a man entrusted with this position has greater or lesser revenues, according to his ability of gaining the confidence of the inhabitants. There are examples of governors in this and other provinces of North America, who by their dissensions with the inhabitants of their respective provinces have lost their whole salary, his Majesty having no power to make them pay it. If a governor had no other resources in such circumstances he would be obliged either to resign his office, to be content with an income too small for his dignity, or else to conform in everything to the inclinations of the inhabitants. But there are several stated profits which in some measure make up for this.

1.   No one is allowed to keep a public house without the governor's leave, which is only to be obtained by the payment of a certain fee, according to the circumstances of the person. Some governors therefore, when the inhabitants refuse to pay them a salary, have hit upon the expedient of doubling the number of inns in their province.

2.   Few people who intend to be married, unless they be very poor, will have their banns published from the pulpit; so instead of this they get licenses from the governor, which empower any minister to marry them. Now for such a license the governor receives about half a guinea, and this collected throughout the whole province amounts to a considerable sum.

3.   The governor signs all passports, and especially of such travellers as go to sea, and this gives him another means of supplying his expenses. There are several other advantages allowed to him, but as they are very trifling I shall omit them.

At the above assembly the old laws are reviewed and amended, and new ones are made, and the regulation and circulation of the coinage together with all other affairs of that kind are there determined. For it is to be observed that each English colony in North America is independent of the other, and that each has its own laws and coinage, and may be looked upon in several lights as a state by itself. Hence it happens that in time of war things go on very slowly and irregularly here; for not only the opinion of one province is sometimes directly opposite to that of another, but frequently the views of the governor and those of the assembly of the same province are quite different; so that it is easy to see that, while the people are quarrelling about the best and cheapest manner of carrying on the war, an enemy has it in his power to take one place after another. It has usually happened that while some provinces have been suffering from their enemies, the neighboring ones have been quiet and inactive, as if it did not in the least concern them. They have frequently taken up two or three years in considering whether or not they should give assistance to an oppressed sister colony, and sometimes they have expressly declared themselves against it. There are instances of provinces which were not only neutral in such circumstances, but which even carry on a great trade with the power which at that very time is attacking and laying waste some other provinces.

The French in Canada, who are but an unimportant body in comparison with the English in America, have by this position of affairs been able to obtain great advantages in times of war; for if we judge from the number and power of the English, it would seem very easy for them to get the better of the French in America.

It is however, of great advantage to the crown of England that the North American colonies are near a country, under the government of the French, like Canada. There is reason to believe that the king never was earnest in his attempts to expel the French from their possessions there; though it might have been done with little difficulty. For the English colonies in this part of the world have increased so much in their number of inhabitants, and in their riches, that they almost vie with Old England. Now in order to keep up the authority and trade of their mother country and to answer several other purposes they are forbidden to establish new manufactures, which would turn to the disadvantage of the British commerce. They are not allowed to dig for any gold or silver, unless they send it to England immediately; they have not the liberty of trading with any parts that do not belong to the British dominion, excepting a few places; nor are foreigners allowed to trade with the English colonies of North America. These and some other restrictions occasion the inhabitants of the English colonies to grow less tender for their mother country. This coldness is kept up by the many foreigners such as Germans, Dutch and French, who live among the English and have no particular attachment to Old England. Add to this also that many people can never be contented with their possessions, though they be ever so large. They will always be desirous of getting more, and of enjoying the pleasure which arises from a change. Their extraordinary liberty and their luxury often lead them to unrestrained acts of selfish and arbitrary nature.

I have been told by Englishmen, and not only by such as were born in America but also by those who came from Europe, that the English colonies in North America, in the space of thirty or fifty years, would be able to form a state by themselves entirely independent of Old England. But as the whole country which lies along the seashore is unguarded, and on the land side is harassed by the French, these dangerous neighbors in times of war are sufficient to prevent the connection of the colonies with their mother country from being quite broken off. The English government has therefore sufficient reason to consider means of keeping the colonies in due submission. But I have almost gone too far from my purpose; I shall therefore finish my observations on New York. . . .

There are two printers in the town and every week some English papers are published, which contain news from all parts of the world.

The winter is much more severe here than in Pennsylvania, it being nearly as cold as in some of the provinces of Sweden: its season, however, is much shorter than with us. The spring is very early and the autumn very late, and the heat in summer is excessive. For this reason the melons planted in the fields are ripe at the beginning of August, whereas we can hardly bring them so soon to maturity under glass and in hotbeds. The cold of the winter I cannot justly determine, as the thermometric observations which were sent to me were all calculated after incorrect thermometers that were placed inside the houses and not in the open air. The snow lies for several months upon the ground, and sleighs are made use of here as in Sweden, but they are rather bulky. The Hudson River is about an English mile and a half broad at its mouth; the difference between the highest flood and the lowest ebb is between six and seven feet; and the water is very brackish. Yet the ice may remain in it for several months and has sometimes a thickness of more than a foot.

Mosquitoes. The inhabitants are sometimes greatly troubled with mosquitoes. They either follow the hay which is made near the town, in the low meadows saturated with salt water, or they accompany the cattle at night when they are brought home. I have myself experienced, and have observed in others, how much these little animals can disfigure a person's face during a single night; for the skin is sometimes so covered over with little swellings from their stings that people are ashamed to appear in public.

The *first colonists* in New York were Dutchmen. When the town and its territories were taken by the English and left to them by the next peace in exchange for Surinam, the old inhabitants were allowed either to remain at New York, and enjoy all the privileges and immunities which they were possessed of before, or to leave the place with all their goods. Most of them chose the former; and therefore the inhabitants both of the town and of the province belonging to it are still for the greatest part Dutch, who still, and especially the old people, speak their mother tongue.

They were beginning however by degrees to change their manners and opinions, chiefly indeed in the town and in its neighborhood; for most of the young people now speak principally English, go only to the English church, and would even take it amiss if they were called Dutchmen and not Englishmen.

Treatment of Germans. Though the province of New York has been inhabited by Europeans much longer than Pennsylvania, yet it is not by far so populous as that colony. This cannot be ascribed to any particular discouragement arising from the nature of the soil, for that is pretty good, but I was told of a very different reason which I shall mention here. In the reign of Queen Anne, about the year 1709, many Germans came hither, who got a tract of land from the government on which they might settle. After they had lived here for some time, and had built houses and churches and cultivated fields and meadows, their liberties and privileges were infringed upon, and under several pretences they were repeatedly deprived of parts of their land. This at last roused the Germans; they returned violence for violence, and beat those who thus robbed them of their possessions. But these proceedings were looked upon in a very bad light by the government: the leading Germans being imprisoned, they were very roughly treated and punished with the utmost rigor of the law. This however so exasperated the rest, that the greater part of them left their houses and fields and went to settle in Pennsylvania. There they were exceedingly well received, got a considerable tract of land, and were granted great privileges in perpetuity. The Germans not satisfied with being themselves removed from New York, wrote to their relations and friends and advised them if ever they intended to come to America not to go to New York, where the government had shown itself so inequitable. This advice had such influence that the Germans, who afterwards emigrated in great numbers to North America, constantly avoided New York and kept going to Pennsylvania. It sometimes happened that they were forced to go on board such ships as were bound for New York; but they had scarcely got on shore, when they hastened on to Pennsylvania, right before the eyes of all the inhabitants of New York.

The Dutch Settlers. But the lack of people in this province may likewise be accounted for in a different manner. As the Dutch, who first cultivated this section, obtained the liberty of staying here by the treaty with England, and of enjoying all their privileges and advantages without the least limitation, each of them took a very large piece of ground for himself, and many of the more powerful heads of families made themselves the possessors and masters of a country of as great territory as would be sufficient to form one of our moderately-sized, and even one of our large, parishes. Most of them being very rich, their envy of the English led them not to sell them any land, but at an excessive rate, a practice which is still punctually observed among their descendants. The English therefore, as well as people of other nations, have but little encouragement to settle here. On the other hand, they have sufficient opportunity in the other provinces to purchase land at a more moderate price, and with more security to themselves. It is not to be wondered then, that so many parts of New York are still uncultivated, and that it has entirely the appearance of a frontier-land. This instance may teach us how much a small mistake in a government can hamper the settling of a country.

Rev. Andrew Burnaby, Travels through the Middle Settlements in North-America. In the Years 1759 and 1760 *(London, 1775), pp. 104-108, 113-114.*

On Wednesday the 9th of July, I crossed over to Staten Island, in the province of New York; and travelled upon it about nine miles to the point which is opposite New York city.

In my way I had an opportunity of seeing the method of making wampum. This, I am persuaded the reader knows is the current money amongst the Indians. It is made of the clam-shell; a shell, consisting within of two colours, purple and white; and in form not unlike a thick oyster-shell. The process of manufacturing it is very simple. It is first clipped to a proper size, which is that of a small oblong parallelopiped, then drilled, and afterward ground to a round smooth surface, and polished. The purple wampum is much more valuable than the white; a very small part of the shell being of that colour.

At the point I embarked for New York; and, after a pleasant passage over the bay, which is three leagues wide; and various delightful prospects of rivers, islands, fields, hills, woods, the Narrows, New York city, vessels sailing to and fro, and innumerable porpoises playing upon the surface of the water; in an evening so serene that the hemisphere was not ruffled by a single cloud, arrived there about the setting of the sun.

This city is situated upon the point of a small island, lying open to the bay on one side, and on the others included between the North and East rivers; and commands a fine prospect of water, the Jerseys, Long Island, Staten Island, and several others, which lie scattered in the bay. It contains between two and three thousand houses, and 16 or 17,000 inhabitants, is tolerably well built, and has several good houses. The streets are paved, and very clean, but in general they are narrow; there are two or three, indeed, which are spacious and airy, particularly the Broad-Way. The houses in this street have most of them a row of trees before them; which form an agreeable shade, and produce a pretty effect. The whole length of the town is something more than a mile; the breadth of it about half an one. The situation is, I believe, esteemed healthy; but it is subject to one great inconvenience, which is the want of fresh water; so that the inhabitants are obliged to have it brought from springs at some distance out of town. There are several public buildings, though but few that deserve attention.

The college, when finished, will be exceedingly handsome: it is to be built on three sides of a quadrangle, fronting Hudson's or North river, and will be the most beautifully situated of any college, I believe, in the world. At present only one wing is finished, which is of stone, and consists of twenty-four sets of apartments; each having a large sitting-room, with a study, and bedchamber. They are obliged to make use of some of these apartments for a master's lodge, library, chapel, hall, &c. but as soon as the whole shall be completed, there will be proper apartments for each of these offices. The name of it is King's College.

There are two churches in New York, the old or Trinity Church, and the new one, or St. George's Chapel; both of them large buildings, the former in the Gothic taste, with a spire, the other upon the model of some of the new churches in London. Besides these, there are several other places of religious worship; namely, two Low Dutch Calvinist churches, one High Dutch ditto, one French ditto, one German Lutheran church, one presbyterian meeting-house, one quakers ditto, one anabaptists ditto, one Moravian ditto, and a Jews synagogue. There is also a very handsome charity-school for sixty poor boys and girls, a good work-house, barracks for a regiment of soldiers, and one of the finest prisons I have ever seen. The court or stadt-house makes no great figure, but it is to be repaired and beautified. There is a quadrangular fort, capable of mounting sixty cannon, though at present there are, I believe, only thirty-two. Within this is the governor's palace, and underneath it a battery capable of mounting ninety-four guns, and barracks for a company or two of soldiers. Upon one of the islands in the bay is an hospital for sick and wounded seamen; and, upon another, a pest-house. These are the most noted public buildings in and about the city.

The inhabitants of New York, in their character, very much resemble the Pensylvanians: more than half of them are Dutch, and almost all traders: they are, therefore, habitually frugal, industrious, and parsimonious. Being, however, of different nations, different languages, and different religions, it is almost impossible to give them any precise or determinate character. The women are handsome and agreeable; though rather more reserved than the Philadelphian ladies. Their amusements are much the same as in Pensylvania; viz. balls, and sleighing expeditions in the winter; and, in the summer, going in parties upon the water, and fishing; or making excursions into the country. There are several houses pleasantly situated upon East river, near New York, where it is common to have turtle-feasts: these happen once or twice in a week. Thirty or forty gentlemen and ladies meet and dine together, drink tea in the afternoon, fish and amuse themselves till evening, and then return home in Italian chaises, (the fashionable carriage in this and most parts of America, Virginia excepted, where they make use only of coaches, and these commonly drawn by six horses), a gentleman and lady in each chaise. In the way there is a bridge, about three miles distant from New York, which you always pass over as you return, called the Kissing-bridge; where it is a part of the etiquette to salute the lady who has put herself under your protection.

Albany

One of the oldest cities in America, Albany exerted an attraction upon 18th-century visitors because of its proximity to the Indian frontier of New York, still largely inhabited by the famous Iroquois nations. What evidence of its Dutch origins still remained in the 18th century? What signs of its frontier position were visible? How important were the Indians to the economic life of the town? What advantages did Albany enjoy in the Indian trade? How was the Albany character treated by foreign visitors? How did they suggest that this character was formed? Whose views do you think are of most worth?

Alexander Hamilton toured the American colonies in 1744 to cure a prolonged illness. It seems that summer travel was regarded more effective than the expert knowledge that this young physician had acquired at the Edinburgh Medical School seven years earlier or in his five years of practice in Annapolis, Maryland. At any rate, the cosmopolitan Scottish bachelor covered 1624 miles on horseback from 30 May to 27 September 1744, leaving us his travel diary which Carl Bridenbaugh has edited under the title of Gentleman's Progress: The Itinerarium of Dr. Alexander Hamilton, 1744 *(Chapel Hill: University of North Carolina Press for the Institute of Early American History and Culture, 1948). The following observations are taken from pp. 71-74 of that edition.*

The city of Albany lyes on the west side of Hudson's River upon a rising hill about 30 or 40 miles below where the river comes out of the lake and 160 miles above New York. The hill whereon it stands faces the south east. The city consists of three pritty compact streets, two of which run parallel to the river and are pritty broad, and the third cuts the other two att right angles, running up towards the fort, which is a square stone building about 200 foot square with a bastion att each corner, each bastion mounting eight or ten great guns, most of them 32 pounders. In the fort are two large, brick houses facing each other where there is lodging for the souldiers. There are three market houses in this city and three publick edifices, upon two of which are cupolos or spires, vizt., upon the Town House and the Dutch church. The English church is a great, heavy stone building without any steeple, standing just below the fort. The greatest length of the streets is half a mile. In the fort is kept a garrison of 300 men under the King's pay, who now and then send reinforcements to Oswego, a frontier garrison and trading town lying about 180 miles south [north] and by west of Albany. This city is inclosed by a rampart or wall of wooden palisadoes about 10 foot high and a foot thick, being the trunks of pine trees rammed into the ground, pinned close together, and ending each in a point at top. Here they call them stockadoes. Att each 200 foot distance round this wall is a block house, and from the north gate of the city runs a thick stone wall down into the river, 200 foot long, att each end of which is a block house. In these block houses about 50 of the city militia keep guard every night, and the word all's well walks constantly round all night long from centry to centry and round the fort. There are 5 or 6 gates to this city, the chief of which are the north and the south gates. In the city are about 4,000 inhabitants, mostly Dutch or of Dutch extract.

The Dutch here keep their houses very neat and clean, both without and within. Their chamber floors are generally laid with rough plank which, in time, by constant rubbing and scrubbing becomes as smooth as if it had been plained. Their chambers and rooms are large and handsom. They have their beds generally in alcoves so that you may go thro all the rooms of a great house and see never a bed. They affect pictures much, particularly scripture history, with which they adorn their rooms. They set out their cabinets and bouffetts much with china. Their kitchens are likewise very clean, and there they hang earthen or delft plates and dishes all round the walls in manner of pictures, having a hold drilled thro the edge of the plate or dish and a loop of ribbon put into it to hang it by. But notwithstanding all this nicety and cleanliness in their houses, they are in their persons slovenly and dirty. They live here very frugally and plain, for the chief merit among them seems to be riches, which they spare no pains or trouble to acquire, but are a civil and hospitable people in their way but, att best, rustick and unpolished. I imagined when I first came there that there were some very rich people in the place. They talked of 30, 40, 50 and 100 thousand pounds as of nothing, but I soon found that their riches consisted more in large tracts of land than in cash. They trade pritty much with the Indians and have their manufactorys for wampum, a good Indian commodity. It is of two sorts —the black, which is the most valuable, and the white wampum. The first kind is a bead made out of the bluish black part of a clam shell. It is valued att 6 shillings York money per 100 beads. The white is made of a conch shell from the W. Indies and is not so valuable. They grind the beads to a shape upon a stone, and then with a well tempered needle dipt in wax and tallow, they drill a hole thro' each bead. This trade is apparently triffling but would soon make an estate to a man that could have a monopoly of it, for being in perpetuall demand among the Indians from their custome of burying quantitys of it with their dead, they are very fond of it, and they will give skins or money or any thing for it, having (tho they first taught the art of making it to the Europeans) lost the art of making it themselves.

They live in their houses in Albany as if it were in prisons, all their doors and windows being perpetually shut. But the reason of this may be the little desire they have for conversation and society, their whole thoughts being turned upon profit and gain which necessarily makes them live retired and frugall. Att least this is the common character of the Dutch every where. But indeed the excessive cold winters here obliges them in that season to keep all snug and close, and they have not summer sufficient to revive heat in their veins so as to make them uneasy or put it in their heads to air themselves. They are a healthy, long lived people, many in this city being in age near or above 100 years, and 80 is a common age. They are subject to rotten teeth and scorbutick gumms which, I suppose, is caused by the cold air and their constant diet of salt provisions in the winter, for in that season they are obliged to lay in as for a sea voyage, there being no stirring out of doors then for fear of never stirring again. As to religion they have little of it among them and of enthusiasm not a' grain. The bulk of them, if any thing, are of the Lutheran church. Their women in generall, both old and young, are the hardest favoured ever I beheld. Their old women wear a comicall head dress, large pendants, short petticoats, and they stare upon one like witches. They generally eat to their morning's tea raw hung beef sliced down in thin chips in the manner of parmezan cheese. Their winter here is excessive cold so as to freeze their cattle stiff in one night in the stables.

To this city belongs about 24 sloops about 50 tons burden that go and come to York. They chiefly carry plank and rafters. The country about is very productive of hay and good grain, the woods not much cleared.

The neighbouring Indians are the Mohooks to the north west, the Canada Indians to the northward, and to the southward a small scattered nation of the Mohackanders.

The young men here call their sweethearts luffees, and a young fellow of 18 is reckoned a simpleton if he has not a luffee; but their women are so homely that a man must never have seen any other luffees else they will never entrap him.

The America of 1750. Peter Kalm's Travels in North America. The English Version of 1770, *edited by Adolph B. Benson (New York, 1937), pp. 340-347.*

Description of Albany. Next to New York Albany is the principal town, or at least the most wealthy, in the province of New York. It is situated on the slope of a hill, close to the western shore of the Hudson River, about one hundred and forty-six English miles from New York. The town extends along the river, which flows here from N.N.E. to S.S.W. The high mountains in the west, above the town, bound the view on that side. There are two churches in Albany, one English and the other Dutch. The Dutch church stands a short distance from the river on the east side of the market. It is built of stone and in the middle it has a small steeple with a bell. It has but one minister who preaches twice every Sunday. The English church is situated on the hill at the west end of the market, directly under the fort. It is likewise built of stone but has no steeple. There is no service at the church at this time because they have no minister, but all the people understand Dutch, the garrison excepted. The minister of this church, has a settled income of one hundred pounds sterling, which he gets from England. The town hall lies to the south of the Dutch church, close by the riverside. It is a fine building of stone, three stories high. It has a small tower or steeple, with a bell, and a gilt ball and vane at the top of it.

The houses in this town are very neat, and partly built of stones covered with shingles of white pine. Some are slated with tile from Holland, because the clay of this neighborhood is not considered fit for tiles. Most of the houses are built in the old Frankish way, with the gable-end towards the street, except a few, which were recently built in the modern style. A great number of houses are built like those of New Brunswick, the gable-end towards the street being of bricks and all the other walls of boards. The outside of the houses is never covered with lime or mortar, nor have I seen it practised in any North American towns which I have visited; and the walls do not seem to be damaged by the weather. The eaves on the roofs reach almost to the middle of the street. This preserves the walls from being damaged by the rain, but it is extremely disagreeable in rainy weather for the people in the streets, there being hardly any means of avoiding the water from the eaves. The front doors are generally in the middle of the houses, and on both sides are porches with seats, on which during fair weather the people spend almost the whole day, especially on those porches which are in the shade. The people seem to move with the sun and the shade, always keeping in the latter. When the sun is too hot the people disappear. In the evening the verandas are full of people of both sexes; but this is rather troublesome because a gentleman has to keep his hat in constant motion, for the people here are not Quakers whose hats are as though nailed to the head. It is considered very impolite not to lift your hat and greet everyone. The streets are broad, and some of them are paved. In some parts they are lined with trees. The long streets are almost parallel to the river, and the others intersect them at right angles. The street which goes between the two churches is five times broader than the others and serves as a marketplace. The streets upon the whole are very dirty because the people leave their cattle in them during the summer nights. There are two marketplaces in town, to which the country people come twice a week. There are no city gates here but for the most part just open holes through which people pass in and out of the town.

The fort lies higher than any other building on a high steep hill on the west side of the town. It is a great building of stone surrounded with high and thick walls. Its location is very bad, as it can serve only to keep off plundering parties without being able to sustain a siege. There are numerous high hills to the west of the fort, which command it, and from which one may see all that is done within it. There is commonly an officer and a number of soldiers quartered in it. They say the fort contains a spring of water.

Trade. The location of Albany is very advantageous in regard to trade. The Hudson River which flows close by it is from twelve to twenty feet deep. There is not yet any quay made for the better landing of the boats, because the people fear it will suffer greatly or be entirely carried away in spring by the ice which then comes down the river. The vessels which are in use here may come pretty near the shore in order to be loaded, and heavy goods are brought to them upon canoes tied together. Albany carries on a considerable commerce with New York, chiefly in furs, boards, wheat, flour, peas, several kinds of timber, etc. There is not a place in all the British colonies, the Hudson's Bay settlements excepted, where such quantities of furs and skins are bought of the Indians as at Albany. Most of the merchants in this town send a clerk or agent to Oswego, an English trading town on Lake Ontario, to which the Indians come with their furs. I intend to give a more minute account of this place in my Journal for the year 1750. The merchants from Albany spend the whole summer at Oswego, and trade with many tribes of Indians who come with their goods. Many people have assured me that the Indians are frequently cheated in disposing of their goods, especially when they are drunk, and that sometimes they do not get one half or even one tenth of the value of their goods. I have been a witness to several transactions of this kind. The merchants of Albany glory in these tricks, and are highly pleased when they have given a poor Indian, a greater portion of brandy than he can stand, and when they can, after that, get all his goods for mere trifles. The Indians often find when they are sober again, that they have for once drunk as much as they are able of a liquor which they value beyond anything else in the whole world, and they are quite insensible to their loss if they again get a draught of this nectar. Besides this trade at Oswego, a number of Indians come to Albany from several places especially from Canada; but from this latter place, they hardly bring anything but beaver skins. There is a great penalty in Canada for carrying furs to the English, that trade belonging to the French West India Company. Notwithstanding that the French merchants in Canada carry on a considerable smuggling trade. They send their furs by means of the Indians to their agent at Albany, who purchases them at the price which they have fixed upon with the French merchants. The Indians take in return several kinds of cloth, and other goods, which may be bought here at a lower rate than those which are sent to Canada from France.

The greater part of the merchants at Albany have extensive estates in the country and a large property in forests. If their estates have a little brook, they do not fail to erect a sawmill upon it for sawing boards and planks, which many boats take during the summer to New York, having scarcely any other cargo.

Many people at Albany make wampum for the Indians, which is their ornament and money, by grinding and finishing certain kinds of shells and mussels. This is of considerable profit to the inhabitants. I shall speak of this kind of money later. The extensive trade which the inhabitants of Albany carry on, and their sparing manner of living, in the Dutch way, contribute to the considerable wealth which many of them have acquired.

The Dutch in Albany. The inhabitants of Albany and its environs are almost all Dutchmen. They speak Dutch, have Dutch preachers, and the divine service is performed in that language. Their manners are likewise quite Dutch; their dress is however like that of the English. It is well known that the first Europeans who settled in the province of New York were Dutchmen. During the time that they were the masters of this province, they seized New Sweden of which they were jealous. However, the pleasure of possessing this conquered land and their own was but of short duration, for towards the end of 1664 Sir Robert Carr, by order of King Charles the second, went to New York, then New Amsterdam, and took it. Soon after Colonel Nicolls went to Albany, which then bore the name of Fort Orange, and upon taking it, named it Albany, from the Duke of York's Scotch title. The Dutch inhabitants were allowed either to continue where they were, and under the protection of the English to enjoy all their former privileges, or to leave the country. The greater part of them chose to stay and from them the Dutchmen are descended who now live in the province of New York, and who possess the greatest and best estates in that province.

The avarice, selfishness and immeasurable love of money of the inhabitants of Albany are very well known throughout all North America, by the French and even by the Dutch, in the lower part of New York province. If anyone ever intends to go to Albany it is said in jest that he is about to go to the land of Canaan, since Canaan and the land of the Jews mean one and the same thing, and that Albany is a fatherland and proper home for arch-Jews, since the inhabitants of Albany are even worse. If a real Jew, who understands the art of getting forward perfectly well, should settle amongst them, they would not fail to ruin him. For this reason nobody comes to this place without the most pressing necessity; and therefore I was asked in several places, both this and the following year, what induced me to make the pilgrimage to this New Canaan. I likewise found that the judgment which people formed of them was not without foundation. For though they seldom see any strangers, (except those who go from the British colonies to Canada and back again) and one might therefore expect to find victuals and accommodation for travellers cheaper than in places where they always resort, yet I experienced the contrary. I was here obliged to pay for everything twice, thrice and four times as much as in any part of North America which I have passed through. If I wanted their assistance, I was obliged to pay them very well for it, and when I wanted to purchase anything or be helped in some case or other, I could at once see what kind of blood ran in their veins, for they either fixed exorbitant prices for their services or were very reluctant to assist me. Such was this people in general. However, there were some among them who equalled any in North America or anywhere else, in politeness, equity, goodness, and readiness to serve and to oblige; but their number fell far short of that of the former. If I may be allowed to declare my conjectures, the origin of the inhabitants of Albany and its neighborhood seems to me to be as follows. While the Dutch possessed this country, and intended to people it, the government sent a pack of vagabonds of which they intended to clear their native country, and sent them along with a number of other settlers to this province. The vagabonds were sent far from the other colonists, upon the borders towards the Indians and other enemies, and a few honest families were persuaded to go with them, in order to keep them in bounds. I cannot in any other way account for the difference between the inhabitants of Albany and the other descendants of so respectable a nation as the Dutch, who are settled in the lower part of New York province. The latter are civil, obliging, just in prices, and sincere; and though they are not ceremonious, yet they are well meaning and honest and their promises may be relied on.

The behavior of the inhabitants of Albany during the war between England and France, which ended with the peace of Aix la Chapelle, has, among several other causes, contributed to make them the object of hatred in all the British colonies, but more especially in New England. For at the beginning of that war when the Indians of both parties had received orders to commence hostilities, the French engaged theirs to attack the inhabitants of New England, which they faithfully executed, killing everybody they met with, and carrying off whatever they found. During this time the people of Albany remained neutral, and carried on a great trade with the very Indians who murdered the inhabitants of New England. Articles such as silver spoons, bowls, cups, etc. of which the Indians robbed the houses in New England, were carried to Albany, for sale. The people of that town bought up these silver vessels, though the names of the owners were engraved on many of them, and encouraged the Indians to get more of them, promising to pay them well, and whatever they would demand. This was afterwards interpreted by the inhabitants of New England to mean that the colonists of Albany encouraged the Indians to kill more of the New England people, who were in a manner their brothers, and who were subjects of the same crown. Upon the first news of this behavior, which the Indians themselves spread in New England, the inhabitants of the latter province were greatly incensed, and threatened that the first step they would take in another war would be to burn Albany and the adjacent parts. In the present war it will sufficiently appear how backward the other British provinces in America are in assisting Albany, and the neighboring places, in case of an attack from the French or Indians. The hatred which the English bear against the people at Albany is very great, but that of the Albanians against the English is carried to a ten times higher degree. This hatred has subsisted ever since the time when the English conquered this section, and is not yet extinguished, though they could never have gotten larger advantages under the Dutch government than they have obtained under that of the English. For, in a manner, their privileges are greater than those of Englishmen themselves.

In their homes the inhabitants of Albany are much more sparing than the English and are stingier with their food. Generally what they serve is just enough for the meal and sometimes hardly that. The punch bowl is much more rarely seen than among the English. The women are perfectly well acquainted with economy; they rise early, go to sleep very late, and are almost superstitiously clean in regard to the floor, which is frequently scoured several times in the week. Inside the homes the women are neatly but not lavishly dressed. The children are taught both English and Dutch. The servants in the town are chiefly negroes. Some of the inhabitants wear their own hair very short, without a bag or queue, because these are looked upon as the characteristics of Frenchmen. As I wore my hair in a bag the first day I came here from Canada, I was surrounded with children, who called me a Frenchman, and some of the boldest offered to pull at my French head dress, so I was glad to get rid of it.

Their food and its preparation is very different from that of the English. Their breakfast is tea, commonly without milk. About thirty or forty years ago, tea was unknown to them, and they breakfasted either upon bread and butter, or bread and milk. They never put sugar into the cup, but take a small bit of it into their mouths while they drink. Along with the tea they eat bread and butter, with slices of dried beef. The host himself generally says grace aloud. Coffee is not usual here. They breakfast generally about seven. Their dinner is buttermilk and bread, to which they add sugar on special occasions, when it is a delicious dish for them, or fresh milk and bread, with boiled or roasted meat. They sometimes make use of buttermilk instead of fresh milk, in which to boil a thin kind of porridge that tastes very sour but not disagreeable in hot weather. With each dinner they have a large salad, prepared with an abundance of vinegar, and very little or no oil. They frequently drink buttermilk and eat bread and salad, one mouthful after another. Their supper consists generally of bread and butter, and milk with small pieces of bread in it. The butter is very salt. Sometimes too they have chocolate. They occasionally eat cheese at breakfast and at dinner; it is not in slices, but scraped or rasped, so as to resemble coarse flour, which they pretend adds to the good taste of cheese. They commonly drink very weak beer, or pure water.

Mrs. Anne [MacVicar] Grant, Memoirs of an American Lady with Sketches of Manners and Scenes in America as They Existed Previous to the Revolution *(London, 1809), vol. 1, pp. 76-80, 83-90*.

In the more ordinary course of things, love, which makes labour light, tamed these young hunters [Albany boys], and transformed them into diligent and laborious traders, for the nature of their trade included very severe labour. When one of the *boys* was deeply smitten, his fowling-piece and fishing rod were at once relinquished. He demanded of his father forty or at most fifty dollars, a negro boy, and a canoe; all of a sudden he assumed the brow of care and solicitude, and began to smoke, a precaution absolutely necessary to repel aguish damps, and troublesome insects. He arrayed himself in a habit very little differing from that of the Aborigines, into whose bounds he was about to penetrate, and in short commenced Indian trader. That strange amphibious animal, who, uniting the acute senses, the strong instincts, and the unconquerable patience and fortitude of the savage, with the art, policy, and inventions of the European, encountered in the pursuit of gain dangers and difficulties equal to those described in the romantic legends of chivalry.

The small bark canoe in which this hardy adventurer embarked himself, his fortune, and his faithful *squire*, (who was generally born in the same house, and predestined to his service,) was launched amidst the tears and prayers of his female relations, amongst whom was generally included his destined bride, who well knew herself to be the motive of this perilous adventure.

The canoe was entirely filled with coarse strouds and blankets, guns, powder, beads, &c. suited to the various wants and fancies of the natives; one pernicious article was never wanting, and often made a great part of cargo. This was ardent spirits, for which the natives too early acquired a relish, and the possession of which always proved dangerous, and sometimes fatal to the traders. The Mohawks bring their furs and other peltry habitually to the stores of their wonted and patrons. It was not in that easy and safe direction that these trading adventures extended. The canoe generally steered northward towards the Canadian frontier. They passed by the Flats and Stonehook in the outset of their journey. Then commenced their toils and dangers at the famous water-fall called the Cohoes, ten miles above Albany, where three rivers, uniting their streams into one, dash over a rocky shelf, and falling into a gulph below with great violence, raise clouds of mist bedecked with splendid rain-bows. This was the Rubicon which they had to cross before they plunged into pathless woods, ingulphing swamps, and lakes, the opposite shores of which the eye could not reach. At the Cohoes, on account of the obstruction formed by the torrent, they unloaded their canoe, and carried it above a mile further upon their shoulders, returning again for the cargo, which they were obliged to transport in the same manner. This was but a prelude to labours and dangers, incredible to those who dwell at ease. Further on, much longer carrying places frequently recurred: where they had the vessel and cargo to drag through thickets impervious to the day, abounding with snakes and wild beasts, which are always to be found on the side of rivers.

Their provision of food was necessarily small, from fear of over loading the slender and unstable conveyance already crouded with goods. A little dried beef and Indian corn-meal was their whole stock, though they formerly enjoyed both plenty and variety. They were in a great measure obliged to depend upon their own skill in hunting and fishing, and on the hospitality of the Indians: for hunting, indeed, they had small leisure, their time being sedulously employed by the obstacles that retarded their progress. In their slight and fragile canoes, they often had to cross great lakes, on which the wind raised a terrible surge. Afraid of going into the track of the French traders, who were always dangerous rivals, and often declared enemies, they durst not follow the direction of the river St. Lawrence; but, in search of distant territories and unknown tribes, were wont to deviate to the east and south-west, forcing their painful way towards the source of "rivers unknown to song," whose winding course was often interrupted by shallows, and oftener still by fallen trees of great magnitude lying across, which it was requisite to cut through with their hatchets before they could proceed. Small rivers which wind through fertile valleys, in this country, are peculiarly liable to this obstruction. The chesnut and hiccory grow to so large a size in this kind of soil, that in time they become top-heavy, and are then the first prey to the violence of the winds; and thus falling, form a kind of accidental bridge over these rivers. . . . It is inconceivable how well these young travellers, taught by their Indian friends, and the experimental knowledge of their fathers, understood every soil and its productions. A boy of twelve years old would astonish you with his accurate knowledge of plants, their properties, and their relation to the soil and to each other. "Here," said he, "is a wood of red oak, when it is grubbed up this will be loam and sand, and make good Indian-corn ground. This chesnut wood abounds with strawberries, and is the very best soil for wheat. The poplar wood yonder is not worth clearing; the soil is always wet and cold. There is a hiccory wood, where the soil is always rich and deep, and does not run out; such and such plants that dye blue, or orange, grow under it."

This is merely a slight epitome of the wide views of nature that are laid open to these people from their very infancy, the acquisition of this kind of knowledge being one of their first amusements; yet those who were capable of astonishing you by the extent and variety of this local skill, in objects so varied and so complicated, never heard of a petal, corolla, or stigma in their lives, nor even of the strata of that soil, with the productions and properties of which they were so intimately acquainted.

Without compass, or guide of any kind, the traders steered through these pathless forests. In those gloomy days when the sun is not visible, or in winter, when the falling snows obscured his beams, they made an incision on the bark on the different sides of a tree; that on the north was invariably thicker than the other, and covered with

moss in much greater quantity. And this never-failing indication of
the polar influence, was to those sagacious travellers a sufficient
guide. They had indeed several subordinate monitors. Knowing so
well as they did the quality of the soil by the trees or plants most
prevalent, they could avoid a swamp, or approach with certainty to
a river or high ground if such was their wish, by means that to us
would seem incomprehensible. Even the savages seldom visited these
districts, except in the dead of winter; they had towns, as they called
their summer dwellings, on the banks of the lakes and rivers in the
interior, where their great fishing places were. In the winter, their
grand hunting parties were in places more remote from our boundaries,
where the deer and other larger animals took shelter from the
neighbourhood of man. These single adventurers sought the Indians
in their spring haunts as soon as the rivers were open; there they had
new dangers to apprehend. It is well known that among the natives
of America, revenge was actually a virtue, and retaliation a positive
duty; while faith was kept with these people they never became
aggressors. But the Europeans, by the force of bad example, and
strong liquors, seduced them from their wonted probity. Yet from the
first their notion of justice and revenge was of that vague and general
nature, that if they considered themselves injured, or if one of their
tribe had been killed by an inhabitant of any one of our settlements,
they considered any individual of our nation as a proper subject for
retribution. This seldom happened among our allies; indeed never, but
when the injury was obvious, and our people very culpable. But the
avidity of gain often led our traders to deal with Indians, among whom
the French possessed a degree of influence, which produced a
smothered animosity to our nation. When at length, after conquering
numberless obstacles, they arrived at the place of their destination,
these daring adventurers found occasion for no little address, patience,
and indeed courage, before they could dispose of their cargo, and
return safely with the profits.

The successful trader had now laid the foundation of his fortune,
and approved himself worthy of her for whose sake he encountered
all these dangers. It is utterly inconceivable, how even a single season,
spent in this manner, ripened the mind, and changed the whole appearance, nay the very character of the countenance of these demi-savages,
for such they seem on returning from among their friends in the forests. Lofty, sedate, and collected, they seem masters of themselves,

and independent of others; though, sun-burnt and austere, one scarce knows them till they unbend. By this Indian likeness, I do not think them by any means degraded. One must have seen these people, (the Indians I mean,) to have any idea what a noble animal man is, while unsophisticated. Of the class of social beings (for such indeed they were) of whom I speak, let us judge from the traders who know their language and customs, and from the adopted prisoners who have spent years among them. How unequivocal, how consistent is the testimony they bear to their humanity, friendship, fortitude, fidelity, and generosity; . . .

The joy that the return of these youths occasioned was proportioned to the anxiety their perilous journey had produced. In some instances the union of the lovers immediately took place before the next career of gainful hardships commenced. But the more cautious went to New York in winter, disposed of their peltry, purchased a large cargo, and another slave and canoe. The next year they laid out the profits of their former adventures in flour and provisions, the staple of the province; this they disposed of at the Bermuda Islands, where they generally purchased one of those light sailing cedar schooners, for building of which those islanders are famous, and proceeding the Leeward Islands, loaded it with a cargo of rum, sugar, and molasses.

They were now ripened into men, and considered as active and useful members of society, possessing a stake in the common weal.

The young adventurer had generally finished this process by the same time he was one or (at most) two and twenty. He now married, or if married before, which pretty often was the case, brought home his wife to a house of his own. Either he kept his schooner, and loading her with produce, sailed up and down the river all summer, and all winter disposed of the cargoes he obtained in exchange to more distant settlers; or he sold her, purchased European goods, and kept a store. Otherwise he settled in the country, and became as diligent in his agricultural pursuits as if he had never known any other.

Boston

As Boston went, so went Massachusetts. How had the character of Boston changed since the 17th century? What vestiges of the old

Puritanism remained? What new influences were visible? Had anything taken the place of religion as a source of social cohesion in the city? What effect did the Revolution have on Boston society?

Gentleman's Progress: The Itinerarium of Dr. Alexander Hamilton, 1744, *edited by Carl Bridenbaugh (Williamsburg, 1948), pp. 144-146.*

I need scarce take notice that Boston is the largest town in North America, being much about the same extent as the city of Glasgow in Scotland and having much the same number of inhabitants, which is between 20 and 30 thousand. It is considerably larger than either Philadelphia or New York, but the streets are irregularly disposed and, in generall, too narrow. The best street in the town is that which runs down towards the Long Wharff which goes by the name of King's Street. This town is a considerable place for shipping and carrys on a great trade in time of peace. There were now above 100 ships in the harbour besides a great number of small craft tho now, upon account of the war, the times are very dead. The people of this province chiefly follow farming and merchandise. Their staples are shipping, lumber, and fish. The government is so far democratic as that the election of the Governour's Council and the great officers is made by the members of the Lower House, or representatives of the people. Mr. [William] Shirly, the present Governour, is a man of excellent sense and understanding and is very well respected there. He understands how to humour the people and, att the same time, acts for the interest of the Goverment. Boston is better fortified against an enimy than any port in North America, not only upon account of the strength of the Castle but the narrow passage up into the harbour which is not above 160 foot wide in the channell att high water.

There are many different religions and perswasions here, but the chief sect is that of the Presbyterians. There are above 25 churches, chapells, and meetings in the town, but the Quakers here have but a small remnant, having been banished the province att the first settlement upon account of some disturbances they raised. The people here have lately been, and indeed are now, in great confusion and much infested with enthusiasm from the preaching of some fanaticks and New Light teachers, but now this humour begins to lessen. The people are generally more captivated with speculative than with practicall religion. It is not by half such a flagrant sin to cheat and cozen one's neighbour as it is to ride about for pleasure on the sabbath day or to neglect going to church and singing of psalms.

The middling sort of people here are to a degree dissingenuous and dissembling, which appears even in their common conversation in which their indirect and dubious answers to the plainest and fairest questions show their suspicions of one another. The better sort are polite, mannerly, and hospitable to strangers, such strangers, I mean, as come not to trade among them (for of them they are jealous). There is more hospitality and frankness showed here to strangers than either att [New] York or at Philadelphia. And in the place there is abundance of men of learning and parts; so that one is att no loss for agreeable conversation nor for any sett of company he pleases. Assemblys of the gayer sort are frequent here; the gentlemen and ladys meeting almost every week att consorts of musick and balls. I was present att two or three such and saw as fine a ring of ladys, as good dancing, and heard musick as elegant as I had been witness to any where. I must take notice that this place abounds with pritty women who appear rather more abroad than they do att York and dress elegantly. They are, for the most part, free and affable as well as pritty. I saw not one prude while I was here.

J. P. Brissot de Warville, New Travels in the United States 1788, *translated by Mara Soceanu Vamos and Durand Echeverria, edited by Durand Echeverria (Cambridge, 1964), pp. 84-86, 90-93, 99-101.*

Boston, July 30, 1788

How joyfully, my dear friend, did I leap ashore to tread this land of liberty! I was weary of the sea, and the sight of woods and towns—even of men—was wonderfully restful to my eyes, tired by the empty desert of the ocean. A refugee from despotism, I was at last to have the happiness of witnessing freedom, of seeing a people whom nature, education, and tradition had endowed with that equality of rights which is everywhere else considered a chimerical dream. With what pleasure did I look upon this city, the first one to shake off the English yoke, the city which had for so long resisted all the seductions and threats of Britain and had endured all the horrors of civil war! What a delight it was to wander along that long street whose

simple wooden houses face Boston's magnificent harbor, and to stroll
past the shops which displayed for sale all the products of the continent I had just left! How I enjoyed watching the shopkeepers, the
workmen, and the seamen at their various tasks! This was not the
noisy, distracting bustle of Paris; the people did not have the tense,
harried look of the French, that intense preoccupation with pleasure,
nor did they display the towering pride of the English. They had
instead the simple and kindly but dignified look of men who are conscious of their liberty and to whom all other men are merely brothers
and equals. Everything on this street seemed to say that here was a
city still in its infancy, but one which even in its infancy was enjoying
a great prosperity. I felt as though I were in Salentum, of which
Fénelon's sensitive pen has left us such an entrancing picture. But
the prosperity of this new Salentum was not the work of a single man,
of a king or of a minister; it was the creation of Liberty, mother of
industry. Under her protection all the achievements of men are rapid,
noble, and enduring. Prosperity brought about by a king or a minister
is as ephemeral as the royal reign or a minister's tenure. Boston is
barely reviving from the horrors of civil war, but its commerce is
flourishing; it is not yet a century old, but its arts, manufactures, products, and learning offer the opportunity for innumerable curious and
interesting observations. I shall write down for you those I made during my first stay after my arrival and during a second visit.

The manners and customs of Boston are not quite like those
described in the *Letters from an American Farmer*, that work so full
of sensibility. [See page 217]   You will no longer find that intran-
sigent Presbyterianism which condemned all pleasure, even that of a
walk, which forbade traveling on Sunday, and which persecuted those
who opposed its doctrines. Bostonians now combine with their simplicity French politeness and that delicacy of manners which renders
virtue all the more amiable. They are courteous to foreigners and
obliging to their friends; they are tender husbands, loving—almost
adoring—fathers, and kind masters. Music, which their preachers formerly proscribed as a diabolical art, is now beginning to form part
of their education. In certain wealthy homes you now hear pianofortes.
This art, it is true, is still only in its infancy, but the young girls
who are learning to play are so sweet, so kind, and so modest that
the pleasure they give you is far greater than any that proud profi-
ciency could offer. God grant that the women of Boston never imitate

French women in their mania for technical perfection! It is attained only at the price of the homely virtues.

Girls here enjoy the same freedom that they have in England and that they used to have in Geneva when that city was a republic and moral standards were respected. This freedom they do not abuse. Their sensitive and open hearts need not fear the deceits practiced by the roués of the Old World, and seductions are very rare. A girl believes an oath pronounced by love, and her young man keeps his word or else is forever disgraced. You see girls go off for a drive in the country with their sweethearts in a chaise, and their innocent pleasures are never beclouded with insulting suspicions.

When they become mothers, the women of Boston grow reserved, but they are just as natural, kind, and sociable as in their youth. Entirely devoted to their households, they care about nothing but making their husbands happy and about bringing up their children well. In cases of adultery the law provides heavy penalties such as the pillory or imprisonment. But these punishments are seldom inflicted, for almost all marriages here are happy, and, being happy, are pure.

Neatness and cleanliness without extravagance are the visible signs of this moral purity, and these qualities are to be seen everywhere in Boston, in the dress of the people, in their houses, and in their churches. Nothing is more agreeable than the sight of a congregation gathered in a meetinghouse on a Sunday. The men are dressed in good cloth coats and the women and children in calicoes and chintzes, without any of those baubles and gewgaws which our French women add out of boredom, whim, or just bad taste. No powder or pomatum ever sully the hair of youths or children, but I am unhappy to say one does see them on the heads of some men, for the art of the hairdresser has, alas, already crossed the seas. . . .

Since the old Puritan austerity is slowly disappearing, one is not surprised to see card games introduced among these good Presbyterians. Men and women filled with evangelical fervor and those who endure religious persecution are never bored; for their minds feed continually on their hatred and their misfortunes. But when life is peaceful and easy there are moments of leisure, and for a people who have no theaters, card games are a natural way to fill such moments. This is particularly true in a country such as this, where men do not spend their time courting women, where they read few books, and where they are even less interested in learning and the sciences. This taste for cards is certainly very unfortunate in a republican state; it is a habit which stultifies the mind. Fortunately, there is no heavy gambling, and you never see heads of families risking their entire fortunes at the card table.

There are several clubs in Boston. M. Chastellux mentions a private club which meets once a week and to which he was invited. I went there several times and was always delighted with the members' politeness to foreigners and with the learning they displayed in their conversations. There are only sixteen members and one can be admitted only by a unanimous vote. Each member may bring one guest. Meetings are held at the home of each member in turn. Clubs no longer meet in taverns, and this is a blessing, for people drink less, drinks are cheaper, and less money is spent. The need to save cash, which was felt at the end of the war, probably led to this change in custom, to the benefit of public morals.

There are no coffeehouses in this city, or in New York or Philadelphia either. There is, however, a single establishment known by this name which serves as a meeting place and exchange for merchants.

One of the principal pleasures of the inhabitants of these cities consists in parties in the country with one's family or a few friends. The favorite drink, especially after dinner, is tea. In this, as in their whole way of life, Bostonians and Americans in general greatly resemble the English. Punch, hot or cold, is drunk before dinner. Excellent beef or mutton, fish, and vegetables of all sorts, as well as Madeira or Spanish wines, and Bordeaux in the summer, are to be found on their bountifully served tables. Spruce beer and the excellent local cider precede the wine. English porter used to be served exclusively, but it has now been replaced by an excellent porter brewed near Philadelphia, which is so similar to the English that even British palates have been deceived. It is a great advantage for America not to have to pay extra to English brewers for their product. This country will soon be self-sufficient in another product when the making of cheese has been perfected. I have tasted some delicious cheeses which can compete with English Cheshire and French Roquefort. Excellent cheeses are made at Weymouth, a small island belonging to the respected former Governor Bowdoin. He used to raise a great many cattle on the island, but during the last war they were all destroyed or stolen by the English. He is now beginning to replace his losses. Soon his Weymouth cheese will become a profitable local industry and will displace the English product, to which rich men are still attached by habit, despite the enormous duties placed on it by the state.

After forcing the English to surrender control of the country, Americans now want to rival them in all fields, and this competitive spirit is visible everywhere. A Mr. Break and several other private investors have built in Boston a superb glass factory—a most useful industry in a country rich enough for good liquors to be within the reach of all citizens and consequently for glass containers to be a necessity, and where window glass is used in an astonishing abundance, even in country houses. A German was supervising the erection of Mr. Break's useful glassworks, built in the form of a rotunda, and his knowledge of chemistry had led to the discovery of a sand which makes better bottles than Europe can provide.

It is this spirit of competition which has opened up for Bostonians so many avenues of foreign trade and is sending them out into the most remote regions of the globe. Two ships have already completed voyages to the East Indies with great success. They carried salt beef, lumber, and other cargo to the Cape of Good Hope and to Ile Bourbon, which they exchanged for dollars and coffee.

Would you care to hear a story illustrating this circular trade? One of their ships returned with 300 barrels of coffee which cost 6 s. per pound; it sold 150 barrels in America and carried 150 to Gothenburg, where it loaded tea, which was sold in Constantinople. Note that these were seas and ports hitherto unknown to Americans. Formerly they sailed only in certain narrowly restricted regions.

> Nil mortalibus arduum est;
> Audax Japeti genus.

> (Nothing is impossible to mortals,
> To the daring race of Japetus.)

If these lines can apply to any people, surely they apply to Free Americans. No danger, no distance, no obstacle stops them. What have they to fear? All nations are their brothers; they wish to be at peace with all men.

The first voyages made to Canton filled the people of Boston with such enthusiasm that to commemorate the achievement they struck a medal in honor of the two captains who made the trips.

It is this spirit of competition which has so increased the number of fine ropewalks in this city and has improved their product; it has likewise created factories for spinning hemp and flax, which provide a good occupation for young people without forcing them to work in crowded groups to the ruin of their health and their morals, and which supply a particularly suitable occupation for women left idle by the long voyages of their seafaring husbands or by other accidents.

To the same spirit of competition and enterprise are due the salt-works now being built, the factories producing wallpaper and nails, the papermills, of which there are many in the state, especially in Watertown, and the distilleries making the cheap rum previously used in the Guinea trade. Much less rum has been consumed since the suppression of this traffic and since the Quakers and the Methodists have begun to preach so fervently to the country people against the use of spirits. As a result distilleries are becoming fewer around Boston. Humanity will be the better for this; and what small loss American industry may suffer by the disappearance of these poison factories will be soon repaired.

At the present moment the American people are afflicted by two ills: the wave of emigration to the West, of which I shall speak later, and the growth of manufacturing. Massachusetts is trying to rival Connecticut and Pennsylvania in its industrial growth, and there has been organized, as in the latter state, a society for the encouragement of manufacturing and industry.

Usually such societies are formed by merchants, farmers and leading government figures in the state. Each member contributes his knowledge and a modest sum of money. Wit or intellect are not in great demand in these groups, which instead stress practical benefits and whose members are trying to be useful. . . .

Besides the societies for the encouragement of agriculture and manufacturing, Bostonians have founded still another by the name of the Humane Society. Its purpose is to revive drowned people, or rather to prevent deaths caused by ignorance. This society, modeled on that of London, which in turn is copied from the one in Paris, knows and practices all the methods used in Europe. It has rendered important services, for you may well imagine that in a seaport accidents occur very frequently. This society has about 153 members, who contribute toward its expenses. It awards prizes to those who have saved the lives of persons in danger of drowning or who have quickly alerted the society in such cases. It has constructed buildings on the three most dangerous points on the coast, where help is given to the shipwrecked.

The Medical Society is no less useful than the Humane Society. It conducts correspondence with all villages and towns to learn of outbreaks of disease, to study the symptoms, to find the best remedies, and to alert the citizens.

Another valuable establishment is the Almshouse. It is intended for those who are unable to make a living either because of illness or old age. I was told that it cares for 150 persons—women, children, and old people.

The Workhouse, or house of correction, is not, you may be sure, so well populated. It is natural that in a young country, in an active port where provisions are very cheap, in short, in a city where virtue prevails, the number of thieves and rogues must be very small. This kind of vermin thrives on poverty and unemployment; here there is no poverty and the supply of work is greater than the supply of workers. . . .

One of the professions which, unfortunately, is quite lucrative in this state is that of the law. There are still preserved here the costly forms of English legal procedure, forms which common sense and a taste for orderly methods will undoubtedly eliminate, but which at present make lawyers necessary. American lawyers have also adopted from their English forefathers the habit of demanding very high fees. But this is not the only harm that lawyers cause this state; they also worm their way into the houses of the legislature and into the administration, which they infiltrate with their vexing disputatiousness.

Employment in government offices and in the legislature is in great demand—in the cities because the pay, which is quite considerable, brings in cash; in the country because in addition it lends prestige. People complain that this pay is much higher than it was under the English government. They do not realize that the English government and its creatures managed to compensate themselves for their inadequate pay by abuses which have now been abolished. The governor of Massachusetts receives £1,100. The governor of New Hampshire, not even £200. The latter state does not spend more than £2,000 for its entire civil list.

In spite of the abuses to which the law is subject, the people of Massachusetts complain very little about their lawyers.

III. THE RELUCTANT AMERICANS

The American conscience has to live with two evils perpetrated in the colonial period of its history: the dispossession of the native American people of their ancestral lands and the enslavement of black people. In the end they were both the product of the attitude that the early colonists held toward people of another color and culture. (See p. 42) What evidence is there that slavery was based more on color than on culture? What was the origin of most slaves in the 18th century? Was it any different in the 17th century? Did slaves receive equal justice with whites? How free were free blacks? free from what? Were American slaves treated better than those in the West Indies? Were different slaves treated differently in the American colonies? Did northern slavery differ from southern slavery? Why were most slaves not educated or Christianized? What forms of resistance did slaves use toward their masters? What arguments did contemporaries use to justify the enslavement of black people? to justify their emancipation?

"Report of the Journey of Francis Louis Michel from Berne, Switzerland, to Virginia, October 2, 1701-December 1, 1702," translated and edited by William J. Hinke, The Virginia Magazine of History and Biography, *24 (1916), pp. 116-117.*

There are many people who have plantations for rent. Two to five pounds secures a good dwelling, and as much land as one can work. Most of the wealth consists in slaves or negroes, for if one has many workmen, much food-stuff and tobacco can be produced. These negroes are brought annually in large numbers from Guiné and

Jamaica, (the latter of which belongs to England) on English ships. They can be selected according to pleasure, young and old, men and women. They are entirely naked when they arrive, having only corals of different colors around their neck and arms. They usually cost from 18-30 pounds. They are life-long slaves and good workmen after they have become acclimated. Many die on the journey or in the beginning of their stay here, because they receive meagre food and are kept very strictly. Both sexes are usually bought, which increase afterwards. The children like the parents must live in slavery. Even if they desire to become Christians, it is only rarely permitted, because the English law prescribes that after seven years' service they are [in that case] to be freed, in accordance with the Mosaic law. When a slave is bought from the captain of a ship, he is not paid at once, but the slave so bought usually plants tobacco, in order that the captain may be paid with it. Lately, before my departure, I was over night on a ship, which several days before had come from Guiné with 230 slaves. They get them there for a small sum, as also gold and ivory, but a hundred of them died on the journey to Virginia. It is said to be a very unhealthy country. Half of the sailors died also, including the brother of the captain, who had sailed along as clerk. The others were sickly and yellow in their faces. It often happens that the ships must be left in Guiné, because everybody dies of sickness. The captain, to whom I refer, was named Schmid. He almost shared the same fate. I was surprized at the animal-like people, The savages [Indians] are a far better breed. Among such people food tastes so badly, that one can hardly stand it. The negro fever is due to this, because it is their common sickness. It clings to people for a long time and emaciates them very much.

The America of 1750. Peter Kalm's Travels in North America. The English Version of 1770, *edited by Adolph B. Benson (New York, 1937), pp. 204-211.*

Servants. The servants which are employed in the English-American colonies are either free persons or slaves, and the former, again, are of two different classes.

1. Those who are entirely free serve by the year. They are not only allowed to leave their service at the expiration of their year, but may

leave it at any time when they do not agree with their masters. However, in that case they are in danger of losing their wages, which are very considerable. A man servant who has some ability gets between sixteen and twenty pounds in Pennsylvania currency, but those in the country do not get so much. A maidservant gets eight or ten pounds a year. These servants have their food besides their wages, but they must buy their own clothes, and whatever they get of these as gifts they must thank their master's generosity for.

Indenture. 2. The second kind of free servants consists of such persons as annually come from Germany, England and other countries, in order to settle here. These newcomers are very numerous every year: there are old and young of both sexes. Some of them have fled from oppression, under which they have labored. Others have been driven from their country by religious persecution, but most of them are poor and have not money enough to pay their passage, which is between six and eight pounds sterling for each person. Therefore, they agree with the captain that they will suffer themselves to be sold for a few years on their arrival. In that case the person who buys them pays the freight for them; but frequently very old people come over who cannot pay their passage, they therefore sell their children for several years, so that they serve both for themselves and for their parents. There are likewise some who pay part of their passage, and they are sold only for a short time. From these circumstances it appears that the price on the poor foreigners who come over to North America varies considerably, and that some of them have to serve longer than others. When their time has expired, they get a new suit of clothes from their master and some other things. He is likewise obliged to feed and clothe them during the years of their servitude. Many of the Germans who come hither bring money enough with them to pay their passage, but prefer to be sold, hoping that during their servitude they may get a knowledge of the language and character of the country and the life, that they may the better be able to consider what they shall do when they have gotten their liberty. Such servants are preferable to all others, because they are not so expensive. To buy a negro or black slave requires too much money at one time; and men or maids who get yearly wages are likewise too costly. But this kind of servant may be gotten for half the money, and even for less; for they commonly pay fourteen pounds, Pennsylvania currency, for a person who is to serve four years, and so on in proportion.

Their wages therefore are not above three pounds Pennsylvania currency per annum. These servants are, after the English, called *servingar* by the Swedes. When a person has bought such a servant for a certain number of years, and has an intention to sell him again, he is at liberty to do so, but is obliged, at the expiration of the term of servitude, to provide the usual suit of clothes for the servant, unless he has made that part of the bargain with the purchaser. The English and Irish commonly sell themselves for four years, but the Germans frequently agree with the captain before they set out, to pay him a certain sum of money, for a certain number of persons. As soon as they arrive in America they go about and try to get a man who will pay the passage for them. In return they give according to their circumstances, one or several of their children to serve a certain number of years. At last they make their bargain with the highest bidder. 3. The *negroes* or blacks constitute the third kind. They are in a manner slaves; for when a negro is once bought, he is the purchaser's servant as long as he lives, unless he gives him to another, or sets him free. However, it is not in the power of the master to kill his negro for a fault, but he must leave it to the magistrates to proceed according to the laws. Formerly the negroes were brought over from Africa, and bought by almost everyone who could afford it, the Quakers alone being an exception. But these are no longer so particular and now they have as many negroes as other people. However, many people cannot conquer the idea of its being contrary to the laws of Christianity to keep slaves. There are likewise several free negroes in town, who have been lucky enough to get a very zealous Quaker for their master, and who gave them their liberty after they had faithfully served him for a time.

At present they seldom bring over any negroes to the English colonies, for those which were formerly brought thither have multiplied rapidly. In regard to their marriage they proceed as follows: in case you have not only male but likewise female negroes, they may intermarry, and then the children are all your slaves. But if you possess a male negro only and he has an inclination to marry a female belonging to a different master, you do not hinder your negro in so delicate a point, but it is of no advantage to you, for the children belong to the master of the female. It is therefore practically advantageous to have negro women. A man who kills his negro is, legally, punishable by death, but there is no instance here of a white man ever having been executed for this crime. A few years ago it happened that a master killed his slave. His friends and even the magistrates secretly advised him to make his escape, as otherwise they could not avoid taking him prisoner, and then he would be condemned to die according to the laws of the country, without any hopes of being saved. This leniency was granted toward him, that the negroes might not have the satisfaction of seeing a master executed for killing his slave. This would lead them to all sorts of dangerus designs against their masters, and to value themselves too much.

The negroes were formerly brought from Africa, as I mentioned before, but now this seldom happens, for they are bought in the West Indies, or American Islands, whither they were originally brought from their own country. It has been found that in transporting the negroes from Africa directly to these northern countries, they have not such good health as when they come gradually, by shorter stages, and are first carried from Africa to the West Indies, and from thence to North America. It has frequently been found, that the negroes cannot stand the cold here so well as the Europeans or whites; for while the latter are not in the least affected by the cold, the toes and fingers of the former are frequently frozen. There is likewise a material difference among them in this point; for those who come immediately from Africa, cannot bear the cold so well as those who are either born in this country, or have been here for a considerable time. The frost easily hurts the hands or feet of the negroes who come from Africa, or occasions violent pains in their whole body, or in some parts of it, though it does not at all affect those who have been here for some time. There are frequent examples that the negroes on their passage from Africa, if it happens in winter, have some of their limbs frozen on board the ship, when the cold is but very moderate and the sailors are scarcely obliged to cover their hands. I was even assured that some negroes have been seen here who had excessive pain in their legs, which afterwards broke in the middle, and dropped entirely from the body, together with the flesh on them. Thus it is the same case with men here as with plants which are brought from the southern countries, before they accustom themselves to a colder climate.

The price of negroes differs according to their age, health and ability. A full grown negro costs from forty pounds to a hundred of Pennsylvania currency. There are even examples that a gentleman has paid a hundred pounds for a black slave at Philadelphia and refused to sell him again for the same money. A negro boy or girl of two or three years old, can hardly be gotten for less than eight or fourteen pounds in Pennsylvania money. Not only the Quakers but also several Christians of other denominations sometimes set their negroes at liberty. This is done in the following manner: when a gentleman has a faithful negro who has done him great services, he sometimes declares him independent at his own death. This is however very expensive; for they are obliged to make a provision for the negro thus set at liberty, to afford him subsistence when he is grown old, that he may not be driven by necessity to wicked actions, or that he may fall a charge to anybody, for these free negroes become very lazy and indolent afterwards. But the children which the free negro has begot during his servitude are all slaves, though their father be free. On the other hand, those negro children which are born after the parent was freed are free. The negroes in the North American colonies are treated more mildly and fed better than those in the West Indies. They have as good food as the rest of the servants, and they possess equal advantages in all things, except their being obliged to serve their whole lifetime and get no other wages than what their master's goodness allows them. They are likewise clad at their master's expense. On the contrary, in the West Indies, and especially in the Spanish Islands, they are treated very cruelly; therefore no threats make more impression upon a negro here than that of sending him over to the West Indies, in case he will not reform. It has likewise been frequently found by experience that when you show too much kindness to these negroes, they grow so obstinate that they will no longer do anything but of their own accord. Therefore a strict discipline is very necessary, if their master expects to be satisfied with their services.

In the year 1620 some negroes were brought to North America in a Dutch ship, and in Virginia they bought twenty of them. These are said to have been the first that came hither. When the Indians, who were then more numerous in the country than at present, saw these black people for the first time, they thought they were a real breed of devils, and therefore they called them *manito* for a long while. This word in their language signifies not only god but also devil. Some time before that, when they saw the first European ship on their coasts, they were quite convinced that God himself was in the ship. This account I got from some Indians, who preserved it among them as a tradition which they had received from their ancestors. Therefore the arrival of the negroes seemed to them to have confused everything; but since that time, they have entertained less disagreeable notions of the negroes, for at present many live among them, and they even sometimes intermarry, as I myself have seen.

The negroes have therefore been upwards of a hundred and thirty years in this country. As the winters here, especially in New England and New York, are as severe as our Swedish winter, I very carefully inquired whether the cold had not been observed to affect the color of the negroes, and to change it, so that the third or fourth generation from the first that came hither became less black than their ancestors. But I was generally answered that there was not the slightest difference of color to be perceived; and that a negro born here of parents who were likewise born in this country, and whose ancestors, both men and women had all been blacks born in this country, up to the third or fourth generation, was not at all different in color from those negroes who were brought directly from Africa. Hence many people concluded that a negro or his posterity did not change color, though they continued ever so long in a cold climate; but the union of a white man with a negro woman, or of a negro man with a white woman had an entirely different result. Therefore to prevent any dis-agreeable mixtures of the white people and negroes, and to hinder the latter from forming too great opinions of themselves, to the disad-vantage of their masters, I am told there was a law passed prohibiting the whites of both sexes to marry negroes, under pain of almost capital punishment, with deprivation and other severer penalties for the cler-gyman who married them. But that the whites and blacks sometimes copulated, appears from children of a mixed complexion, which are sometimes born.

It is likewise greatly to be pitied that the masters of these negroes in most of the English colonies take little care of their spititual wel-fare, and let them live on in their pagan darkness. There are even some who would be very ill pleased [with negro enlightenment], and would in every way hinder their negroes from being instructed in the doctrines of Christianity. To this they are led partly by the conceit of its being shameful to have a spiritual brother or sister among so despicable a people; partly by thinking that they would not be able to keep their negroes so subjected afterwards; and partly through fear of the negroes growing too proud on seeing themselves upon a level with their masters in religious matters.

Several writings are well known which mention that the negroes in South America have a kind of poison with which they kill each other, though the effect is not sudden, and takes effect a long time after the person has taken it. The same dangerous art of poisoning is known by the negroes in North America, as has frequently been experienced. However, only a few of them know the secret, and they likewise know the remedy for it; therefore when a negro feels himself poisoned and can recollect the enemy who might possibly have given him the poison, he goes to him, and endeavors by money and entreaties to move him to deliver him from its effects. But if the negro is malicious, he not only denies that he ever poisoned him, but likewise that he knows an antidote for it. This poison does not kill immediately, as I have noted, for sometimes the sick person dies several years afterward. But from the moment he has the poison he falls into a sort of consumption state and enjoys but few days of good health. Such a poor wretch often knows that he is poisoned the moment he gets it. The negroes commonly employ it on such of their brethren as behave well [toward the whites], are beloved by their masters, and separate, as it were, from their countrymen, or do not like to converse with them. They have likewise often other reasons for their enmity; but there are few examples of their having poisoned their masters. Perhaps the mild treatment they receive, keeps them from doing it, or perhaps they fear that they may be discovered, and that in such a case, the severest punishments would be inflicted on them.

They never disclose the nature of the poison, and keep it inconceivably secret. It is probable that it is a very common article, which may be had anywhere in the world; for wherever the blacks are they can always easily procure it. Therefore it cannot be a plant, as several learned men have thought, for that is not to be found everywhere. I have heard many accounts here of negroes who have been killed by this poison. I shall only mention one incident which happened during my stay in this country. A man here had a negro who was exceedingly faithful to him, and behaved so well that he would not have exchanged him for twenty other negroes. His master likewise showed him a peculiar kindness, and the slave's conduct equalled that of the best servant. He likewise conversed as little as possible with the other negroes. On that account they hated him to excess, but as he was scarcely ever in company with them they had no opportunity of conveying the poison to him, which they had often tried. However, on coming to town during the fair (for he lived in the country) some other negroes invited him to drink with them. At first he would not but they pressed him till he was obliged to comply. As soon as he came into the room, the others took a pot from the wall and pledged him, desiring him to drink likewise. He drank, but when he took the pot from his mouth, he said: "what beer is this? It is full of . . ." I purposely omit what he mentioned, for it seems undoubtedly to have been the name of the poison with which the malicious negroes do so much harm, and which is to be met with almost everywhere. It might be too much employed to wicked purposes, and it is therefore better that it remains unknown. The other negroes and negro women began laughing at the complaints of their hated countryman, and danced and sang as if they had done an excellent thing, and had at last won the point so much wished for. The innocent negro went away immediately, and when he got home asserted that the other negroes had certainly poisoned him: he then fell into a decline, and no remedy could prevent his death.

Mrs. Anne [MacVicar] Grant, Memoirs of an American Lady with Sketches of Manners and Scenes in America as They Existed Previous to the Revolution *(London, 1809), vol. 1, pp. 51-55, 57-60.*

In the society I am describing [Albany], even the dark aspect of slavery was softened into a smile. And I must, in justice to the best possible masters, say, that a great deal of that tranquillity and comfort, to call it by no higher name, which distinguished this society from all others, was owing to the relation between master and servant being better understood here than in any other place. Let me not be detested as an advocate for slavery when I say that I think I have never seen people so happy in servitude as the domestics of the Albanians. One reason was, (for I do not now speak of the virtues of their masters), that each family had few of them, and that there were no field negroes. They would remind one of Abraham's servants, who were all born in the house; this was exactly their case. They were baptized too, and shared the same religious instruction with the children of the family; and, for the first years, there was little or no difference with regard to food or clothing between their children and those of their masters.

When a negroe-woman's child attained the age of three years, it was solemnly presented, the first New Year's Day following, to a son or daughter, or other young relative of the family, who was of the same sex with the child so presented. The child to whom the young negro was given immediately presented it with some piece of money and a pair of shoes; and from that day the strongest attachment grew between the domestic and the destined owner. I have no where met with instances of friendship more tender and generous than that which here subsisted between the slaves and their masters and mistresses. Extraordinary proofs of them have been often given in the course of hunting or of Indian trading; when a young man and his slave have gone to the trackless woods together, in the case of fits of the ague, loss of a canoe, and other casualties happening near hostile Indians. The slave has been known, at the imminent risk of his life, to carry his disabled master through unfrequented wilds, with labor and fidelity scarce credible; and the master has been equally tender on similar occasions of the humble friend who stuck closer than a brother; who was baptized with the same baptism, nurtured under the same roof, and often rocked in the same cradle with himself. These gifts of domestics to the younger members of the family, were not irrevocable: yet they were very rarely withdrawn. If the kitchen family did not increase in proportion to that of the master, young children were purchased from some family where they abounded, to furnish those attached servants to the rising progeny. They were never sold without consulting their mother, who, if expert and sagacious, had a great deal to say in the family, and would not allow her child to go into any family with whose domestics she was not acquainted. These negro-women piqued themselves on teaching their children to be excellent servants, well knowing servitude to be their lot for life, and that it could only be sweetened by making themselves particularly useful, and excelling in their department. If they did their work well, it is astonishing, when I recollect it, what liberty of speech was allowed to those active and prudent mothers. They would chide, reprove, and expostulate in a manner that we would not endure from our hired servants; and sometimes exert fully as much authority over the children of the family as the parents, conscious that they were entirely in their power. They did not crush freedom of speech and opinion in those by whom they knew they were beloved, and who watched with incessant care over their interest and comfort. Affectionate and faithful as these home-bred servants were in general, there were some instances (but very few) of those who, through levity of mind, or a love of liquor or finery, betrayed their trust, or habitually neglected their duty. In these cases, after every means had been used to reform them, no severe punishments were inflicted at home. But the terrible sentence, which they dreaded worse than death, was passed—they were sold to Jamaica. The necessity of selling them was bewailed by the whole family as a most dreadful calamity, and the culprits were carefully watched on their way to New York, lest they should evade the sentence by self-destruction.

Amidst all this mild and really tender indulgence to their negroes, these colonists had not the smallest scruple of conscience with regard to the right by which they held them in subjection. Had that been the case, their singular humanity would have been incompatible with continued injustice. But the truth is, that of law the generality of those people knew little; and of philosophy, nothing at all. They sought their code of morality in the Bible, and imagined they there found this hapless race condemned to perpetual slavery; and thought nothing remained for them but to lighten the chains of their fellow Christians, after having made them such. I neither "extenuate," nor "set down in malice," but merely record the fact. At the same time it is but justice to record also a singular instance of moral delicacy distinguishing this settlement from every other in the like circumstances, though, from their simple and kindly modes of life, they were from infancy in habits of familiarity with their negroes, yet being early taught that nature had placed between them a barrier, which it was in a high degree criminal and disgraceful to pass, they considered a mixture of such distinct races with abhorrence, as a violation of her laws. This greatly conduced to the preservation of family happiness and concord. An ambiguous race, which the law does not acknowledge; and who (if they have any moral sense, must be as much ashamed of their parents as these last are of them), are certainly a dangerous, because degreaded part of the community. How much more so must be those unfortunate beings who stand in the predicament of the bat in the fable, whom both birds and beasts disowned? I am sorry to say that the progress of the British army, when it arrived, might be traced by a spurious and ambiguous race of this kind. But of a mulatto born before their arrival I only remember a single instance; and from the regret and wonder it occasioned, considered it as singular. Colonel

Schuyler, of whom I am to speak, had a relation so weak and defective in capacity, that he never was intrusted with any thing of his own, and lived an idle bachelor about the family. In process of time a favorite negro-woman, to the great offence and scandal of the family, bore a child to him, whose colour gave testimony to the relation. The boy was carefully educated; and when he grew up, a farm was allotted to him well stocked and fertile, but in "depth of woods embraced," about two miles back from the family seat. A destitute white woman, who had somehow wandered from the older colonies, was induced to marry him; and all the branches of the family thought it incumbent on them now and then to pay a quiet visit to Chalk (for so, for some unknown reason, they always called him). I have been in Chalk's house myself, and a most comfortable abode it was; but considered him as a mysterious and anomalous being.

About the Frenchman who toured the American colonies for five months in 1777, we know nothing but what he reveals of his attitudes and impressions in his journal. The following has been reprinted from On the Threshold of Liberty: Journal of a Frenchman's Tour of the American Colonies in 1777, *Edward D. Seeber, trans., Copyright © 1959 Indiana University Press, Bloomington. Reprinted by permission of the publisher. The following excerpt is found on pp. 13-15, 122-127 of that edition.*

The white population of Charles-Town is not large, consisting at the most of some 2500 or 3000 families. But the Negroes are more numerous; one meets seven or eight men of color for every European. Although I do not wish to draw a comparison here between the Negroes that one finds in the French colonies and those in the Anglo-American colonies, I must point out one noticeable difference. The latter, bent like ours under the oppressive yoke of slavery, do not assuredly deplore their lot as do the West Indian slaves; they do not have that fear and terror of white men which causes all the Negroes in the French colonies to assume a servile respectfulness in the presence of white men, who, one might say, always carry a hidden whip with which to mistreat them or rob them of their subsistence or pleasures.

Then, too, without affecting the senseless arrogance of our freed Negroes, the Anglo-American slaves have a peculiar kind of pride and bearing; without degenerating into insolence, it at least gives the impression that they regard a man who is not their master simply as a man, not a tyrant. Thus in Santo-Domingo and in other places every Negro slave is, so to speak, the slave of the first-comer: he must be prompt in saluting him, must execute respectfully his orders, and, if it pleases the white man to beat him, receive without murmur or attempt to protect himself the blows which the white man is entitled, as such, to deliver.

This pride, so shocking to the French who come here from the Indies, probably results either from the education that the Negroes receive as they become more civilized and adjusted to the manners and way of life of the colonists, or from the moderation and protection of the laws; but the latter principle, which limits and restrains the despotism of the masters, can have no effect unless the former principle offers its aid and fulfills the desires and intentions of the law-makers. This is evident in our French colonies: the law contains some provisions in favor of the Negro slaves, yet one sees the whites redouble their ferocity in evading its benefits or in extending its severity. Thus the Negroes' proud bearing or serenity, in the presence of a white man, can be explained by their treatment at the hands of the colonists; and this manner of treatment results from a certain way of thinking and living, as we shall see when speaking of the agriculture of the independent provinces as compared with that of the French possessions in the Indies. Let us hope that this parallel will not unduly disparage the manners and way of life of our French colonists in America.

Colonial agriculture is very interesting to consider from the standpoint of the colonists themselves and of those who have aided them continually in rendering their farms fertile. The first colonists had to bear, as you know, the labors and adversities involved in clearing the land. They managed, not without great effort, alone and without the help of day-laborers, to add to their land as needed for their subsistence; but when, as time passed, they or their children gradually became wealthy or at least in easier circumstances, they acquired more leisure and, to get some relief, purchased white bondsmen from the government or black slaves from the West Indies. In some cases they would hire, for the same purpose, unfortunates who had fled from their homeland to escape tyranny, or sectarians who had come to these humble cottages seeking refuge from persecution.

This additional supply of farmers did not for the moment increase the number of landowners, although it did make them rich. Later it gave them both rivals and friends, for when the white laborers, free or enslaved, had through their savings acquired enough money to stand the expense of new clearings or to buy their freedom, they became landowners in their turn. Then, if their efforts were blessed with good fortune, they could become the equals or at least the intimates of those under whom they had suffered enslavement, or with whom they had shared the bread of adversity.

Only the Negroes do not enjoy this good fortune, so deserved and so well earned by those who make the land fruitful and enrich their masters. Sold by those who had snatched them from their homeland, they did not become slaves conditionally or for fixed terms like the whites sent over from Europe as punishment; they had no more hope of becoming free than did their fellow blacks who cultivated the Antilles. For that reason, there are very few free Negroes here, whereas in the West Indies, where there are more slaves in proportion to the whites, there are, proportionally, many more freedmen. It is equally true that the slaves in the Indies are plunged more deeply into affliction and adversity. The reason for this is readily apparent. In the colonies of the Antilles, most of the colonists are people who have left their homeland with the intention of rebuilding their fortunes. Far from settling in the islands, they look upon them merely as a land of exile, never as a place where they plan to live, prosper, and die. On the other hand, the Anglo-American colonists are permanent, born in the country and attached to it; they have no motherland save the one they live in; and, although London formerly was so considered, they have clearly proved that they held it in less esteem than they did the prosperity, tranquility, and freedom of their own country.

As the result of the opinions occupying the minds of the colonists of the two regions I have spoken of, the West Indians must have regarded their slave laborers as instruments necessary to their prosperity; and, since success never came to them very swiftly, they had to arm themselves with whips and rods in order to accelerate pitilessly the activity of these unfortunate humans, crushed beneath the weight of slavery and prostrated under the burden of their daily life and woes. Thenceforth there was to be no show of respect, no pity or commiseration; avarice alone became the colonists' god, and in spite of the kindheartedness brought with them from France, which made them rebel in the early days against the barbarity of despotic masters, they checked the progress of this sentiment and themselves became, thanks to the projects of fortune-building that had brought them there, quite as tyrannical as the others, if not more callous over the trials and sufferings of their fellowmen of another color. The Anglo-American colonists, on the other hand, settled and acclimatized by the love that the English have for the place where they are born and raised, must have looked upon these Negro cultivators as obligatory instruments of their fortunes, it is true, but also as much needed ones whose perpetuation was important to their wealth, and who must be spared rather than crushed beneath the yoke of servitude and physical misfortune. Hence the greater respect, pity, and commiseration, and, finally, this noticeable difference between the blacks of the American colonies and those of the islands of the Mexican Archipelago.

This widespread commiseration not only did them honor; it profited them as well. Land cultivated by slaves under a gentle, humane master was better attended to and produced more than land cultivated under a harsh and cruel master. Escapes, so easy in a continent developed and populated ajacent to the Indians' clearings, were less common under a merciful regime. The slaves, better cared for, better clothed and less oppressed, enjoyed superior health, made the land produce more uniformly, and were more strongly attached to the soil upon which they had to live and to which they were bound. Their numbers further enriched their masters with a commodity precious in the sight of all humane farmers whose hearts tell them how far they may profit from the advantages which the tyranny of the laws and of the *Code noir* [Black code, enacted in 1685 by the French chief minister Colbert] give them over their fellowmen. As reason enlightens men, it teaches them how to behave according to their best interests; and these interests, when properly directed, tend naturally toward humane and benevolent practices.

I now permit you, my friend, to judge the relative goodness of heart displayed by the French colonists in America and by the Anglo-Americans. See for yourself which merits the greater praise, he who increases his wealth as he endears himself, or he who profits by tyrannical laws to accelerate his fortune, goes about afterwards preaching good deeds, playing the decent gentleman or shamelessly hoisting the banner of luxury, and bequeaths to like-minded farmers who come after him his example, methods, and cruelty.

This same humane treatment of Negro slaves has been practiced consistently toward the Americans' indentured white servants. Most of these shared in the labors and pursuits of their masters; and, after satisfying as prescribed by law and society the sentences pronounced against them by reason of their misdeeds or misfortunes, they often became the friends, equals, or voluntary servants of those who had spared them the torments, shame, and humiliations of servitude. They commonly received financial aid from them, and, even oftener, thrived on their advice and assistance. Is it any wonder that the class of farmers has increased in so short a time, and that this land, formerly the accustomed and precarious abode of the Indians, is now so populous and well cultivated? Can one cite in the course of history a people so diligent and noble, and who do so much honor to the English and colonists alike as the natural consequence of heroism, social virtues, and beneficence? O love of liberty! O true English spirit!

Johann David Schoepf, Travels in the Confederation [1783-84], *translated by Alfred J. Morrison (Philadelphia, 1911), pp. 147-152, 220-222.*

The day after our arrival [in Wilmington, N.C.] we attended a public auction held in front of the Court-house. House-leases for a year were offered for sale, and very indifferent houses in the market street, because advantageously placed for trade, were let for 60, 100, and 150 Pd. annual rent.

After this, negroes were let for 12 months to the highest bidder, by public cry as well. A whole family, man, wife, and 3 children, were hired out at 70 Pd. a year; and others singly, at 25, 30, 35 Pd., according to age, strength, capability, and usefulness. In North Carolina it is reckoned in the average that a negro should bring his master about 30 Pd. Current a year (180 fl. Rhenish). In the West Indies the clear profit which the labor of a negro brings his master, is estimated at 25-30 guineas, and in Virginia, according to the nature of the land, at 10-12-15 guineas a year. The keep of a negro here does not come to a great figure, since the daily ration is but a quart of maize, and rarely a little meat or salted fish. Only those negroes kept for house-service are better cared for. Well-disposed masters clothe their negroes once a year, and give them a suit of coarse woollen cloth, two rough shirts, and a pair of shoes. But they who have the largest droves keep them the worst, let them run naked mostly or in rags, and accustom them as much as possible to hunger, but exact of them steady work. Whoever hires a negro, gives on the spot a bond for the amount, to be paid at the end of the term, even should the hired negro fall sick or run off in the meantime. The hirer must also pay the negro's head-tax, feed him and clothe him. Hence a negro is capital, put out at a very high interest, but because of elopement and death certainly very unstable.

Other negroes were sold and at divers prices, from 120 to 160 and 180 Pd., and thus at 4-5 to 6 times the average annual hire. Their value is determined by age, health, and capacity. A cooper, indispensable in pitch and tar making, cost his purchaser 250 Pd., and his 15-year old boy, bred to the same work, fetched 150 Pd. The father was put up first; his anxiety lest his son fall to another purchaser and be separated from him was more painful than his fear of getting into the hands of a hard master. "Who buys me," he was continually calling out, "must buy my son too," and it happened as he desired, for his purchaser, if not from motives of humanity and pity, was for his own advantage obliged so do do. An elderly man and his wife were let go at 200 Pd. But these poor creatures are not always so fortunate; often the husband is snatched from his wife, the children from their mother, if this better answers the purpose of buyer or seller, and no heed is given the doleful prayers with which they seek to prevent a separation.

One cannot without pity and sympathy see these poor creatures exposed on a raised platform, to be carefully examined and felt by buyers. Sorrow and despair are discovered in their look, and they must anxiously expect whether they are to fall to a hard-hearted barbarian or a philanthropist. If negresses are put up, scandalous and indecent questions and jests are permitted. The auctioneer is at pains to enlarge upon the strength, beauty, health, capacity, faithfulness, and sobriety of his wares, so as to obtain prices so much the higher. On the other hand the negroes auctioned zealously contradict everything good that is said about them; complain of their age, longstanding misery or sickness, and declare that purchasers will be selling themselves in buying them, that they are worth no such high bids: because they know well that the dearer their cost, the more work will be required of them.

For the betterment of the condition of this class of mankind especially the Quakers in America have for a long time worked, but in vain. Only recently one of them, a member of the Virginia Assembly, had courage and philanthropy enough to make a public proposal for freeing the negro slaves; but this time he did not succeed. However, while the Quakers have been looking forward to a time when the civil powers should give ear to their repeated philanthropical representations, and by general ordinances entirely do away with the thraldom of the Africans, individual members of their society have held it a matter of conscience to encourage others by example to so praiseworthy an end. But their benevolent and noble purposes have commonly been thwarted by the corrupt state of mind prevalent among the negroes themselves, a result due to nothing but their rude bringing-up and the absolute neglect of their instruction. A rich old Quaker, who lives near Richmond in Virginia, gave all his slaves their freedom, but under the condition that they should remain with him and work for very fair day's wages. All of them solemnly promised, but as soon as they had got their free papers, most of them left him. Another rich Virginia Quaker set his negroes free likewise, and gave each family a bit of land on which they could support themselves, paying annual rent like other tenants; this indeed they began to do, but no longer feeling under strict oversight, and moral and religious principles (of which they knew nothing) not keeping them in order, to which they had previously been accustomed by force alone, the good Quaker's designs were not carried out, and he soon saw his lands and himself deserted of his free negroes. One hears of many such instances, cited to prove that the negroes generally are incapable of making any good use of freedom, and to support the quite ungrounded opinion that they are destined by nature for servitude. But as many examples might be given of free negroes who live decently, orderly, and industriously; and that so much may not be said of all of them, and certainly it may not, is to be explained solely on the ground of the great and intentional neglect of the education of their children; and the disposition to indolence, thievery, and untruth laid to their charge is the inevitable consequence of slavery. They are let grow up like other cattle, and taught no rule but the will of their master, have no motive to action other than the whip. It is said that the negro is by nature trifling and can be accustomed to work only by compulsion and rigid oversight, and hence, if left to himself, would be nothing but a useless member of the community and a burden therein.

It is very likely that the African, blessed at home by kind Nature with almost everything he needs for his support, has brought with him thence no great inclination for severe and painfully continuous labor; but no good reason can be given why the negro, forcibly transferred to America, should do zealously and with pleasure what the American planter himself does not like to do—why the one, in the sweat of his brow and on very scant rations, should till the fields so that the other may spend his days in peace and good-living. "Were I to defend the rights of Europeans to make the negroes their slaves," says Montesquieu, "I could give only these reasons: The Europeans, having driven out and exterminated the native Americans, are compelled to bring the Africans under the yoke in order to till such great tracts of land. Sugar, indigo, rice, &c. would be too dear if produced otherwise than by bondmen. These creatures are so black and their noses are so flat, it is impossible to compassionate them. It is difficult of belief that a wise and good Creator should have placed a soul, much less a worthy soul, in such black, ugly bodies. The negroes think beads of greater value than gold,—which plainly shows that they are unreasoning beings. It is not possible we should regard these creatures as men, for so we make ourselves no Christians." Montesquieu has here said everything that the defenders of negro slavery are wont to say, whether clearly or ambiguously. . . .

The condition of the Carolina negro-slaves is in general harder and more troublous than that of their northern brethren. On the rice-plantations, with wretched food, they are allotted more work and more tedious work; and the treatment which they experience at the hands of their overseers and owners is capricious and often tyrannical. In Carolina (and in no other of the North American states) their severe handling has already caused several uprisings among them. There is less concern here as to their moral betterment, education, and instruction, and South Carolina appears little inclined to imitate the praiseworthy and benevolent ordinances of its sister states in regard to the negro. It is sufficient proof of the bad situation in which these creatures find themselves here that they do not multiply in the same proportion as the white inhabitants, although the climate is more natural to them and agrees with them better. Their numbers must be continually kept up by fresh importations; to be sure, the constant taking up of a new land requires more and more working hands, and the pretended necessity of bringing in additional slaves is thus warranted in part; but close investigation makes it certain that the increase of the blacks in the northern states, where they are handled more gently, is vastly more considerable. The gentlemen in the country have among their negroes, as the Russian nobility among their serfs, the most necessary handicraftsmen, cobblers, tailors, carpenters, smiths, and the like, whose work they command at the smallest possible price, or for nothing almost. There is hardly any trade or craft which has not been learned and is not carried on by negroes, partly free, partly slave; the latter are hired out by their owners for day's wages. Charleston swarms with blacks, mulattoes, and mestizos; their number greatly exceeds that of the whites, but they are kept under strict order and discipline, and the police has a watchful eye upon them. There may nowhere assemble together more than 7 male negro slaves; their dances and other assemblies must stop at 10 o'clock in the evening; without permission of their owners none of them may sell beer or wine or brandy. There are here many free negroes and mulattoes. They get their freedom if by their own industry they earn enough to buy themselves off, or their freedom is given them at the death of their masters or in other ways. Not all of them know how to use their freedom to their own advantage: many give themselves up to idleness and dissipations which bring them finally to crafty deceptions and thievery. They are besides extraordinarily given to vanity, and love to adorn themselves as much as they can and to conduct themselves importantly.

The feast of the Sunday is strictly observed at Charleston. No shop may keep open; no sort of game or music is permitted, and during the church service watchmen go about who lay hold upon any one idling in the streets, (any not on urgent business or visiting the sick), and compel him to turn aside into some church or pay 2 shillings 4 pence; no slave may be required to work on this day.

J.P. Brissot de Warville, New Travels in the United States of America 1788, translated by Mara Soceanu Vamos and Durand Echeverria, *edited by Durand Echeverria (Cambridge, 1964), pp. 232-238.*

In the four Northern [New England] states and in the Southern [Middle?] states, free Negroes are either domestic servants, small

shopkeepers, or farmers. Some work on coasting vessels, but few dare
to ship on long voyages because they are afraid of being carried off
and sold in the West Indies.

Physically, these Negroes are in general vigorous. They have good
constitutions, are able to perform the hardest labor, and are generally
active. As servants, they are sober and faithful. All these traits are
equally characteristic of Negro women. I have not seen any distinction
made in respect to these qualities between Negro and white servants,
though the latter always treat Negroes with contempt as if they
belonged to an inferior race.

Those who are shopkeepers earn a moderate living but never expand
their businesses beyond a certain point. The simple reason is that,
although Negroes are everywhere treated humanely, the whites, who
have the money, are not willing to lend a Negro the capital necessary
for a big commercial establishment. Moreover, to succeed in a larger
enterprise, a certain amount of preliminary experience is necessary
and one must have had training in a countinghouse; but the forces
of reason have not yet opened to Negroes the doors of countinghouses,
in which they are not allowed to sit down alongside a white man.
If, then, Negroes here are limited to the small retail trade, let us not
attribute it to their lack of ability but rather to the prejudices of the
whites, who put obstacles in their way.

For the same reasons Negroes in the country cannot own large
farms. Their fields are small but usually well cultivated. European
travelers are impressed by their good clothes, their well-kept log
houses, and their many children, while the eye of the philospher lingers with pleasure on these homes where tyranny causes no tears to
flow.

In this part of America [the North] Negroes are certainly happy,
but let us have the courage to admit that their happiness and their
abilities have not reached the levels they are capable of attaining.
There still is too great a distance between them and the whites, especially in the eye of public opinion, and this humiliating barrier frus-
trates all the efforts they make to elevate themselves. This discrimina-
tion is apparent everywhere. For instance, Negro children are admitted
to public schools but they cannot cross the threshold of a college.
They themselves, even though they are free and independent, are still
in the habit of considering themselves inferior to the whites, who have

rights they do not have. Thus, it would not be fair to estimate the nature and extent of Negroes' abilities on the basis of the achievements of the free Negroes in the North.

Yet when we compare them with the slaves in the Southern states, what a tremendous difference we find! The brutalized and degraded condition of the latter is difficult to describe. Many are naked, underfed, and forced to sleep on straw in miserable huts. They receive no education and no religious instruction whatsoever. They are not married, but coupled. The result is that they are brutish and lazy, lack energy, and have no ideas. They will not go to any trouble to get themselves clothes or better food, preferring to wear rags rather than mend them. Sunday, their day of rest, they spend doing absolutely nothing. Total inactivity is their supreme happiness, and as a consequence they do little work and perform their tasks listlessly.

In all fairness, I must admit that Southerners do not treat their slaves harshly; this is one of the effects of the general diffusion of the idea of liberty. Everywhere the slave works less, but that is all. Neither his food, nor his clothing, nor his morality, nor his thinking has improved; thus the master is the loser but the slave gains nothing. If Southerners followed the example set by Northerners, both slaves and masters would benefit by the change.

In describing Negroes of the South, a careful distinction must be made between those who work in the fields and those who work as house servants. The preceding description applies only to the former; the others, few in number, are generally better clad, more energetic, and less ignorant.

It has been popularly believed until recently that Negroes are intellectually inferior to whites. Even respectable writers have supported this theory. This prejudice is now beginning to disappear, and the Northern states can furnish examples to prove its falsity. I shall cite only two striking cases, the first proving that through education Negroes can be made fit for any profession, and the second showing that a Negro's brain can accomplish the most astonishing mathematical calculations and can, therefore, deal with all the sciences.

During my stay in Philadelphia I saw a Negro named James Derham, a doctor who practices in New Orleans. His life story, confirmed by several doctors, is as follows: He was born in a family in Philadelphia, in which he was taught to read and write, and instructed in the principles of Christianity. When a boy he was transferred by his master to the late Dr. John Kearsley, Jr. of Philadelphia, who employed him to compound medicines and to administer them to his patients. Upon the death of Dr. Kearsley, he became (after passing through several hands) the property of Dr. George West, surgeon to the Sixteenth British Regiment, under whom, during the late war in America, he performed many of the menial duties of medicine. At the close of the war, he was sold by Dr. West to Dr. Robert Dove of New Orleans, who employed him as an assistant in his business, in which capacity he gained so much of his master's confidence and friendship that Dr. Dove consented to liberate him, after two or three years, upon easy terms. By his numerous opportunities of improving in medicine Derham became so well acquainted with the healing art as to commence practicing in New Orleans with success. He is now about twenty-six years of age, has a wife but no children and does business to the amount of $3,000, or about 16,000 livres, a year.

"I conversed with him," Dr. [Caspar] Wistar told me, "upon the acute and epidemic diseases of the country where he lives and found him perfectly acquainted with the modern simple mode of practice in these diseases. I expected to have suggested some new medicines to him; but he suggested many more to me." He is very modest and engaging in his manners. He speaks French fluently and has some knowledge of the Spanish language. By some accident, although born in a religious family, he was not baptized in his infancy, in consequence of which he applied to Dr. [William] Whithe [White] to receive baptism. He found him qualified, both by knowledge and moral conduct, to be admitted to baptism.

The other case was reported to me by Dr. [Benjamin] Rush, a famous doctor and writer of Philadelphia, who has published an account of it. Several of the details have since been confirmed by the wife of the immortal Washington, in whose neighborhood this Negro has long been living.

Thomas Fuller was born in Africa and can neither read nor write. He is now seventy years old and has lived all his life on Mrs. Cox's plantation, four miles from Alexandria. Two gentlemen, natives of Pennsylvania, Messrs. [William H.] Hartshorne and Samuel Coates, having heard in traveling in Virginia of his extraordinary powers in arithmetic, sent for him, and had their curiosity sufficiently gratified by the answers which he gave to the following questions:

First. Upon being asked how many seconds there are in a year and a half, he answered, in about two minutes, 47,304,000, counting 365 days in the year.

Second. On being asked how many seconds a man has lived who is seventy years, seventeen days and twelve hours old, he answered, in a minute and a half, 2,210,500,800. One of the gentlemen, who employed himself with his pen in making these calculations, told him he was wrong, and that the sum was not so great as he said. This was true, because Fuller had overlooked the leap years, but with the greatest speed he corrected his figures.

Third. Suppose a farmer has six sows and each sow has six female pigs the first year, and they all increase in the same proportion to the end of eight years, how many sows will the farmer then have? In ten minutes, he answered 34,588,806. The difference of time between his answering this and the two former questions was occasioned by a trifling mistake he had made from a misapprehension of the question.

After he had correctly answered all the questions, he told how he had discovered and developed his arithmetical talent. He began his application to figures by counting ten, and then when he was able to count a hundred, he thought himself (to use his own words) "a very clever fellow." He next amused himself counting, grain by grain, a bushel of wheat. From this he was led to calculate how many rails were necessary to enclose and how many grains of corn were necessary to sow a certain quantity of ground. From this application of his talents his mistress has often derived considerable benefit, and he spoke of her with great respect and mentioned in a particular manner his obligations to her for refusing to sell him, which she had been tempted to do by offers of large sums of money. He said his memory was beginning to fail him. When one of the gentlemen remarked in his presence that it was a pity he had not had an education equal to his genius, he said: "No, massa, it is best I got no learning; for many learned men be great fools."

These examples prove beyond a doubt that the mental capacity of Negroes is equal to any task, and that all they need is education and freedom. The difference between those who are free and educated and those who are not can also be seen in their work. The lands of both whites and Negroes in the free states, as for example in Connecticut or Pennsylvania, are infinitely better cultivated, produce larger crops, and present in general an impression of well-being and contentment.

But cross over into Maryland and Virginia, and, as I have said before, you think you are in a different world. No longer will you see well-cultivated fields, neat and even elegant farm-houses, large, well-designed barns, and big herds of fat, healthy cattle. Everything in Maryland and in Virginia bears the stamp of slavery: the parched soil, the badly managed farming, the ramshackled houses, and the few scrawny cattle that look like walking skeletons. In short, you find real poverty existing alongside a false appearance of wealth.

Even in the Southern states men are beginning to see that it is poor economy to feed a slave badly, and that capital invested in slaves does not pay its interest. The introduction of free labor into a part of Virginia, in the area along the lovely Shenandoah River, may be due more to these considerations and particularly to the economic impossibility of importing more slaves than to humanitarian motives. When you see the Shenandoah you think you are still in Pennsylvania.

Let us hope that all of Virginia will look like this in the perhaps not distant future, when it is no longer sullied by slavery. There are slaves in Virginia only because it is believed that they are necessary for raising tobacco. But this crop is decreasing every day in this state and will continue to decrease. The tobacco grown near the Ohio and Mississippi is infinitely more plentiful, of better quality, and requires less labor. When it finds an outlet to the European market, Virginians will be forced to abandon this crop and raise instead wheat, potatoes, and cattle. Intelligent Virginians are anticipating this change and are beginning to grow wheat.

Chief among them must be listed that astonishing man who, though a beloved general, had the courage to be a sincere republican and who is the only one not to remember his own glory, a hero whose unique destiny it will be to save his country twice and to open for it the road to prosperity after having set it on the road to liberty. Now *wholly* occupied with improving his land, developing new crops, and building roads, he is giving to his fellow citizens a useful example which will no doubt be followed. Nevertheless he does own, I am forced to say, large numbers of Negro slaves. They are, however, most humanely treated. Well fed, well clothed, and required to do only a moderate amount of work, they continually bless the master God gave them. It would undoubtedly be fitting that such a lofty, pure, and disinterested soul be the one to make the first step in the abolition of slavery in Virginia. This great man, when I had the honor to talk with him, told me that he admired everything that was being done in the other states and that he desired the extension of the movement in his own. But he did not conceal the fact that there are still many obstacles and that it would be dangerous to make a frontal attack on a prejudice which is beginning to decrease. "Time, patience, and education," he said, "and it will be overcome. Nearly all Virginians," he added, "are convinced that the general emancipation of Negroes cannot occur in the near future, and for this reason they do not wish to organize a society which might give their slaves dangerous ideas." Another obstacle which he pointed out is that most of this part of the country is made up of large plantations and people live far apart, so that it is difficult to hold meetings.

"Virginians are wrong," I told him. "It is evident that sooner or later Negroes will win their freedom everywhere, and that this revolution will extend to Virginia. It is therefore to the interest of your fellow citizens to prepare for it and to try to reconcile the restitution of the Negroes' rights with their own right to property. The necessary steps can only be worked out by a society, and it would be fitting that the savior of America be its head and restore liberty to 300,000 unhappy inhabitants of his country." This great man told me that he was in favor of the formation of such a society and that he would support it, but that he did not believe the moment was favorable. No doubt there were greater problems which demanded his attention and preoccupied him at the time; America's destiny was about to be placed a second time in his hands.

IV. DENOMINATIONS

The character of American religion in the 18th century was the product of the character of the American population. Its variety was a direct reflection of the variety of cultures and peoples whose emigrations populated the colonies, as was its toleration of religious differences. Why was this mutual toleration necessary? Were all religious opinions and practices tolerated equally? What were the consequences of this denominationalism for the strength of religion in general? How did visiting Catholics react to American Protestant churches and services? How was the American clergy supported? Did this form of support have any effect on the quality or independence of religious leadership provided by the clergy? What effect did Sabbatarianism—"Keep the Seventh Day holy"—have on American social life? What role did the clergy play in politics or government? Has this had any effect on the general health of religion in America?

The America of 1750. Peter Kalm's Travels in North America. The English Version of 1770, *edited by Adolph B. Benson (New York, 1937), pp. 20-25, 129-130.*

Among the public buildings [of Philadelphia] I shall first mention churches, of which there are several, for God is served in various ways in this country.

1. The *English established church* stands in the northern part of the town, at some distance from the market, and is the finest of all. It has a small, insignificant steeple, in which a bell is rung when it is time to go to church, and at burials. It has likewise a clock which

strikes the hours. This building, which is called Christ Church, was founded towards the end of the last century, but has lately been rebuilt and more adorned. It has two ministers who get the greatest part of their salary from England. In the beginning of this century the Swedish minister, the Rev. Mr. Rudman, performed the functions of a clergyman in the English congregation for nearly two years during the absence of their own clergyman.

2. The *Swedish church*, which is otherwise called the Church of Wicaco, is in the southern part of the town, almost outside of it on the riverside, and its location is therefore more agreeable than that of any other. I shall have an opportunity of describing it more exactly when I speak of the Swedes who live in this place.

3. The *German Lutheran church* is on the northwest side of the town. On my arrival in America it had a little steeple, but having been put up by an ignorant builder before the walls of the church had become quite dry, the latter were forced out by its weight and the steeple had to be pulled down again in the autumn of the year 1750. About that time the congregation received a fine organ from Germany. They have only one minister, who also preaches at another Lutheran church in Germantown. He preaches alternately one Sunday in that church, and the other in this. The first clergyman which the Lutherans had in this town was the Rev. Mr. Mühlenberg who laid the foundations of the church in 1743, and being called to another place afterwards, the Rev. Mr. Brunnholtz, a Dane from Schleswig, was his successor, and he is still there. Both these gentlemen were sent here from Halle in Saxony, and have been of great value to the church by their peculiar talent of preaching in an edifying manner. A little while before this church was built the Lutheran Germans had no clergyman of their own so that the much-beloved Swedish minister at Wicaco, Mr. Dylander, preached to them also. He therefore gave three sermons every Sunday; the first early in the morning to the Germans: the second to the Swedes; and the third in the afternoon to the English. Besides this he went all week into the country and instructed the scattered Germans who lived there. He frequently preached sixteen sermons a week. And only after his death, which happened in November, 1741, did the Germans write to Germany for a clergyman. This congregation is at present very large, so that every Sunday the church is crowded. It has two galleries but no vestry. They

do not sing the collects but read them before the altar. The sermon is given from the pulpit.

4. The *Old Presbyterian church* is not far from the market and on the south side of Market Street. It is of a middling size and built in the year 1704, as the inscription on the northern pediment shows. The roof is built almost hemispherical, or at least forms a half-hexagon. The building stands north and south, for the Presbyterians are not so particular as other people whether their churches face a certain point of the heavens or not.

5. The *New Presbyterian church* was built in the year 1750 by the "New-lights" in the northwestern part of the town. By the name of New-lights are understood the people who have, from different religions, become proselytes of the well-known [George] Whitefield, who in the years 1739, 1740, and likewise in 1744 and 1745, travelled through almost all the English colonies in North America. His delivery, his extraordinary zeal, and other talents so well adapted to the intellects of his hearers, made him so popular that he frequently, especially in the two first years got an audience of from eight to twenty thousand people. His intention in these travels, was to collect money for an orphans' hospital which had been erected in Georgia. Here he frequently collected seventy pounds sterling at one sermon; nay, at two sermons which he preached in the year 1740, both on one Sunday, at Philadelphia, he received a hundred and fifty pounds. The proselytes of this man, or the above-mentioned "New-lights", are at present merely a sect of Presbyterians. For though Whitefield was originally a clergyman of the English church, he deviated little by little from her doctrines, and on arriving in the year 1744 at Boston in New England the Presbyterians argued with him about their teachings so much that he embraced them almost entirely. For Whitefield was no great disputant and could therefore easily be led by these cunning people whithersoever they would have him. This also, during his latter stay in America, caused his audience to be less numerous than during the first. The New-lights first built in the year 1741 a large house in the western part of the town in which to hold divine service. But a division arising amongst them after the departure of Whitefield, and also for other reasons, the building was sold to the town in the beginning of the year 1750 and destined for a school. The New-lights then built a church which I call the new Presbyterian one. On its east-

ern pediment is the following inscription, in golden letters: *Templum Presbyterianum, annuente numine, erectum, Anno Dom. MDCCL.*

6. The *Old German Reformed* (Calvinistic) *church* is built in the west-northwest part of the town and looks like the church in Ladugårdsgärdet near Stockholm. It is not yet finished, though for several years the congregation has kept up divine service in it. These Germans attended the German service at the Swedish church whilst the Swedish minister Mr. Dylander lived.—But as the Lutherans procured a clergyman of their own on the death of the last, those of the Reformed church likewise made preparations to obtain one from Dordrecht, Holland, and the first who was sent to them was the Rev. Mr. Slaughter whom I found on my arrival. But in the year 1750, another clergyman of the Reformed church arrived from Holland and by his artful behavior so insinuated himself into the favor of the Rev. Mr. Slaughter's congregation that the latter lost almost half of his audience. The two clergymen then disputed for several Sundays about the pulpit; nay, people relate that the newcomer mounted the pulpit on a Saturday and stayed in it all night, the other being thus excluded. The two parties in the audience made themselves the subject both of the laughter and of the scorn of the whole town by beating and bruising each other and committing other excesses. The affair was inquired into by the magistrates and decided in favor of the Rev. Mr. Slaughter, the person who had been abused.

7. The *New Reformed church* was built at a little distance from the old one by the party of the clergyman who had lost his cause. The newcomer, however, had influence enough to bring over to his party almost the whole audience of his antagonist at the end of the year 1750, and therefore this new church will soon be useless.

8. & 9. The *Quakers* have two meeting-houses, one in the market and the other in the northern part of the town. Among them, according to their custom, there are neither altars nor pulpits nor any other ornament usual in churches, but only seats and some sconces. They meet thrice every Sunday in them, and besides that at certain times every week or every month. I shall mention more about them hereafter.

10. The *Anabaptists* have their service in the northern part of the town.

11. The *Roman Catholics* have in the southwest part of the town a large building which is well adorned within and has an organ.

12. The *Moravian or Zinzendorfian Brethren* have hired a large

house in the northern part of the town, in which they perform service both in German and English, not only twice or three times every Sunday but every night after it has grown dark. In the winter of the year 1750 they were obliged to drop their evening meeting, some wanton young fellows having several times disturbed the congregation by an instrument sounding like the note of a cuckoo; for this noise they made in a dark corner not only at the end of every stanza but likewise at that of every line whilst they were singing a hymn.

Those of the English church, the New-lights, the Quakers, and the Germans of the Reformed religion have their burying places out of town and not near their churches, though the first of these sometimes makes an exception. All the others bury their dead in their church-yards, and the Moravian Brethren bury where they can. The negroes are buried in a separate place out of town.

The Jews. Besides the different sects of Christians, many Jews have settled in New York, who possess great privileges. They have a synagogue, own their dwelling-houses, possess large country-seats and are allowed to keep shops in town. They have likewise several ships, which they load and send out with their own goods. In fine, they enjoy all the privileges common to the other inhabitants of this town and province.

A daughter of one of the richest Jews had married a Christian after she had renounced the Jewish religion. Her sister did not wish either to marry a Jew, so went to London to get a Christian husband.

During my residence in New York, both at this time and for the next two years, I was frequently in company with Jews. I was informed among other things that these people never boiled any meat for themselves on Saturday, but that they always did it the day before, and that in winter they kept a fire during the whole Saturday. They commonly eat no pork; yet I have been told by several trustworthy men that many of them (especially the young Jews) when travelling, did not hesitate the least about eating this or any other meat that was put before them, even though they were in company with Christians. I was in their synagogue last evening for the first time, and to-day at noon I visited it again, and each time I was put in a special seat which was set apart for strangers or Christians. A young rabbi read the divine service, which was partly in Hebrew and partly in the Rabbinical dialect. Both men and women were dressed entirely in the English fashion; the former had their hats on, and did not once take them off during the service. The galleries, I observed, were reserved for the ladies, while the men sat below. During prayers the men spread a white cloth over their heads, which perhaps is to represent sackcloth. But I observed that the wealthier sort of people had a much richer cloth than the poorer ones. Many of the men had Hebrew books, in which they sang and read alternately. The rabbi stood in the middle of the synagogue and read with his face turned towards the east; he spoke however so fast as to make it almost impossible for any one to understand what he said.

On the Threshold of Liberty: Journal of a Frenchman's Tour of the American Colonies in 1777, *translated and edited by Edward D. Seeber (Bloomington, Indiana, 1959), pp. 20-27.*

For a papist [Roman Catholic], accustomed only to churches overladen with paintings and decoration, the Anglo-American churches and all the Protestant ones must of a certainty be objects of surprise and astonishment. . . .

Imagine, then, a long rectangular building, usually without a porch, and pierced by enough windows to light the interior; two or three doors on the sides, with steps leading up to the lower floor; a tower with a very tall spire and fancy exterior decoration, placed at the rear and at one side of the edifice; the high ceiling and inside walls well whitewashed or wainscoated on all four sides; and the parishioners' benches, built high enough so that one cannot see, when seated, either his neighbors or those who are entering or leaving—such is the usual appearance of the main body of the church and the nave.

Picture to yourself also a somewhat higher part, panelled in wood, and candles or chandeliers suspended over a table or unaffected pulpit; this is what we call the sanctuary. As for the choir, imagine at one end of the church and at the same pulpit which I have just mentioned, an individual absolutely no different in appearance from the other people present, who sits facing the congregation and intones a stanza of a Psalm of David rendered in English verse; and, at the other side, the congregation, who answer him alternately until the Psalm is ended. That is about the extent of the divine service, and I can assure you that nothing is more impressive than this noble and majestic simplicity; but, as tribute must be paid one way or another to human weakness, I must add that when one, two, or three men whose zeal matches that of the Intoner, or when he himself has sung a certain number of Psalms, a black-robed man with a large wig suddenly and mysteriously appears from behind one end of a wooden screen which seems to be merely a decoration. Dressed exactly like an attorney, he begins a heated harangue lasting three quarters of an hour or more without pausing, coughing, or blowing his nose; he recites or reads a discourse on the Bible and its moral teachings, often very eloquent and well received—and often quite as fanatical as some of ours.

When he is done or feels that he is about to conclude, and at a signal apparently prearranged between himself and one of his listeners, he pauses a moment. A man comes holding in his hand a long pole with the preacher's square cap suspended at the end quite like a fish net. This he presents to the people while recommending the orator to their generosity. As soon as the collection, ample or otherwise, is over, he resumes his seat and signals the clergyman to continue; he does so, but not, I think, without having taken notice of the number of hands advanced to hover over the cap. Thus the discourse ends sooner or later; and at the very moment when you believe that the speaker is catching his breath, or seeking new matters on which to hold forth, you are surprised to find that he is no longer there, or to see him disappear quite as amusingly and suddenly as he came.

Such is the general nature of the Sunday preaching and church service. From the standpoint of the Scriptures and their precepts, it certainly conforms to the rule of the Founder of Christianity: preach and pray; but does it not seem to carry things somewhat to extremes and to go too far in avoiding the pomp and display that divine worship would ostensibly permit? The black-robed man who appears and disappears without one's knowing whence he came and where or for what reason he makes his exit, becomes, through exaggerated simplicity and abhorrence of religious pageantry, a ridiculous affectation. This has another consequence, for it makes one forget the seriousness of the sacred mysteries; and one must be blessed with great composure, or else quite accustomed to the proceedings, not to burst into laughter at the appearance and disappearance of the apostle.

This overaffectation goes even farther. A church, be it Catholic, Lutheran, Protestant, Jewish, or what not, should in every respect have the appearance of what it is—namely, a church—just as a grocer's shop looks like a grocer's shop, not a silk-mercer's or a hosier's. But no; the hatred or scorn of images makes the Americans carry this new bigotry so far that if one of them were to go by chance into a French courtroom, he would mistake it for a church; and a Frenchman would rightly take one of their churches to be a temple of pettifoggery. This error is neither impossible nor purely imaginery, since nothing—not even a sculptured ornament or an inscription—announces what the place is or even might be. I should not consider it strange (if the like were found in France) that litigants of the Paris diocese should mistake it for a court of law, and the minister for an attorney or a bailiff. Any man's common sense would spare him this blunder if he but saw some inscription or suggestive ornamentation. An American visiting the Grand' Chambre in Paris, would be similarly misled if the fleurs-de-lis, paintings, and fireplaces were removed from it.

. . . It would be only partially reprehensible if the English in America, whom we believe so little given to superstition, would content themselves with this affectation of simplicity in their rites; but you cannot imagine how far they carry their fanatical respect for the Sabbath. Beginning Saturday evening, they cannot sing, laugh, work, or do anything, in short, that the Catholics forbid only on Sunday morning. The observance of Sunday itself is even more rigid. The cafés, taverns, and cabarets are deserted; private houses and shops are closed, with their lower windows half shut. In other words, an Anglican Sunday reminds one exactly of a French city in the deepest mourning.

In private or within the home, there is the same strictness and arbitrary rigor: you cannot, either noisily or quietly, laugh, sing, dance, play at games, or, in fact, indulge in any profane activity even after the close of the church service. If you did, certain citizens appointed by the judiciary would be authorized to remove you from your home and throw you charitably into prison, where you would remain a fortnight and be released only on the payment of a stiff fine. This is carried so far that if you were overheard in the street saying "By God!" these new-style inquisitors and soldiers of the Santa Hermandad, who might be strolling by or making their rounds, would have the same authority as though they had caught you singing, dancing, or drinking; and imprisonment and a fine would be the consequence of their charity and zeal.

In all this, they are not guided completely by blind superstition; whereas the cafés, taverns, and dance halls in the city are deserted on Sunday, in the country sections they are full of imbibers gravely celebrating the sanctity of the Sabbath and managing at the same time to get good and drunk. In short, apart from the lack of clamor, songs, and gaiety inspired by wine, the same disorder reigns as on any other day. Such, my friend, is another of the abuses found in the Anglican religion. Those of the Roman Church are well known to you, but you will at least admit that they are more sensible. Under the Anglican religion, Sunday offers sailors and laborers nothing better than the boredom of melancholy intoxication, and only on workdays can they find varied amusement suited to their humor—which they invariably do. In the Roman Church, on the other hand, Sunday is a day of pleasure and diversion once the divine service is over; workingmen can then enjoy any pleasures they wish, and if they do not return to work on Monday, at least they cannot claim, "We've no way of amusing ourselves except on weekdays." Thus on working-days the cafés and taverns are full of people spending their money, who would be ahead if they were free to spend it on Sunday.

To finish this description of Sunday: those who do not visit the roadhouses outside the town, return home and there idly pass the fine summer day or the long winter evening in boredom; or they read their Bibles or meditate piously instead of congregating with mutual friends, walking abroad in nice weather, or indulging in those moderate pursuits of leisure time sanctioned by wisdom and reason. The women follow mechanically in their husbands' ways and spend in complete boredom the only hours, one might say, that would be set apart for their pleasure in any other country. And so you see them, wasting their time during the pleasant days of summer and dying of tedium on Sunday, with nothing better to do than listen to sermons and deck themselves out in the extravagant finery they all wear to church, and which they put away as soon as they come home.

Johann David Schoepf, Travels in the Confederation [1783-84], *translated by Alfred J. Morrison (Philadelphia, 1911), pp. 66-69, 111-112.*

Pensylvania, and in consequence Philadelphia, assures freedom to all religious sects; men of all faiths and many of none, dwell together in harmony and peace. Tolerance, the advantages of which are only now beginning to be felt in several of the kingdoms of Europe, has been for a hundred years the foundation-stone of this flourishing state. Whoever acknowledges a God can be a citizen and has part in all the privileges of citizenship. Whoever is a member of any of the Christian congregations is eligible to petty office, and can be elected also to the Assembly, to the governorship, or to the Congress. Inspiration is left out of the account, except among the Quakers who look for everything from that source, and without it a man may be a good citizen and senator of Pensylvania. By such laws as these the Jews enjoy every right of citizenry and, provided they own property enough, vote for members of the Assembly. This everywhere oppressed and burdened nation can here and throughout America follow any civil business, and is restricted in hardly any way. The spirit of tolerance has gone so far that different religious sects have assisted one another in the building of houses of worship. At the present time there are in Philadelphia more than thirty such buildings, which if not all equally of a size and comeliness are in every case of a simple and neat construction; costly and artistic decoration is not to be found in them. Of these churches and meeting-houses, the Quakers own five, including their new meeting-house—there are three churches, using the English liturgy and ceremonies, which formerly were under the care of the English bishops—there are two Scotch Presbyterian churches—two German Lutheran, of which the one in Fourth-street is large and handsome—one German Reformed church—two Roman Catholic chapels, the one directed by a former Jesuit from Ireland and the other by a German priest, the two parishes numbering probably more than 1000 souls—there is a Swedish church at Wikakoa near the city—there is a synagogue—and there are other meeting-houses belonging to the Anabaptists, Methodists, Moravian Brethren, &c.

In the German Lutheran congregation there are baptized yearly some 400 children, and perhaps half as many burials are made. This difference is due to the fact that people living at a distance from

Philadelphia bring in their children to be baptized, on occasions of market or other business; but with the dead the case is that they are buried quietly in the country, behind the houses they have lived in—for many landowners in America have a family burying-ground in their gardens. The priesthood gains nothing by the dead, unless their services are desired at burials. You may (if the father in the case consents) be born for nothing, and you may die gratis—as you like; only while you live must taxes be paid. . . .

The clergy of the German nation, it was to be expected, would scatter not only the seeds of the gospel but those of scientific enlightenment as well. However, among the few ministers in all America a few only can give their mind to these things and fewer yet will. With the exception of several worthy men, chiefly in the larger towns, the services of the clergy are very ambiguous. Their position is not an agreeable one. They depend absolutely on the caprice of their congregations who (to use their own expression) hire a pastor from year to year at 20-30 or more pounds.—And so the ministers are often obliged to take charge of several congregations if they are to earn a passable support. Many of them, after the manner of the Apostles, have to carry on another occupation for a living. Mr. Kunze recently paid a visit to a worthy colleague beyond the Schuylkill. When he came into the house the pastor's wife asked him, 'do you wish to see the pastor or the cobbler?'—the pastoral office not bringing in enough to support the little family, the son added to the income by shoemaking, in which his father lent a hand. Congregations may dismiss their ministers so soon as they have the misfortune to displease. But before that pass, much must happen; the pastor preaching no strict morality, out of recompense and Christian love little faults on his part are overlooked.

To be sure, all the clergy in America (outside the English establishment) were without support from the civil authorities, which not inducting them left them to their congregations entirely. Each sect was permitted to dance as it would and manage the whistling as it could —for if the state interfered in church affairs in America there would be no end, and only evil could come of it. The Presbyterians indeed are not exposed to the blind choice or dismission of a freakish congregation, their discipline depending on an assembly of all the ministers. Only the ministers of the English establishment (because consecrated by some one of the English bishops and paid by the King) had under the old régime a closer connection with the state. The German Lutheran ministers, however, meet together at times in Synods to discuss general questions; at such meetings the office of President passes from one to another, since they are all equally independent.

Travels in North America in the Years 1780, 1781 and 1782 by the Marquis De Chastellux, *translated and edited by Howard C. Rice, Jr. (Chapel Hill, North Carolina, 1963), pp. 522-525.*

December 11, 1782: Bethlehem—Kalf's Tavern

The 11th, at half past eight, I went out with a Moravian, given me by the landlord. He was not much better informed and only served me as a guide. This man is a seaman, who happens to have some talent for drawing; for, since the war, he has quitted the sea, although he has sent his son there. He subsists on a small estate he has at Reading, but lives at Bethlehem, where he and his wife board in a private family. We went first to visit the house for "single women." This edifice is spacious, and built of stone. It is divided into several large chambers, all heated with stoves; here the girls work, some at coarse tasks, such as spinning cotton, hemp, and wool, while others do more tasteful and even very fine, fancywork, such as embroidery, either in silk or linen; they excel particularly in working ruffles, little pocketbooks, pincushions, etc., very much as our French nuns do. The superintendent of this house came to receive me. She is a woman of rank, born in Saxony, whose name is Madame von Gersdorf; but she does not presume upon her birth, and she even appeared surprised to see that I offered her my hand, whenever we went up and down stairs. She took me to the first [second] floor, where she had me enter a large vaulted room, spotlessly clean, in which all the residents of the house sleep; each one has a separate bed, in which there is no lack of feathers. There is never any fire in this room, and although it is high and very airy, they have built into the ceiling a ventilator like those in our playhouses. The kitchen is not large, but it is clean and well arranged; you see there immense kettles placed on stoves, as in our hospitals. The residents of the house dine in the refectory, and have meat and vegetables every day; the price they pay is three shillings and sixpence per week, about eight *sols* per day; they are not given supper, and I believe the house furnishes only bread for breakfast. After this expense and what they pay for heat and light are deducted, they enjoy the fruit of their labor, which is more than sufficient to maintain them. This house also has a place of worship [the Sisters' Chapel], which serves only for evening prayers, for they go to the church on Sundays. There is an organ in this chapel, and I saw several musical instruments hanging from hooks. I took leave of Madame von Gersdorf very well pleased with her reception, and then went to the church, which is simple and differs little from the one I had seen at Moravian Mill. Here also several religious pictures can be seen.

From the church I went to the house of the "Single men." I entered the intendant's apartment, and found him busy copying music. He had in his room a rather indifferent *forte piano*, made in Germany. I talked music with him, and discovered that he was not only a performer, but a composer as well; so when we went into the chapel together, I asked him to play the organ. He played some improvisations, into which he introduced a great deal of harmony and chords in the base. This man, whose name I have forgotten, was born in New York, but resided seven years in Germany, whence he had recently arrived. I found him better informed than the others, yet it was with some difficulty that I got from him the following details: The Moravian brethren, in whatever quarter of the world they live, are under the rule of their Metropolitans, who reside in Germany. It is from there that the directors of the Society send out commissioners to manage their different settlements. These same Metropolitans advance the necessary funds, which are repaid as the colonies prosper; thus the income from the mills I have spoken of, as well as from the farms and manufacture of Bethlehem, are employed in the first instance to pay the expenses of the community, and afterwards to reimburse the interest and principal of the funds advanced from Europe. Bethlehem, for example, posesses lands purchased by the Moravians in Europe; this property consists of fifteen hundred acres of land, forming a vast farm, which is managed by a steward, who is responsible to the community. If an individual wants a lot of land, he must purchase it from the public, but under this restriction, that in case of defection from the sect, or emigration from the place, he shall restore it to the community, which will then reimburse him the original payment. As to their opinions, this sect is closer to the Lutherans than to the Calvinists; differing, however, from the latter, by admitting music, pictures, etc. into their churches, and from the former, by having no bishops, and being governed by a synod. Their regulations and discipline have something monastic about them, since they recommend celibacy, although not requiring it, and keep the women very much separated from the men. There is a special house, also, for the widows, which I did not visit. The two sexes being thus habitually separated, none of those familiar connections exist between them, which lead to marriage; it is even contrary to the spirit of this sect to marry from inclination. If a young man finds himself sufficiently at his ease to have a house of his own and to maintain a wife and children, he presents himself to the commissioner and asks him for a girl; this official proposes one to him, whom he may, in fact, refuse to accept; but it is contrary to custom to select or choose a wife for himself. Consequently the Moravian colony has been far from multiplying in the same proportion as the other American colonies. At Bethlehem there is a colony of about six hundred persons, more than half of whom live in a state of celibacy; nor does it appear to have increased for several years past. Furthermore every precaution is taken to provide for the livelihood of the brethren, and in the houses destined for the unmarried of both sexes, there are masters who teach them different trades.

The house of the single men which I saw in detail, does not differ from that of the single women; I shall mention but one thing which seems to me worthy of notice, that is a very convenient method they have devised of being waked up at the hour they want to arise: all the beds are numbered, and near the door is a slate, on which all the numbers are written. A man who wishes to be awakened early, at five o'clock in the morning for example, has only to write a figure 5 under his number; the servants who take care of the room are thus informed, and the next morning, at the time indicated, they go straight to the number of the bed without needing to know the sleeper's name.

J.P. Brissot de Warville, New Travels in the United States of America 1788, *translated by Mara Soceanu Vamos and Durand Echeverria, edited by Durand Echeverria (Cambridge, 1964), pp. 86-90.*

I shall never recall without emotion the pleasure I felt one day [in Boston] when I heard a sermon by the Reverend Mr. [John] Clarke, successor to the famous Doctor [Samuel] Cooper, to whom every good Frenchman and every lover of liberty owes a debt of gratitude for the affection he bore the French and the zeal with which he preached and defended American independence. Mr. Clarke's rather large congregation displayed the same look of well-being which I have mentioned, that air of serious meditation produced by a tradition of solemnity in the presence of the Almighty, that reverent decorum which is equally removed from superstitious, groveling idolatry and from the impudent, wanton airs of those Europeans who go to church as they would to a theater.

> Spectatum veniunt; veniunt spectentur ut ipsae.
> [They come to see, and they come also that they may be seen.]

To crown my happiness, I saw none of those livid, ragged wretches that one sees in Europe, who, soliciting our compassion at the foot of the altar, seem to bear witness against Providence, against our inhumanity, and against the chaos of our society. Sermon, prayer, ritual—everything had the same simplicity. The sermon was instinct with the highest moral thoughts and the congregation listened to it with attention.

This kind of superior moral tone chracterizes almost all the sermons of all the sects on this continent. Rarely do the ministers speak of dogma; tolerance, born with American independence, has banished dogmatic preaching, which always leads to disputes and quarrels. Only the preaching of viture, which is the same for all sects, is accepted as being suitable in a great society of brothers.

This tolerance is most striking in Boston, in this very city which once witnessed such bloody persecutions, in particular those suffered by the Quakers. Now there are Friends—indeed, in very small number—in this place where several of their predecessors paid with their lives for their perseverance in their religious opinions. Just Heaven! How is it possible that men who sincerely believed in God could have been barbarous enough to put to death a woman, the intrepid [Mary] Dyer, because she thee'd and thou'd God and men, because she did not believe in priests, and because she tried to follow the Gospel literally? But let us draw a curtain over these scenes of horror; they will undoubtedly never again defile this new continent destined by Heaven to be the haven of liberty and humanity. Today in Boston everyone worships God in his own way; Anabaptists, Methodists, Quakers, and even Catholics, all freely profess their opinions. There is as yet no Catholic chapel, but one will soon be built by a Protestant minister recently converted to Catholicism. The Reverent Dr. [John] Thayer, son of a Bostonian, has been traveling in France and in Italy. He says that the life and miracles of the blessed Labre, who for the love of God let himself be devoured by vermin, made him see the light, which he intends to preach in America. He has sent ahead to Boston chasubles, chalices, and all the other articles of Catholic ritual. His mission, which twenty years ago would have incited persecution, now merely excites the curiosity. The Puritans may make fun in the newspapers of the converted minister and of the "miracle" of his conversion, but they will certainly not persecute him.

The ministers of the various sects live in such harmony that they substitute for each other when private business detains any one of them from his pulpit.

This indifference to religious disputes is the result of a war during which Americans came into contact with men from many countries and, as a consequence, broke loose from their old habits and prejudices. When they saw that other men with religious opinions different from their own could none the less be virtuous, they understood that it was possible to be a good man whether one believed or not in transubstantiation or in the divinity of Christ. So they concluded that they should tolerate one another, and that this was the kind of worship most agreeable to God.

Before these ideas had become widespread, another essential principle was generally accepted, namely, the necessity of simplifying divine worship as much as possible, of freeing it from all the superstitious ceremonies which formerly gave it the appearance of idolatry, and particularly of refraining from paying their ministers salaries which would permit them to live in luxury and idleness. In a word, they believed in the need to restore evangelical simplicity. In this they have succeeded.

In the country, land is set aside for the support of the church, but in Boston the ministers are supported entirely by the collections made each Sunday and by the rents paid for pews. This is an excellent practice which induces the ministers to be learned and to fulfill conscientiously their functions, for those whose sermons are most popular are in the greatest demand and have the largest incomes; in contrast, in

France ignorant and corrupt priests are just as sure as learned and virtuous ones of their emoluments. Another consequence of this practice is that the unbeliever is not assessed. Is it not tyranny to force men to pay for the support of a religion they have rejected?

Bostonians have become so philosophical on the subject of religion that they have recently appointed a man as minister even though he had been refused regular ordination. The members of the sect to which he belonged installed him in their church and empowered him to teach and to preach; and he does teach and preach with considerable skill, for the people rarely make a mistake in their choices.

This canonical ordination, unprecedented except in the primitive church, has been censured by those who still believe in the tradition of the apostolic succession. But Bostonians are so close to believing that every man can be his own priest that the apostolic doctrine has not found very strong advocates. Ministers in America will soon be in the position which M. D'Alembert assigned to the pastors of Geneva, ["reduced almost to the adoration of one God"].

The Quakers

Visitors to 18th-century America were intrigued by the history and strength of the Quakers, a small band of persecuted believers who had become the dominant political and social force in the most American of the colonies. For what were the Quakers chiefly criticized? For what were they praised? Why were they criticized and defended so vigorously? Did the critics and defenders hold essentially the same view of the Quakers, adding only different value judgements about what they saw? In what did their religious strength lie? their social strength? their political power?

On the Threshold of Liberty: Journal of a Frenchman's Tour of the American Colonies in 1777, *translated and edited by Edward D. Seeber (Bloomington, Indiana, 1959), pp. 30-33.*

All these [34] sects [in Philadelphia] can, for practical purposes, be reduced to four or five: Protestants, Lutherans, Presbyterians, and

Quakers. The rest are so unimportant by comparison that, although they enjoy the right of representation in governmental bodies, the number of voices raised up through fanaticism against their candidates makes their efforts fruitless. At the same time, these representatives are not denied the right to nominate and vote for those who are called to the office of the magistracy.

It follows that each person, lest he diminish his own sect and expand another, refuses insofar as possible to become a member of the family of a different sectarian; and, consistent with this behavior, he has business dealings and does his buying only within his own communion. In a city, this results necessarily in indifference and, sometimes, animosity. Such are those Quakers so highly praised by the celebrated abbé R[aynal], who has invariably deified them because he has not had a close look at them: they are, says he, kind to all people individually, benevolent toward those they know, generous beyond all imagining, and eager to be of service. Most of them (though not all) are at the present time the most hard-hearted, ungrateful people once they are dissociated from sectarian interests. Would you believe that a sect calculated to be the wellspring of virtue and the model of humaneness, which assumes the equality of all men, subjects and rulers, valets and masters; which bases its belief and duty on humility, beneficence and kindness; which, finally, proscribes pride among its followers, and turns them into the simplest and best of men when they conform to its precepts—would you believe, I ask, that this is the sect that shows the greatest desire to dominate, that displays the readiest resources of vengeance and obduracy, that employs oaths, perjury, usury, and hypocrisy as the commonest means for the execution of any project calculated to strengthen it or to guarantee the pleasure of seeing itself in complete control of the civil and military administration? To think that this is the sect set apart by its founders' precepts from worldly vanities and involvements!

Perhaps you will think that, because I am biased against them (as most people are), I have been carried away by public opinion. Not at all. No Frenchman is a more enthusiastic partisan of Quakerism; yet I have had to admit the truth. In the midst of the turmoil of civil war, or the combat of the weak against the strong, the Quakers were privileged to decide whether to wage war or not, to pay taxes or not, to flee from the country with their cash assets, or to abide there peacefully, shielded from the tumults of a war being waged at their very doorstep. At the same time they gave written guarantees that they would remain neutral; they were asked to furnish neither hostages nor any security other than their good faith. But it became as clear as day to me, as it did to others, that they who had agreed to remain neutral because their religion forbids warfare, and who had given their sworn promise to serve neither one side nor the other, were, great and small, rich or poor, repudiating their oaths and their word, trafficking in and betraying all the decisions of Congress, and plotting to deliver it into the hands of General Howe. What is more, they were stripping themselves of their own wealth by offering seven or eight paper guineas for one of gold in order to destroy the credit of the continental paper currency; they were even supplying the enemy with their scarcely ripened crops and paying for guides who would furnish them ready knowledge of defiles and fording-places in creeks and rivers. One can but accept the evidence and recognize in all this the weakness of humankind which, unmindful of the labyrinth of iniquity into which it is plunging, abandons itself blindly to transports of vengeance and no longer holds anything sacred whenever it is found either to serve or to harm its interests.

In spite of their slowness in making decisions when a firm stand is called for, their hatred of bloodshed and their fanatical devotion to the precepts of their faith which forbids it even under special circumstances, and their scorn and aversion for soldiers and everything connected with their profession (which they call the scourge of humanity and the lash of despotism), the Quakers, had they been able to win a majority in the Congress and see their party become the strongest, would have vied with each other in trampling beneath their feet this cherished idol, and, in brief, done as much against King George as they now do so enthusiastically for him. To this degree, in the accomplishing of their projects, are vengeance and party spirit blind in their choices, inconsiderate in their reasoning, and perfidious in their conduct—and there you have my much vaunted Quakers!

Travels in North America in the Years 1780, 1781 and 1782 by the
Marquis De Chastellux, *translated and edited by Howard C. Rice,
Jr. (Chapel Hill, North Carolina, 1963), pp. 165-168.*

December 9, 1780: Philadelphia

Our young folks needing some rest after their travels and their late
hours, did not appear at breakfast. In their stead, we had an old
Quaker by the name of [Anthony] Benezet, whose small stature and
humble and unimposing looks formed a perfect contrast to Mr. Pendle-
ton. This Mr. Benezet may rather be regarded as the model, than as
a specimen of the sect of Quakers: wholly occupied with the welfare
of mankind, his charity and generosity brought him great consideration
in happier times, when the virtues alone sufficed to render a citizen
illustrious. At present, the loud clash of arms deafens ears to the small
voice of charity, and love of country has prevailed over the love of
mankind. Benezet, however, still continues to exercise his benevo-
lence: he had come to ask me for some information respecting the
new methods invented in France for restoring drowned persons to life.
I promised not only to send him this information from Newport, but
to transmit to him one of the boxes such as our government has distributed in the seaport towns. Confidence being established between
us, we fell on the topic of the miseries of war.

"Friend," he said to me, "I know thou art a man of letters, and
a member of the French Academy. The men of letters have written
a great many good things of late; they have attacked errors and prejudices and, above all, intolerance; will they not endeavor, too, to
disgust men with the horrors of war, and to make them live together
like friends and brethren?" "Thou art not deceived, Friend," I
replied, "when thou buildest some hope on the progress of enlightened
philosophy. Many active hands are laboring at the great edifice of
public happiness; but vainly will they employ themselves in finishing
some parts of it, as long as there is a deficiency at the base, and
that base, thou hast said it, is universal peace. As for intolerace and
persecution, it is true that these two enemies of the human race are
not yet bound by strong enough chains; but I will whisper a word
in thy ear, of which thou wilt not perhaps feel all the force, though
thou art well acquainted with French: *elles ne sont plus à la mode*,
they are no longer fashionable; I should even believe them to be on
the point of annihilation, but for certain little circumstances thou art

not informed of; which are, that they who attack them are sometimes imprisoned, and that livings of a hundred thousand *livres* a year are bestowed upon those who favor them."

"A hundred thousand *livres* a year!" cried Benezet. "But that is enough to build hospitals and establish manufactures; this doubtless is the use they make of their riches." "No, Friend," I replied, "persecution needs bribes; though it must be confessed that it is but indifferently paid and that the most splendid of these persecutors content themselves with giving a pension of ten or twelve hundred *livres* to a few satirical poets, or journalists, enemies of letters, whose works are widely read but little sold." "Friend," the Quaker said to me, "this persecution is a strange thing: I can hardly believe what has happened to myself. My father was a Frenchman, and I was born in thy country. It is now sixty years since he was obliged to seek an asylum in England, taking with him his children, the only treasure he could save in his misfortunes. Justice, or what is so called in thy country, ordered him to be hung in effigy, because he explained the Gospel differently from thy priests. My father was not much better pleased with those of England; wishing to get out of the way of all hierarchy, he came and settled in this country, where I had a happy life until this war broke out. I have long forgotten all the persecutions my family underwent. I love thy nation, because it is mild and sensible, and as for thee, Friend, I know that thou servest humanity as much as in thy power. When thou shalt be again in Europe, engage thy brethren to second thee and, in the meantime, permit me to place under thy protection our brethren of Rhode Island." He then recommended to me specifically the Quakers living in that state, and who are pretty numerous; after which he took leave, asking my permission to send me some pamphlets of his making, which were principally apologies for his sect. I assured him I would read them with great pleasure, and he did not fail to send them to me the next morning.

To whatever sect he belongs, a man burning with zeal and love of humanity is, let there be no doubt of it, a being worthy of respect; but I must confess that it is difficult to bestow upon this sect in general that esteem which cannot be refused to some individuals. The law observed by many of them, of saying neither *you* nor *sir*, is far from giving them a tone of simplicity and candor. I know not whether it be to compensate for this sort of rusticity that they often assume a smooth and wheedling tone which is altogether Jesuitical. Nor does their conduct belie this resemblance: concealing their indifference for the public welfare under the cloak of religion, they are indeed sparing of blood, especially of their own, but they trick both parties out of their money, and that without either shame or decency. It is a commonplace maxim in trade, to beware of them, and this opinion, which is well founded, will become still more so. In fact, nothing can be worse than religious enthusiasm in its decline; for what can be its substitute, but hypocrisy? This monster, so well known in Europe, finds but too easy an access to all religions. It found none, however, into a company of young ladies, who were invited, as well as myself, to drink tea with Mrs. Cunningham [Conyngham?]. They were well dressed, seemed desirous of pleasing, and it must be assumed that their private sentiments did not belie their appearance. The mistress of the house is amiable, and her conversation graceful and interesting. This assembly recalled to my mind in every respect those of Holland and of Geneva, where one meets with gaiety without indecency, and the wish to please without coquetry.

December 10, 1780: Philadelphia

On Sunday the 10th I had resolved to make a circuit through the churches and different places of worship. Unfortunately the different sects, who agree on no other point, have chosen the same hour to assemble the faithful, so that in the morning I was only able to visit the Quakers' meeting, and in the afternoon the Anglicans. The hall where the Quakers meet is square; there are, on all sides and parallel to the walls, benches and desks, so that people are placed facing each other, without either altar or pulpit to attract the attention. As soon as they are assembled, one of the more elderly makes an impromptu prayer, just as it comes to his mind; silence is then observed until some man or woman feels inspired and rises to speak. Travelers must be taken at their word, however extraordinary their tales may be. Like Ariosto, I shall be recounting wonders, *dirò maraviglia:* but the fact is that I arrived just as a woman had stopped talking. She was followed by a man who talked a great deal of nonsense about inner grace, the illumination of the spirit, and the other dogmas of his sect, which he kept repeating but avoided explaining; at length his discourse ended to the great satisfaction of the brethren and the sisters, who all looked inattentive and bored. After seven or eight minutes of silence, an old man went on his knees, dealt us out a very commonplace prayer, and dismissed the audience.

After this dreary and rustic assembly, the service of the Anglicans appeared to me a sort of opera, both because of the music and the scenery: a handsome pulpit placed before a handsome organ; a handsome minister in that pulpit, reading, speaking, and singing with truly theatrical grace; a number of young women responding melodiously from the pit and the boxes (for the two side galleries are much like boxes); soft and agreeable singing, alternating with excellent sonatas played on the organ; all this, compared to the Quakers, the Anabaptists, the Presbyterians, etc., appeared to me more like a little paradise in itself than as the road to it. If however we consider these many different sects, some of them strict and others lax, but all of them imperious and all of them self-opinionated, we seem to see men reading in the great book of Nature, like illiterate Montauciel at his lesson. The letters as written actually spell *"vous êtes un blanc bec"* (you are a simpleton), but he persists in misreading them as fanciful nonsense of his own imagining. There is not one chance in a million that he can guess correctly a line of writing without knowing his letters; should he, however, come to implore your help, beware of giving it; better far to leave him in error than to cut throats with him!

Johann David Schoepf, Travels in the Confederation [1783-84], *translated by Alfred J. Morrison (Philadelphia, 1911), pp. 62-65.*

I remember once reading in some book of travels that Philadelphia was a city of Quakers and beautiful gardens. Brief enough, and for the time probably true. Quakers from the beginning have been the most numerous, the most respectable, and the richest among the inhabitants; in the government of the state they have had an important, perhaps the weightiest, influence; and their manners, through imitation, have become general among the people. Quakers purchased and peopled the country; they made with the aborigines peaceable treaties, as Voltaire observes, the only treaties between Indians and Christians, unsworn-to and not broken. The greatest part of the useful institutions and foundations owe their origin to this sect. By it chiefly was the police organized and maintained. This temperate and originally virtue-seeking brotherhood takes no part in impetuous and time-consuming pleasures which worldliness and idleness bring other, baptized Christians into. Their religion, giving them a coat with no buttons or creases, denies them play and the dance. Thus they gain much time for pondering useful regulations which do honor to their society and are advantageous to the community. For the same reason, where circumstances are equally favorable, Quakers are invariably better-off than their neighbors, because they bring order into their domestic affairs, undertake nothing without the most careful forethought, and prosecute everything with constant zeal. In Philadelphia the large Hospital and the Workhouse are standing examples of their benevolent views. Also, the field of the sciences has them to thank; the American Philosophical Society was founded by them, and their sect furnishes to it many worthy members. For gradually the Quakers are giving over their former depreciation of the sciences, since they find that increased intelligence does not injure the well-being of a community, and that everything is not to be expected from immediate revelation. In their outward conduct, and in their relations with their fellow-citizens of other beliefs, they are beginning to recede from the strict attitude of an earlier time. No longer does the hat sit quite so square, and many young Quakers venture to half-tilt the round hat, gently, so that the brims are brought into a position, doubtful as yet, half perpendicular and half horizontal. But the 'Thou' and 'Thee,' which in our title-seeking Germany was the chief hindrance in the spread of Quakerism, they still find it well to retain.

It is against the principles of the Quakers to take part in any feud whatsoever, because as Christians they consider it their duty to love their enemies. Hence, neither in former wars nor in this last war would they let themselves be placed in ranks and companies with murderous weapons in their hands, although the Jews themselves have not in America declined such service. In former times it was the easier to abjure all participation in war, since the Proprietors, the Governors, all the more important citizens and officers of state were of that sect. Besides, it happened that the unbaptized blood-shy Friends stayed quietly at their plantations or their towns in lower Pensylvania while in the farther regions the poorer, baptized Christians were being murdered and scalped by the Indians or the French. To be sure they did not cease to deprecate these grewsome contrivances of jealous and land-hungry monarchs; but they excused themselves on the ground that the Brotherhood never waged war, and would the rather suffer everything at the hands of an enemy insatiable. How long a state could exist, composed entirely of Quakers and therefore inimical to war, may be easily imagined. Adjoining states must be Quakers as well or the supposed state less rich than Quakers commonly are. The leaders of the now free American states very clearly perceived that by the virtues of Quakerism no victories could be won: so, during the war the Brotherhood was left in undisturbed inactivity, but was doubly taxed. But the Quakers resisted payment of these taxes because they regarded them as mediate contributions in the effecting of bloody designs—for which they professed an absolute hatred, but the results of which were entirely to their liking. In the circumstances, a part of the property of those refusing to pay was seized, and sold below value in the name of the state. Eventually, most of them became amenable, if only to preserve the appearance of the peace-loving and non-paying Quaker, and when the tax-gatherer came, (in America the farmer does not seek him out), they fell into a custom of laying a piece of gold on the table, which could be taken for tax—the part of conscience or duty, perhaps also the part of wisdom. Those Quakers within the compass of the royal English army conducted themselves in like manner during the war. They never gave a horse, or a wagon, or a servant, or anything which might be demanded of them for the maintenance of the troops, but they looked on unconcerned if without further question such things were taken as needed.

During the late war, however, certain of the Quakers permitted themselves to be led astray by the spirit of schism and took an active part in the war; but these, with their friends and adherents, were excluded from the meetings of the genuine, orthodox Quakers. Upon that, they built themselves a meeting-house of their own, in Arch-street, between Fourth and Fifth-street, where they will, like the others, quietly await the moving of the same spirit. Their number is not large and they are distinguished by the name of Fighting Quakers. It might perhaps have been possible, by compliance on either side, to avoid a separation; but since this is never the case in matters of opinion and faith, and since the break has gone so far as the erection of a new meeting-house, there will be no re-union, if only because the building would then have been raised to no purpose: and so Philadelphia gains a new rubric in the list of its sects. A certain Matlock is one of the most conspicuous of these fighting Quakers, or quaking fighters, and made no scruple of accepting a colonelcy in the American army. He had always been an enterprising genius, and as a consequence had debts. When he was just made Colonel, and with his sword at his side, was walking the streets, an acquaintance met him—'Friend, what doest thee with that thing at thy side?' 'Protecting Liberty and Property,' (two words very current in England and America), answered the Colonel. 'Eh,' said his friend, 'as for property I never knew thee had any, and liberty, that thee hast by the indulgence of the brethren.'

J.P. Brissot de Warville, New Travels in the United States of America 1788, *translated by Mara Soceanu Vamos and Durand Echeverria, edited by Durand Echeverria (Cambridge, 1964), pp. 298-307.*

I have promised you, my dear friend, a letter specially devoted to this worthy society, and today I shall keep my word.

You recall the insulting frivolity with which M. Chastellux discussed the Quakers in his most superificial *Travels.* You will also recall my stern criticism of his errors, lies, and calumnies, the underhanded persecution I suffered for this criticism, and the attempts to block its success made by that clever marquis and some Academicians seeking to tyrannize public opinion and inflate their own reputations. Nor will you have forgotten those petty letters published in the *Journal de Paris,* a sheet which served the cause of every sort of despot, in which the Quakers were pitilessly lacerated while the biased censors and journalists cravenly suppressed every reply to these virulent diatribes.

I now have had the opportunity, my friend, to compare the portrait I formerly made of the Quakers with the Quakers I have seen in America, and I am convinced that, with the exception of a few details, I did not flatter them. You will be convinced of this as you read the following observations and impressions. I have tried as much as possible not to be influenced by the flattering manner in which they received me because of their gratitude for the apology of their sect which I had published. It has been translated into English here in America by some worthy members of the Society and has been widely distributed among the Friends. I was happy to see that my work had helped to dispel the unfortunate prejudices against our nation which had been occasioned by the indiscretion, boasting, and indecent sarcasm of that frivolous Academician.

I first must quote from the general description I wrote when in England of the private conduct and public morals of the Quakers. You yourself have had opportunity to become more intimately acquainted with Quakers during your frequent trips to England and your extended stay in Ireland. I wrote as follows:

Simplicity, candor, and honesty characterize their actions and speech. They are not affectionate, but they are sincere; they are not polite, but they are humane; they lack the scintillating wit without which a man cannot exist in France and with which he can do anything, but they have common sense, balanced judgment, integrity, and honest hearts. In short, for friends and associates, give me Quakers; for diverting companions, give me the French. As for their women, they are what all women ought to be: faithful to their husbands, tender with their children, simple in their dress, and thrifty and conscientious housewives. Their main characteristic is that they are not in the least interested in courting the attention of other individuals or of the world at large. Their whole life is directed inward, not outward.

There are still a few countries where such simplicity of manners exists; it is preserved, for instance, by the Arabs, who lead the nomadic life of the early patriarchs. I cannot repeat too often that it is only among people following this way of life that one finds happy families and public virtue. We, unhappy and diseased in the mist of our civilization and polite manners, have renounced these virtues. And indeed, who among us is happy except the man who has the strength to return to nature and live as did the good people of ancient times? . . .

I shall not repeat here everything that M. Crèvecoeur wrote about the Quakers; I wish to tell you only what he did not say.

Simplicity is the Quakers' main virtue, and the men still adhere quite closely to Penn's advice: "Choose thy clothes by thine own eyes, not another's. The more plain and simple they are, the better. Neither unshapely, nor fantastical; and for use and decency, not for pride . . . If thou art clean and warm, it is sufficient; for more doth but rob the poor and please the wanton."

I have seen James Pemberton, one of the wealthiest Quakers and a man whose virtues place him among the most respected of their leaders. His coat was threadbare but spotless; he prefers to clothe the poor and spend his money in defense of the Negroes rather than have a large wardrobe.

You are familiar with Quaker dress: a round hat, almost always white; a coat of fairly good cloth; cotton or woolen stockings; and their hair cut round and without powder. A Quaker usually carries in his pocket a small comb in a case, and if his hair is in disorder when he enters a house he simply combs it in front of the first mirror he finds.

The white hat which the Quakers prefer has recently become more common since Franklin has proved its advantages over black ones. They still insist on not wearing buttons on their hats. They have nothing against this custom in itself, but since they despise vanity and superfluity and wish to have only well-tried members who are above the fear of appearing ridiculous, they require of all Quakers that they do not dress as other men. A test at first, this practice ends by becoming a distinctive sign of the truly devout.

The country Quakers usually wear homespun cloth. It was called to my attention that at their General Meeting in September of this year nine tenths of the nearly 1,500 persons present wore this domestic cloth, thus setting a good example for other sects to follow.

There are Quakers who dress with greater care and elegance, who wear powder, silver buckles, and ruffled cuffs. They are called "Wet Quakers" and are regarded by the others as schismatic or weak. Though allowed to attend the Sunday Meetings, they are never permitted at the Monthly or Quarterly Meetings.

Not more than fifteen years ago it was still considered a sort of crime by all the sects in America to wear powder. A mother would send her daughter to the theater and forbid her to wear any. Since the last war, however, manners have changed in almost all sects because of the influence of the European armies. Let it be said to the honor of the Quakers that theirs have changed less, because of the strictness with which they adhere to their discipline and repudiate those who stray from it.

On the fifteenth of September Quakers put on woolen stockings. This is part of their sytem of discipline, which applies even to their clothing, and they attribute their longevity to the regular observance of this custom. There is also another fact which I forgot to mention, and which proves that they are right. Of the Quakers who were Penn's contemporaries in 1693, there are six who are still alive at the moment I write. One named Drinker, born in 1680, lived to be a hundred. It is this deep-seated conviction of the advantages of their ways that causes the Quakers to keep their dress unchanged. Their so-called eccentricities are in reality customs inspired by the counsel of reason and by long experience. Yet writers who are presumed to be serious have had the effrontery to ridicule their simple dress.

Quaker women usually dress more warmly than other American women and consequently are less subject to diseases, as I have already noted. Age and wealth do, however, introduce differences in their dress which are far more noticeable than in men's clothing. The matrons wear very dark, even dismal, colors and small black bonnets, with their hair simply brushed up. On the other hand, the young women often curl their hair with so much care that they spend as much time, I am told, as they might on the most elegant toilettes. I noticed with sorrow that they wear small hats covered with silk or satin. These young Quakeresses, who are so well endowed with natural beauty and whose charms have so little need of artifices or added adornments, make themselves conspicuous by their choice of the finest linens, muslins, and silks. Their fingers play with elegant fans, and the luxury of the Orient would not disdain their fine linen. Is all this in accordance with Penn's precepts? "Meekness and modesty," he said, "are the rich and charming attire of the soul; and the plainer the dress, the more distinctly, and with greater lustre, their beauty shines."

Since I will not flatter even my friends, I must say frankly to the Quakers (for I am sure they will read me and I know they always profit by good counsel) that if anything can discredit their principles abroad it is this gradual and imperceptible relaxation of their morals and customs. Their liking for fine cloth appears as an ill-disguised and hypocritical love of luxury, which is, to say the least, inconsistent with their loud professions of simplicity and austerity.

Luxury begins where utility ends. Now, of what use is fine linen to the body? And to what use could not be put the money which is spent on this luxury! There are so many good deeds to be done! So many people in need!

Luxury in simple things betrays even more vanity than the usual sort of luxury, for it appears to be a measure of that very wealth which the Quakers would have us believe they scorn to parade. Such luxury proclaims that the mind is no longer imbued with great moral principles; it proves that one believes that happiness depends on appearances and show rather than on virtue.

What a poor example the Quakers, who have been the models of simplicity, set for other Americans! The United States does not now nor will it for a long time manufacture fine linens, delicate fabrics, and almost transparent muslins; these must be imported from the foreign countries on which Americans already rely for so many other more essential needs. Thus these luxury goods drain away money which is badly needed for extending the settlements and establishing new industries. Let the Quakers who read this letter meditate on my words; may they realize that the use of rum, which they so strongly oppose, cannot harm America any more than will the introduction of luxury into their society. I have noticed the same sort of thing in the furniture of wealthy Quakers; it seems plain, but there are many fine and expensive pieces.

Fortunately this luxury has not yet found its way to the tables of the Quakers. I must describe a dinner given by one of the richest men of the sect at the time of the General Meeting in September; it presents a curious contrast with our splendid French banquets. At the time of this meeting Philadelphia is filled with Quakers from the country and the neighboring towns, and their brethren lodge and feed them and welcome them with the most affectionate hospitality. About twenty guests were gathered around the table, the master of the house sitting at one end and the mistress at the other. Before the meal was served there was a moment of silence during which the Quakers silently gave thanks to the Supreme Being. The first course consisted of a large piece of beef placed at one end of the table, a ham placed in the middle, a leg of lamb at the other end, two soups, and four dishes of potatoes, cabbage, vegetables, etc., as well as cider, Philadelphia porter, and beer. The master of the house spoke to each Friend, saying: "Help thyself, ask for what thou likest, make thyself at home." The second course consisted merely of various kinds of pies and cakes, two bowls of cream, two dishes of cheese, and two of butter. The servant then poured a glass of wine for each guest, but there were none of those tiresome toasts which are more incitements to drunkenness than expressions of patriotism. We chatted quietly. It is true that at this simple meal there was none of the sparkle and gaiety of our noisy French dinners and suppers. But everybody seemed happy and comfortable and felt at home. Good Thomas—seemed very happy indeed to be able to welcome in this way his brothers from the country.

Those who have reproached Quaker men and women for being sad and morose can have known them only superficially and not intimately. I, who have been received by them as their own son and have shared their family life, have found that they have moments of open, frank emotion and of gaiety, as well as periods of pleasant and affectionate conversation. They do not lead lives of mad joy, but they are serene and happy, and, if gaiety is the expression of the happiness of the soul, they are gay.

We Frenchmen have the reputation of being gay because we laugh at everything and find consolation for misfortune in a vaudeville. This is not gaiety but folly. Laughter is the sign of gaiety, and gaiety is the outward expression of pleasurable sensations, or of a sense of well-being, or of thoughts which awaken such pleasurable sensations. One should therefore not be gay except when one is happy. A man who is gay in the midst of misfortune is mad; but if he is serene and imperturbable he is wise. One should not be crushed by misfortune, nor should one laugh at it; the former is weakness, the latter madness or stupidity. . . .

The composure of the Quakers in their gaiety is also theirs in the midst of misfortune, during their discussions, and in all their undertakings. This they owe to their special training, which teaches them at an early age to curb their passions, and especially to check hasty temper or anger. Their aim is to make themselves, as they say, "immovable," that is, impervious to sudden emotions, impassive, imperturbable. As a result, they are at all times complete masters of themselves, and so in discussions they have a great advantage over those who lose their tempers. "Nothing does reason more right," Penn said in his manual, "than the coolness of those that offer it; for truth often suffers more by the heat of its defenders than from the arguments of its opposers."

I have seen in my friend Miers Fisher, whom I have mentioned before, a sample of the excellent effects of this coolness in discussion. I must first tell you something about his life. He was born a Quaker and belongs to one of the largest and most respected families in Philadelphia, among whom there are several distinguished merchants.

He first went into trade and then studied and practiced law. During the last war he consistently adhered to the pacifist neutrality of the Quakers and refused to side either with the Americans or the English. As a result he became most unpopular. He was one of the Quakers who were exiled to Virginia, and he lost at that time a large part of his fortune. After the peace he returned to Philadelphia, where he continues to practice law. Even his enemies think highly of his ability, and not only in legal matters. This estimable man has a great fund of information, which is rare among Quakers, who rather study the Bible and moral questions, and is indeed rare among Americans generally. His political sentiments, however, still make him an object of considerable suspicion, and we can only hope that this hostility will vanish and that he will someday play the part in Congress for which his talents and virtues have created him. I heard him in the Pennsylvania General Assembly defend the cause of the pilots, who were opposing a bill to reduce their fees. Clarity, close reasoning, and erudition were the distinctive marks of his plea, which was successful. He constantly maintained his calm even though interrupted by sudden and sometimes rather sharp attacks from members of the Assembly.

This composure accompanies Quakers to the very edge of their graves. Even the women do not lose it at this sad moment. It is the fruit both of their religious principles and of right conduct constantly maintained. After a death the survivors seem either to abandon themselves to grief less than do most people or else to contain it within themselves. They hold Heaven their home and do not believe that death, which leads to it, can be a misfortune.

You must understand, however, that this habitual composure in no way diminishes their sensibility. The worthy James Pemberton described to me the death of his beloved daughter on the very next day after this misfortune had struck him. I saw steal down from his eye a tear, which reflection immediately wiped away. He loved to talk to me of her virtues and of her resignation during her long suffering. "She was an angel," he said, "and she is now in her home."

This good father did not exaggerate. In this society you will find a far greater number of those happy, angelic faces on which you can read serenity, the sign of peace of soul, and therefore of virtue.

I cannot explain why, but it is true that with a pure soul, a great soul, I am at once at ease. I feel that we have known one another for centuries; we understand each other without speaking. But a corrupt man, a rake, a man of the world, immediately produces upon me the opposite impression. My soul shrinks and recoils like a sensitive plant. In the company of Quakers I have almost always experienced the first of these two impressions.

The portrait I have given of the Quakers is a summary not only of my own observations, but also of information I have gathered from the best-informed men, including ones of other sects.

Once, in company, I asked: "Is there greater purity of morals, more simplicity, and more honesty and integrity among the Quakers than in any other sect?" A man distinguished for his knowledge and his devotion to the new constitution answered me, "Although I was born a Presbyterian, I must admit that the Quakers excel all other sects in these respects."

Of course, they are not all pure and irreproachable, and there have been rascals among them, for the use to which their reputation can be put has inevitably drawn to them hypocritical proselytes and knaves. A man would rather counterfeit a guinea than a halfpenny. But Quakers are very strict in expelling from their community those who have been found guilty not only of crimes but even of breaches of delicacy and probity that are not punishable by law. The public is often unaware of these expulsions because the rejected Quaker continues to attend Sunday Meetings. The Quakers cannot prevent him from doing so, but they no longer consider him a member of their society, and he is no longer admitted to their Monthly and Quarterly Meetings.

V. WHAT IS AN AMERICAN?

From John Winthrop's sermon on board the *Arbella* in 1630, Europeans have been pondering what it is to be an American. The question became particularly sensitive in the 18th century when the colonies' independence from the mother country became first inevitable and then actual. What role did frontier life play in forming the American character as seen by 18th-century visitors? Was that character solely the product of the frontier (as opposed to the town or the city)? Was there more than one kind of frontier? If so, was there more than one American character? How efficient was the state of agriculture in the 18th century? Did the existence of unlimited free land to the west impede agricultural improvement? (Did it contribute to the ecological crisis of the 20th century?) Was America a *melting* pot or only a supermarket of immigrant variety? What made an immigrant an American? Was the American character something singular or only the cumulation of the cultural characteristics of its immigrants? How important an ingredient was religion in the American character? How did geography and climate affect the development of the colonies?

The America of 1750. Peter Kalm's Travels in North America. The English Version of 1770, *edited by Adolph B. Benson (New York, 1937), pp. 56, 211-212.*

Aging of Americans. It is remarkable that the inhabitants of this country commonly acquire understanding sooner but likewise grow old sooner than the people in Europe. It is nothing uncommon to see little children giving sprightly and ready answers to questions that are proposed to them, so that they seem to have as much understanding as old men. But they do not attain to such an age as the Europeans, and it is an almost unheard-of thing that a person born in this country lives to be eighty or ninety years of age. But I only speak of the Europeans that settle here; for the savages, or first inhabitants, frequently attain a great age, though at present such instances are uncommon, which is chiefly attributed to the great use of brandy which the Indians have learned of the Europeans. Those who are born in Europe attain a greater age than those who are born here of European parents. In the last war it plainly appeared that these new Americans were by far less hardy than the Europeans in expeditions, sieges and long sea voyages, and died in large numbers. It is very difficult for them to accustom themselves to a climate different from their own. The women cease bearing children sooner than in Europe. They seldom or never have children after they are forty or forty-five years old, and some leave off in their thirties. I inquired into the causes of this, but none could give me a good answer. Some said it was owing to the affluence in which the people live here. Some ascribed it to the inconstancy and changeableness of the weather and believed that there was hardly a country on earth in which the weather changed so often in a day as it does here. For if it were ever so hot, one could not be certain whether in twenty-four hours there would not be a piercing cold. Nay, sometimes the weather would change five or six times a day.

Large Families. It does not seem difficult to find out the reasons why the people multiply faster here than in Europe. As soon as a person is old enough he may marry in these provinces without any fear of poverty. There is such an amount of good land yet uncultivated that a newly married man can, without difficulty, get a spot of ground where he may comfortably subsist with his wife and children. The taxes are very low, and he need not be under any concern on their account. The liberties he enjoys are so great that he considers himself as a prince in his possessions. I shall here demonstrate by some plain examples what these conditions accomplish.

Mans Keen, one of the Swedes in Raccoon, [New Jersey] was now near seventy years old. He had many children, grandchildren, and great-grandchildren; so that of those who were yet alive he could count forty-five persons. Besides them, several of his children and grandchildren died young, and some at a mature age. He had, therefore, been uncommonly well blessed. Yet his happiness is not comparable to that which is to be seen in the following examples, which I have taken from the Philadelphia newspapers.

In the year 1732, January the 24th, there died at Ipswich, in New England, Mrs. Sarah Tuthil, a widow, aged eighty-six years. She had brought thirteen children into the world, and from seven of them only she had seen one hundred and seventy-seven grandchildren and great-grandchildren.

In the year 1739, May the 30th, the children, grandchildren and great-grandchildren, of Mr. Richard Buttington, in the parish of Chester, in Pennsylvania, were assembled in his house. They made together one hundred and fifteen persons. Mr. Buttington was born in England, and was then entering his eighty-fifth year. He was at that time quite healthy and active, and had a good memory. His eldest son, then sixty years old, was the first Englishman born in Pennsylvania.

In the year 1742, on the 8th of January, there died at Trenton, in New Jersey, Mrs. Sarah Furman, a widow, aged ninety-seven years. She was born in New England; and left five children, sixty-one grandchildren, one hundred and eighty-two great-grandchildren, and twelve great-great-grandchildren, who were all alive when she died.

In the year 1739, on the 28th of January, there died at South Kingston, in New England, Mrs. Maria Hazard, a widow, in the hundredth year of her age. She was born in Rhode Island, and was a grandmother of the then vice-governor of that colony, Mr. George Hazard. She could count altogether five hundred children, grandchildren, great-grandchildren, and great-great-grandchildren. When she died, two hundred and five of them were alive; a granddaughter of hers had already been grandmother near fifteen years.

In this manner the usual wish or blessing in our liturgy, that newly married couples may see their grandchildren till the third and fourth generation, has been literally fulfilled in regard to some of these persons.

Rev. Andrew Burnaby, Travels through the Middle Settlements in North-America. In the Years 1759 and 1760. *(London, 1775), pp. 154-162.*

I must beg the reader's indulgence, while I stop for a moment, and as it were from the top of a high eminence, take one general retrospective look at the whole—An idea, strange as it is visionary, has entered into the minds of the generality of mankind, that empire is travelling westward; and every one is looking forward with eager and impatient expectation to that destined moment, when America is to give law to the rest of the world. But if ever an idea was illusory and fallacious, I will venture to predict, that this will be so.

America is formed for happiness, but not for empire: in a course of 1200 miles I did not see a single object that solicited charity; but I saw insuperable causes of weakness, which will necessarily prevent its being a potent state.

Our colonies may be distinguished into the southern and northern; separated from each other by the Susquehannah and that imaginary line which divides Maryland from Pensylvania.

The southern colonies have so many inherent causes of weakness, that they never can possess any real strength.—The climate operates very powerfully upon them, and renders them indolent, inactive, and unenterprizing; this is visible in every line of their character. I myself have been a spectator, and it is not an uncommon sight, of a man in the vigour of life, lying upon a couch, and a female slave standing over him, wafting off the flies, and fanning him, while he took his repose.

The southern colonies (Maryland, which is the smallest and most inconsiderable, alone excepted) will never be thickly seated: for as they are not confined within determinate limits, but extend to the westward indefinitely; men, sooner than apply to laborious occupations, occupations militating with their dispositions, and generally considered too as the inheritance and badge of slavery, will gradually retire westward, and settle upon fresh lands, which are said also to be more fertile; where, by the servitude of a Negroe or two, they may enjoy all the satisfaction of an easy and indolent independency: hence the lands upon the coast will of course remain thin of inhabitants.

The mode of cultivation by slavery, is another insurmountable cause of weakness. The number of Negroes in the southern colonies is upon the whole nearly equal, if not superior, to that of the white men; and they propagate and increase even faster.—Their condition is truly pitiable; their labour excessively hard, their diet poor and scanty, their treatment cruel and oppressive: they cannot therefore but be a subject of terror to those who so inhumanly tyrannize over them.

The Indians near the frontiers are a still farther formidable cause of subjection. The southern Indians are numerous, and are governed by a sounder policy than formerly: experience has taught them wisdom. They never make war with the colonists without carrying terror and devastation along with them. They sometimes break up intire counties together.—Such is the state of the southern colonies.—

The northern colonies are of stronger stamina, but they have other difficulties and disadvantages to struggle with, not less arduous, or more easy to be surmounted, than what have been already mentioned. Their limits being defined, they will undoubtedly become exceedingly populous: for though men will readily retire back towards the frontiers of their own colony, yet they will not so easily be induced to settle beyond them, where different laws and polities prevail, and where, in short, they are a different people: but in proportion to want of territory, if we consider the proposition in a general and abstract light, will be want of power.—But the northern colonies have still more positive and real disadvantages to contend with. They are composed of people of different nations, different manners, different religions, and different languages. They have a mutual jealousy of each other, fomented by considerations of interest, power, and ascendency. Religious zeal too, like a smothered fire, is secretly burning in the hearts of the different sectaries that inhabit them, and were it not restrained by laws and superior authority, would soon burst out into a flame of universal persecution. Even the peaceable Quakers struggle hard for pre-eminence, and evince in a very striking manner, that the passions of mankind are much stronger than any principles of religion.

The colonies, therefore, separately considered, are internally weak; but it may be supposed, that, by an union or coalition, they would become strong and formidable: but an union seems almost impossible: one founded in dominion or power is morally so: for, were not England to interfere, the colonies themselves so well understand the policy of preserving a balance, that, I think, they would not be idle spectators, were any one of them to endeavour to subjugate its next neighbour. Indeed, it appears to me a very doubtful point, even supposing all the colonies of America to be united under one head, whether it would be possible to keep in due order and government so wide and extended an empire; the difficulties of communication, of intercourse, of correspondence, and all other circumstances considered.

A voluntary association or coalition, at least a permanent one, is almost as difficult to be supposed: for fire and water are not more heterogeneous than the different colonies in North-America. Nothing can exceed the jealousy and emulation, which they possess in regard to each other. The inhabitants of Pensylvania and New York have an inexhaustible source of animosity, in their jealousy for the trade of the Jerseys. Massachusets-Bay and Rhode Island, are not less interested in that of Connecticut. The West Indies are a common subject of emulation to them all. Even the limits and boundaries of each colony, are a constant source of litigation. In short, such is the difference of character, of manners, of religion, of interest, of the different colonies, that I think, if I am not wholly ignorant of the human mind, were they left to themselves, there would soon be a civil war, from one end of the continent to the other; while the Indians and Negroes would, with better reason, impatiently watch the opportunity of exterminating them all together.

After all, however, supposing what I firmly believe will never take place, a permanent union or alliance of all the colonies, yet it could not be effectual, or productive of the event supposed; for such is the extent of coast settled by the American colonies, that it can never be defended but by a martime power: America must first be mistress of the sea, before she can be independent, or mistress of herself. Suppose the colonies ever so populous; suppose them capable of maintaining 100,000 men constantly in arms, (a supposition in the highest degree extravagant), yet half a dozen frigates would, with ease, ravage and lay waste the whole country from end to end, without a possibility of their being able to prevent it; the country is so intersected by rivers, rivers of such magnitude as to render it impossible to build bridges over them, that all communication is in a manner cut off. An army under such circumstances could never act to any purpose or effect; its operations would be totally frustrated.

Further, a great part of the opulence and power of America depends upon her fisheries, and her commerce with the West Indies; she cannot subsist without them; but these would be intirely at the mercy of that power, which might have the sovereignty of the seas. I conclude therefore, that England, so long as she maintains her superiority in that respect, will also possess a superiority in America; but the moment she loses the empire of the one, she will be deprived of the sovereignty of the other: for were that empire to be held by France, Holland, or any other power, America, I will venture to foretell, will be annexed to it.—New establishments formed in the interior parts of America, will not come under this predicament. I should therefore think it the best policy to enlarge the present colonies, but not to establish fresh ones; for to suppose interior colonies to be of use to the mother country, by being a check upon those already settled, is to suppose what is contrary to experience, and the nature of things, viz. that men removed beyond the reach of power will be subordinate to it.

Except by naturalization and sympathy, the author of Letters from an American Farmer *was not an American, and he was definitely no ordinary farmer. "J. Hector Saint-John" de Crèvecoeur—the romanticized pen name of Michel-Guillaume-Jean de Crèvecoeur—was born into the minor French nobility of Normandy in 1735. He received his first education at his father's townhouse in Caen and the Jesuit Collège du Mont, and then was sent to school in England near Salisbury with a distant relative. At nineteen or twenty he entered General Montcalm's French army in Canada, where he advanced to the rank of lieutenant as a military engineer. When Quebec fell to the English in 1759, Crèvecoeur began to drift into the southern colonies. In 1764 he received his naturalization papers at New York and five years later married a Yonkers girl to help him run his farms in New Jersey and New York. Until 1780, when he returned to France, he lived the life of an American farmer through peace, war, and revolution. The first edition of the* Letters *was published in London in 1782. The following chapter on the American character is found on pp. 45-58, 63-73 of that edition.*

I wish I could be acquainted with the feelings and thoughts which must agitate the heart and present themselves to the mind of an enlightened Englishman, when he first lands on this continent. He must greatly rejoice that he lived at a time to see this fair country discovered and settled; he must necessarily feel a share of national pride, when he views the chain of settlements which embellishes these extended shores. When he says to himself, this is the work of my countrymen, who, when convulsed by factions, afflicted by a variety of miseries and wants, restless and impatient, took refuge here. They brought along with them their national genius, to which they principally owe what liberty they enjoy, and what substance they possess. Here he sees the industry of his native country displayed in a new manner, and traces in their works the embryos of all the arts, sciences, and ingenuity which flourish in Europe. Here he beholds fair cities, substantial villages, extensive fields, an immense country filled with decent houses, good roads, orchards, meadows, and bridges, where an hundred years ago all was wild, woody, and uncultivated! What a train of pleasing ideas this fair spectacle must suggest; it is a prospect which must inspire a good citizen with the most heartfelt pleasure. The difficulty consists in the manner of viewing so extensive a scene. He is arrived on a new continent; a modern society offers itself to his contemplation, different from what he had hitherto seen. It is not composed, as in Europe, of great lords who possess everything, and of a herd of people who have nothing. Here are no aristocratical families, no courts, no kings, no bishops, no ecclesiastical dominion, no invisible power giving to a few a very visible one; no great manufacturers employing thousands, no great refinements of luxury. The rich and the poor are not so far removed from each other as they are in Europe. Some few towns excepted, we are all tillers of the earth, from Nova Scotia to West Florida. We are a people of cultivators, scattered over an immense territory, communicating with each other by means of good roads and navigable rivers, united by the silken bands of mild government, all respecting the laws, without dreading their power, because they are equitable. We are all animated with the spirit of an industry which is unfettered and unrestrained, because each person works for himself. If he travels through our rural districts he views not the hostile castle, and the haughty mansion, contrasted with the clay-built hut and miserable cabin, where cattle and men help to keep each other warm, and dwell in meanness, smoke, and indigence. A pleasing uniformity of decent competence appears throughout our habitations. The meanest of our log-houses is a dry and comfortable habitation. Lawyer or merchant are the fairest titles our town afford; that of a farmer is the only appellation of the rural inhabitants of our country. It must take some time ere he can reconcile himself to our dictionary, which is but short in words of dignity, and names of honour. There, on a Sunday, he sees a congregation of respectable farmers and their wives, all clad in neat homespun, well mounted, or riding in their own humble waggons.

There is not among them an esquire, saving the unlettered magistrate. There he sees a parson as simple as his flock, a farmer who does not riot on the labour of others. We have no princes, for whom we toil, starve, and bleed: we are the most perfect society now existing in the world. Here man is free as he ought to be; nor is this pleasing equality so transitory as many others are. Many ages will not see the shores of our great lakes replenished with inland nations, nor the unknown bounds of North America entirely peopled. Who can tell how far it extends? Who can tell the millions of men whom it will feed and contain? for no European foot has as yet travelled half the extent of this mighty continent!

The next wish of this traveller will be to know whence came all these people? they are a mixture of English, Scotch, Irish, French, Dutch, Germans, and Swedes. From this promiscuous breed, that race now called Americans have arisen. The eastern provinces must indeed be excepted, as being the unmixed descendants of Englishmen. I have heard many wish that they had been more intermixed also: for my part, I am no wisher, and think it much better as it has happened. They exhibit a most conspicuous figure in this great and variegated picture; they too enter for a great share in the pleasing perspective displayed in these thirteen provinces. I know it is fashionable to reflect on them, but I respect them for what they have done; for the accuracy and wisdom with which they have settled their territory; for the decency of their manners; for their early love of letters; their ancient college, the first in this hemisphere; for their industry; which to me who am but a farmer, is the criterion of everything. There never was a people, situated as they are, who with so ungrateful a soil have done more in so short a time. Do you think that the monarchical ingredients which are more prevalent in other governments, have purged them from all foul stains? Their histories assert the contrary.

In this great American asylum, the poor of Europe have by some means met together, and in consequence of various causes; to what purpose should they ask one another what countrymen they are? Alas, two thirds of them had no country. Can a wretch who wanders about, who works and starves, whose life is a continual scene of sore affliction or pinching penury; can that man call England or any other kingdom his country? A country that had no bread for him, whose fields procured him no harvest, who met with nothing but the frowns of the rich, the severity of the laws, with jails and punishments; who owned not a single foot of the extensive surface of this planet? No! urged by a variety of motives, here they came. Every thing has tended to regenerate them; new laws, a new mode of living, a new social system; here they are become men: in Europe they were as so many useless plants, wanting vegetative mould, and refreshing showers; they withered, and were mowed down by want, hunger, and war; but now by the power of transplantation, like all other plants they have taken root and flourished! Formerly they were not numbered in any civil lists of their country, except in those of the poor; here they rank as citizens. By what invisible power has this surprising metamorphosis been performed? By that of the laws and that of their industry. The laws, the indulgent laws, protect them as they arrive, stamping on them the symbol of adoption; they receive ample rewards for their labours; these accumulated rewards procure them lands; those lands confer on them the title of freemen, and to that title every benefit is affixed which men can possibly require. This is the great operation daily performed by our laws. From whence proceed these laws? From our government. Whence the government? It is derived from the original genius and strong desire of the people ratified and confirmed by the crown. This is the great chain which links us all, this is the picture which every province exhibits, Nova Scotia excepted. There the crown has done all; either there were no people who had genius, or it was not much attended to: the consequence is, that the province is very thinly inhabited indeed; the power of the crown in conjunction with the musketos has prevented men from settling there. Yet some parts of it flourished once, and it contained a mild harmless set of people. But for the fault of a few leaders, the whole were banished. The greatest political error the crown ever committed in America, was to cut off men from a country which wanted nothing but men!

What attachment can a poor European emigrant have for a country where he had nothing? The knowledge of the language, the love of a few kindred as poor as himself, were the only cords that tied him: his country is now that which gives him land, bread, protection, and consequence: *Ubi panis ibi patria* [Where there is bread, there is my country] is the motto of all emigrants. What then is the American, this new man? He is either an European, or the descendant of an European, hence that strange mixture of blood, which you will find in no other country. I could point out to you a family whose grandfather was an Englishman, whose wife was Dutch, whose son married a

French woman, and whose present four sons have now four wives of different nations. *He* is an American, who, leaving behind him all his ancient prejudices and manners, receives new ones from the new mode of life he has embraced, the new government he obeys, and the new rank he holds. He becomes an American by being received in the broad lap of our great *Alma Mater*. Here individuals of all nations are melted into a new race of men, whose labours and posterity will one day cause great changes in the world. Americans are the western pilgrims, who are carrying along with them that great mass of arts, sciences, vigour, and industry which began long since in the east; they will finish the great circle. The Americans were once scattered all over Europe; here they are incorporated into one of the finest systems of population which has ever appeared, and which will hereafter become distinct by the power of the different climates they inhabit. The American ought therefore to love this country much better than that wherein either he or his forefathers were born. Here the rewards of his industry follow with equal steps the progress of his labour; his labour is founded on the basis of nature, *self-interest;* can it want a stronger allurement? Wives and children, who before in vain demanded of him a morsel of bread, now, fat and frolicsome, gladly help their father to clear those fields whence exuberant crops are to arise to feed and to clothe them all; without any part being claimed, either by a despotic prince, a rich abbot, or a mighty lord. Here religion demands but little of him; a small voluntary salary to the minister, and gratitude to God; can he refuse these? The American is a new man, who acts upon new principles; he must therefore entertain new ideas, and form new opinions. From involuntary idleness, servile dependence, penury, and useless labour, he has passed to toils of a very different nature, rewarded by ample subsistence.—This is an American.

British America is divided into many provinces, forming a large association, scattered along a coast 1500 miles extent and about 200 wide. This society I would fain examine, at least such as it appears in the middle provinces; if it does not afford that variety of tinges and gradations which may be observed in Europe, we have colours peculiar to ourselves. For instance, it is natural to conceive that those who live near the sea, must be very different from those who live in the woods; the intermediate space will afford a separate and distinct class.

Men are like plants; the goodness and flavour of the fruit proceeds from the peculiar soil and exposition in which they grow. We are nothing but what we derive from the air we breathe, the climate we inhabit, the government we obey, the system of religion we profess, and the nature of our employment. Here you will find but few crimes; these have acquired as yet no root among us. I wish I was able to trace all my ideas; if my ignorance prevents me from describing them properly, I hope I shall be able to delineate a few of the outlines, which are all I propose.

Those who live near the sea, feed more on fish than on flesh, and often encounter that boisterous element. This renders them more bold and enterprising; this leads them to neglect the confined occupations of the land. They see and converse with a variety of people; their intercourse with mankind becomes extensive. The sea inspires them with a love of traffic, a desire of transporting produce from one place to another; and leads them to a variety of resources which supply the place of labour. Those who inhabit the middle settlements, by far the most numerous, must be very different; the simple cultivation of the earth purifies them, but the indulgences of the government, the soft remonstrances of religion, the rank of independent freeholders, must necessarily inspire them with sentiments, very little known in Europe among people of the same class. What do I say? Europe has no such class of men; the early knowledge they acquire, the early bargains they make, give them a great degree of sagacity. As freemen they will be litigious; pride and obstinacy are often the cause of law suits; the nature of our laws and governments may be another. As citizens it is easy to imagine, that they will carefully read the news-papers, enter into every political disquisition, freely blame or censure governors and others. As farmers they will be careful and anxious to get as much as they can, because what they get is their own. As northern men they will love the cheerful cup. As Christians, religion curbs them not in their opinions; the general indulgence leaves every one to think for themselves in spiritual matters; the laws inspect our actions, our thoughts are left to God. Industry, good living, selfish-ness, litigiousness, country politics, the pride of freemen, religious indifference, are their characteristics. If you recede still farther from the sea, you will come into more modern settlements; they exhibit the same strong lineaments, in a ruder appearance. Religion seems to have still less influence, and their manners are less improved.

Now we arrive near the great woods, near the last inhabited districts; there men seem to be placed still farther beyond the reach of government which in some measure leaves them to themselves. How can it pervade every corner; as they were driven there by misfortunes, necessity of beginnings, desire of acquiring large tracts of land, idleness, frequent want of economy, ancient debts; the re-union of such people does not afford a very pleasing spectacle. When discord, want of unity and friendship; when either drunkenness or idleness prevail in such remote districts; contention, inactivity, and wretchedness must ensue. There are not the same remedies to these evils as in a long established community. The few magistrates they have, are in general little better than the rest; they are often in a perfect state of war; that of man against man, sometimes decided by blows, sometimes by means of the law; that of man against every wild inhabitant of these venerable woods, of which they are come to dispossess them. There men appear to be no better than carnivorous animals of a superior rank, living on the flesh of wild animals when they can catch them, and when they are not able, they subsist on grain. He who would wish to see America in its proper light, and have a true idea of its feeble beginnings and barbarous rudiments, must visit our extended line of frontiers where the last settlers dwell, and where he may see the first labours of settlement, the mode of clearing the earth, in all their different appearances; where men are wholly left dependent on their native tempers, and on the spur of uncertain industry, which often fails when not sancitified by the efficacy of a few moral rules. There, remote from the power of example and check of shame, many families exhibit the most hideous parts of our society. They are a kind of forlorn hope, preceding by ten or twelve years the most respectable army of veterans which come after them. In that space, prosperity will polish some, vice and the law will drive off the rest, who uniting again with others like themselves will recede still farther; making room for more industrious people, who will finish their improvements, convert the loghouse into a convenient habitation, and rejoicing that the first heavy labours are finished, will change in a few years that hitherto barbarous country into a fine fertile, well regulated district. Such is our progress, such is the march of the Europeans toward the interior parts of this continent. In all societies there are off-casts; this impure part serves as our precursors or pioneers; my father himself was one of that class, but he came upon honest principles, and was therefore one of the few who held fast; by good conduct and temperance, he transmitted to me his fair inheritance, when not above one in fourteen of his contemporaries had the same good fortune.

Forty years ago this smiling country was thus inhabited; it is now purged, a general decency of manners prevails throughout, and such has been the fate of our best countries.

Exclusive of those general characteristics, each province has its own, founded on the government, climate, mode of husbandry, customs, and peculiarity of circumstances. Europeans submit insensibly to these great powers, and become, in the course of a few generations, not only Americans in general, but either Pennsylvanians, Virginians, or provincials under some other name. Whoever traverses the continent must easily observe those strong differences, which will grow more evident in time. The inhabitants of Canada, Massachusetts, the middle provinces, the southern ones will be as different as their climates; their only points of unity will be those of religion and language. . . .

But to return to our back settlers. I must tell you, that there is something in the proximity of the woods, which is very singular. It is with men as it is with the plants and animals that grow and live in the forests; they are entirely different from those that live in the plains. I will candidly tell you all my thoughts but you are not to expect that I shall advance any reasons. By living in or near the woods, their actions are regulated by the wildness of the neighbourhood. The deer often come to eat their grain, the wolves to destroy their sheep, the bears to kill their hogs, the foxes to catch their poultry. This surrounding hostility immediately puts the gun into their hands; they watch these animals, they kill some; and thus by defending their property, they soon become professed hunters; this is the progress; once hunters, farewell to the plough. The chase renders them ferocious, gloomy, and unsociable; a hunter wants no neighbour, he rather hates them, because he dreads the competition. In a little time their success in the woods makes them neglect their tillage. They trust to the natural fecundity of the earth, and therefore do little; carelessness in fencing often exposes what little they sow to destruction; they are not at home to watch; in order therefore to make up the deficiency, they go oftener to the woods. That new mode of life brings along with it a new set of manners, which I cannot easily describe. These new manners being grafted on the old stock, produce a strange sort of lawless profligacy, the impressions of which are indelible. The manners of the Indian natives are respectable, compared with this European medley. Their wives and children live in sloth and inactivity; and having no proper pursuits, you may judge what education the latter receive. Their tender minds have nothing else to contemplate but the example of their parents; like them they grow up a mongrel breed, half civilised, half savage, except nature stamps on them some constitutional propensities. That rich, that voluptuous sentiment is gone that struck them so forcibly; the possession of their freeholds no longer conveys to their minds the same pleasure and pride. To all these reasons you must add, their lonely situation, and you cannot imagine what an effect on manners the great distances they live from each other has! Consider one of the last settlements in its first view: of what is it composed? Europeans who have not that sufficient share of knowledge they ought to have, in order to prosper; people who have suddenly passed from oppression, dread of government, and fear of laws, into the unlimited freedom of the woods. This sudden change must have a very great effect on most men, and on that class particularly. Eating of wild meat, whatever you may think, tends to alter their temper: though all the proof I can adduce, ɔ, that I have seen it: and having no place of worship to resort to, ʼhat little society this might afford is denied them. The Sunday meet-ᵤgs, exclusive of religious benefits, were the only social bonds that might have inspired them with some degree of emulation in neatness. Is it then surprising to see men thus situated, immersed in great and heavy labours, degenerate a little? It is rather a wonder the effect is not more diffusive. The Moravians and the Quakers are the only instances in exception to what I have advanced. The first never settle singly, it is a colony of the society which emigrates; they carry with them their forms, worship, rules, and decency: the others never begin so hard, they are always able to buy improvements, in which there is a great advantage, for by that time the country is recovered from its first barbarity. Thus our bad people are those who are half cultivators and half hunters; and the worst of them are those who have degenerated altogether into the hunting state. As old ploughmen and new men of the woods, as Europeans and new made Indians, they contract the vices of both; they adopt the moroseness and ferocity of a native, without his mildness, or even his industry at home. If manners are not refined, at least they are rendered simple and inoffensive by tilling the earth; all our wants are supplied by it, our time is divided between labour and rest, and leaves none for the commission of great misdeeds. As hunters it is divided between the toil of the chase, the idleness of repose, or the indulgence of inebriation. Hunting is but a licentious idle life, and if it does not always pervert good dispositions; yet, when it is united with bad luck, it leads to want: want stimulates that propensity to rapacity and injustice, too natural to needy men, which is the fatal gradation. After this explanation of the effects which follow by living in the woods, shall we yet vainly flatter ourselves with the hope of converting the Indians? We should rather begin with converting our backsettlers; and now if I dare mention the name of religion, its sweet accents would be lost in the immensity of these woods. Men thus placed are not fit either to receive or remember its mild instructions; they want temples and ministers, but as soon as men cease to remain at home, and begin to lead an erratic life, let them be either tawny or white, they cease to be its disciples.

Thus have I faintly and imperfectly endeavoured to trace our society from the sea to our woods! yet you must not imagine that every person who moves back, acts upon the same principles, or falls into the same degeneracy. Many families carry with them all their decency of conduct, purity of morals, and respect of religion; but these are scarce, the power of example is sometimes irresistible. Even among these backsettlers, their depravity is greater or less, according to what nation or province they belong. Were I to adduce proofs of this, I might be accused of partiality. If there happens to be some rich intervals, some fertile bottoms, in those remote districts, the people will there prefer tilling the land to hunting, and will attach themselves to it; but even on these fertile spots you may plainly perceive the inhabitants to acquire a great degree of rusticity and selfishness.

It is in consequence of this straggling situation, and the astonishing power it has on manners that the backsettlers of both the Carolinas, Virginia, and many other parts, have been long a set of lawless people; it has been even dangerous to travel among them. Government can do nothing in so extensive a country, better it should wink at these irregularities, than that it should use means inconsistent with its usual mildness. Time will efface those stains: in proportion as the great body of population approaches them they will reform, and become polished and subordinate. Whatever has been said of the four

New England provinces, no such degeneracy of manners has ever tarnished their annals; their back-settlers have been kept within the bounds of decency, and government, by means of wise laws, and by the influence of religion. What a detestable idea such people must have given to the natives of the Europeans! They trade with them, the worst of people are permitted to do that which none but persons of the best characters should be employed in. They get drunk with them, and often defraud the Indians. Their avarice, removed from the eyes of their superiors, knows no bounds; and aided by the little superiority of knowledge, these traders deceive them, and even sometimes shed blood. Hence those shocking violations, those sudden devastations which have so often stained our frontiers, when hundreds of innocent people have been sacrificed for the crimes of a few. It was in consequence of such behaviour, that the Indians took the hatchet against the Virginians in 1774. Thus are our first steps trod, thus are our first trees felled, in general, by the most vicious of our people; and thus the path is opened for the arrival of a second and better class, the true American freeholders; the most respectable set of people in this part of the world: respectable for their industry, their happy independence, the great share of freedom they possess, the good regulation of their families, and for extending the trade and the dominion of our mother country.

Europe contains hardly any other distinctions but lords and tenants; this fair country alone is settled by freeholders, the possessors of the soil they cultivate, members of the government they obey, and the farmers by their own laws, by means of their representatives. This is a thought which you have taught me to cherish; our difference from Europe, far from diminishing, rather adds to our usefulness and consequnce as men and subjects. Had our forefathers remained there, they would only have crowded it, and perhaps prolonged those convulsions which had shook it so long. Every industrious European who transports himself here, may be compared to a sprout growing at the foot of a great tree; it enjoys and draws but a little portion of sap; wrench it from the parent roots, transplant it, and it will become a tree bearing fruit also. Colonists are therefore entitled to the consideration due to the most useful subjects; a hundred families barely existing in some parts of Scotland, will here in six years, cause an annual exportation of 10,000 bushels of wheat: 100 bushels being but a common quantity for an industrious family to sell, if they cultivate good land. It is here then that the idle may be employed, the useless become useful, and the poor become rich; but by riches I do not mean gold and silver, we have but little of those metals; I mean a better sort of wealth, cleared lands, cattle, good houses, good clothes, and an increase of people to enjoy them.

There is no wonder that this country has so many charms, and presents to Europeans so many temptations to remain in it. A traveller in Europe becomes a stranger as soon as he quits his own kingdom; but it is otherwise here. We know, properly speaking, no strangers; this is every person's country; the variety of our soils, situations, climates, governments, and produce, hath something which must please everybody. No sooner does an European arrive, no matter of what condition, than his eyes are opened upon the fair prospect; he hears his language spoke, he retraces many of his own country manners, he perpetually hears the names of families and towns with which he is acquainted; he sees happiness and prosperity in all places disseminated; he meets with hospitality, kindness, and plenty everywhere; he beholds hardly any poor, he seldom hears of punishments and executions; and he wonders at the elegance of our towns, those miracles of industry and freedom. He cannot admire enough our rural districts, our convenient roads, good taverns, and our many accommodations; he involuntarily loves a country where everything is so lovely. When in England, he was a mere Englishman; here he stands on a larger portion of the globe, not less than its fourth part, and may see the productions of the north, in iron and naval stores; the provisions of Ireland, the grain of Egypt, the indigo, the rice of China. He does not find, as in Europe, a crowded society, where every place is over-stocked; he does not feel that perpetual collision of parties, that difficulty of beginning, that contention which oversets so many. There is room for everybody in America; has he any particular talent, or industry? he exerts it in order to procure a livelihood, and it succeeds. Is he a merchant? the avenues of trade are infinite; is he eminent in any respect? he will be employed and respected. Does he love a country life? pleasant farms present themselves; he may purchase what he wants, and thereby become an American farmer. Is he a labourer, sober and industrious? he need not go many miles, nor receive many informations before he will be hired, well fed at the table of his employer, and paid four or five times more than he can get in Europe. Does he want uncultivated lands? thousands of acres present themselves, which he may purchase cheap. Whatever be his talents or inclinations, if they are moderate, he may satisfy them. I do not mean that every one who comes will grow rich in a little time; no, but he may procure an easy, decent maintenance, by his industry. Instead of starving he will be fed, instead of being idle he will have employment; and these are riches enough for such men as come over here. The rich stay in Europe, it is only the mid-'ling and the poor that emigrate. Would you wish to travel in independent idleness, from north to south, you will find easy access, and the most cheerful reception at every house; society without ostentation, good cheer without pride, and every decent diversion which the country affords, with little expense. It is no wonder that the European who has lived here a few years, is desirous to remain; Europe with all its pomp, is not to be compared to this continent, for men of middle stations, or labourers.

An European, when he first arrives, seems limited in his intentions, as well as in his views; but he very suddenly alters his scale; two hundred miles formerly appeared a very great distance, it is now but a trifle; he no sooner breathes our air than he forms schemes, and embarks in designs he never would have thought of in his own country. There the plenitude of society confines many useful ideas, and often extinguishes the most laudable schemes which here ripen into maturity. Thus Europeans become Americans.

On the Threshold of Liberty: Journal of a Frenchman's Tour of the American Colonies in 1777, *translated and edited by Edward D. Seeber (Bloomington, Indiana, 1959), pp. 41-48.*

Although composed of all kinds and classes of men, as you have seen, the Americans numbered more Englishmen than any other nationality; they were living, what is more, under British law, and were bound in the long run to become completely English in their way of life, thinking, dress, and speech. And so they have done. They speak English more or less correctly depending on their racial backgrounds; they live like Anglo-Europeans, but possess to a higher degree that spirit of liberty which the constitution bestows and which enthusiasm excites. In peace and in war, their natural concern over liberty, though incompletely enjoyed, furnishes the main subject and heart of their conversations. This spirit of liberty, which their successes against France in the late war, the severity of the mother country, the discreet avowal of their own strength, and their distance from Europe and from danger—these things have little by little had a telling effect in the present revolution, abetted by secret and hired agents of the nation that is the rival of Great Britain [France].

I may only be imagining this, but it seems to me perfectly clear and verified that, although the French, Germans, Flemish, and others who have become Anglicized during the past century still preserve something of their former language, national customs, and, especially, facial traits (which are very distinct from those of the true English), they differ nowise from the latter in their spirit of liberty and in their manners. This demonstrates how perfectly a doctrine like liberty, which energizes the human spirit and which ought to produce pleasure, easily becomes congenial and close to us, imparting not only the ideas and the manners, but also the mode of thinking of those from whom we derive it.

The Anglo-Americans, then, are similar to Europeans in all respects; they are generous, brusque, sincere, thrifty, active, and, in spite of what people say, very likable if viewed without French prejudices. One must cast one's own prejudices aside in order not to be offended by theirs.

At the very mention of liberty, fatherland, and patriotism, the Swiss of the poorest cantons fall into ridiculous ecstasy and blind conceit over their mountains and forests; but the Americans boast rationally of the beauties of their land, just as they sensibly find fault with its defects; they argue with insight over the mistakes of the present and past governments, criticize the errors or oversights of its early efforts, and honestly admit all the vices, secret or not, that reason, rather than bitterness, might detect or encounter in the administration of their Republic. In a word, they are at all times good citizens; and with whatever success their undertaking be crowned, anyone living among them is forced to admit that they alone know the meaning of true patriotism, and put it into practice.

Englishwomen here, like those in Europe, are very reserved and serious, and above all extremely circumspect in their conversation; moreover, they are good mothers, they nurse their children and teach their daughters to be humble and retiring. Some, in Boston, Annapolis, Philadelphia, etc., successfully operate business houses.

In short, most of them are what we call in France "real mothers and helpmeets." There are a few, however, who betray these usual good qualities; but, as with men, they do not constitute the rule, and, irrespective speak of their occupations when the day's business is over. Since they are all farmers or merchants, commerce is their basic theme of conversation—this and the affairs of the day. But at the same time there are among them very good men of letters, learned chemists, great mathematicians, etc. These are less numerous than in France, yet sufficiently so to permit one to say that this country, with due allowance for its size, is second neither to England or France in wealth, importance, or sciences.

All that I have said thus far about these people is not enough to enable you to know them well. They act according to their humor, and each man is very much an individualist; but they are all alike in their concern for the public good, their love of country, their preoccupation with their resources as they increase the wealth of the nation, and with agriculture, commerce, the education of children, the care of the infirm, and the spirit of democracy which, long restrained by the Royalist government, has broken its bonds in spite of difficulties and impediments.

Men who make their own fortune should value it much more highly than if it was handed down from their fathers. This is as it should be, for the one is merely a gift of fate, the other, the fruit of our labors. For that reason, the appreciation and enjoyment of such fortunes must vary markedly. This truth is well exemplified in America; the citizens or colonists who made her what she is, have as their only concern the pleasure of seeing her prosper and thrive, which is time well spent both for themselves and for their country.

Manufacturing, the clearing of the land, and the expenditures and first costs that these entail, are effected, promoted, and sustained with a zeal and indefatigable ardor that has penetrated the national spirit so deeply that even the women restricted themselves to wearing and using only cloth of local manufacture. Their purpose was to encourage the manufactories, which made a point of utilizing only the products of this country in supplying necessary or unnecessary luxury goods. Also, the men resolved to do without everything that originated abroad and which their own country could supply, such as wood products, engravings, sculpture, designs, etc., in short, all that England was supplying or could supply. That is why a much smaller quantity of foreign goods was being worn shortly before the separation than twenty-five years earlier. This is a real advantage, for it preserves from a life of emptiness and misery those men who are forced to give up farming—a small group, to be sure, but useful in stemming the ruinous tide of foreign luxuries.

Attention to the aggrandizement of one's fortune has not, then, been totally unassociated with solicitude for the public interest; it has made all members of this society eager not only to improve their own lot, but, even more, to set themselves up in business and enjoy, if they could, the facilities offered by the government (which, though wanting in power, aided by advancing funds) and by industriousness, when one could manage by one's self that which government aid might have made possible. Such are the resources drawn upon to clear the land in all the provinces, and the resulting success has come up to the expectations of both the benefactor and the farmer.

There is nothing more astonishing here than the growth of cultivated and productive land. Cities, it is true, are still a rarity in the provinces; but, on the other hand, the highways can be compared to a continuous succession of farms or settlements situated quite close to each other, and which ornament the surface of the land, according to my taste, quite as much as the aspect of a countryside embellished in a few places by sumptuous buildings, and where all or most of the farmers' houses (if wretched cottages can be so called) are crowded into one dirty, stinking, unhealthy hole in the manner of our poor French villages, market towns, and hamlets.

J. P. Brissot de Warville, New Travels in the United States of America 1788, translated by Mara Soceanu Vamos and Durand Echeverria, edited by Durand Echeverria (Cambridge, 1964), pp. 413-415, 418-421, 423-424.

I wish, my friend, I had the time to describe those new western territories that settlers enthusiastically call the Empire of the West. Although this empire is at present completely unknown to Europeans, by the very nature of things it will someday come to deserve its title, and there is no doubt that in less than a century the industrial and trading nations of Europe will be eager to establish commercial and political ties with this area. Since space is limited, I shall describe to you these astonishing settlements only in broad lines, and I shall leave for another time both the details and the broad conclusions that a speculative philosopher can draw from them.

The United States, which cover the eastern region along the Atlantic seaboard, constitute only one third of the vast area that now belongs to the Free Americans, while the immense Western Territory constitutes the other two thirds.

From the foot of the Alleghenies, whose summits do not threaten the heavens as do those of the Andes and the Alps, spreads an immense plain, intersected by gently sloping hills and covered with topsoil three to seven feet deep. It is a fertile land with few or no stones, quite different from that on this side of the Alleghenies, and suitable for every kind of crop, including tobacco, hemp, and Indian corn. These voracious plants grow to prodigious size, and cattle multiply rapidly and require almost no attention.

It is here that have been established a number of prosperous settlements which are attracting many emigrants—Kentucky, Franklin, Cumberland, Holston, Muskingum, and Scioto.

The oldest and most beautiful is Kentucky. . . . In spite of the atrocities suffered by the first settlers at the hands of the Indians, its population has grown rapidly. Kentucky began to be settled only in 1775; by 1782, it had seven to eight thousand inhabitants; by 1787, fifty thousand; and by 1790, seventy thousand. This territory will be shortly declared a free and independent state.

Cumberland [Tennessee], situated near Kentucky and just coming into statehood, counts eight thousand inhabitants. Holston [in northeastern Tennessee] has five thousand, and Franklin [eastern Tennessee] twenty-five thousand. Cumberland will shortly become a separate state. Franklin used to be a state, but could not raise sufficient revenue to subsist on its own and merged with Virginia. . . .

When you behold the speed with which men settle new territories, and when you compare this speed with the slow development of colonies founded by despots, how grand the idea of liberty appears! Liberty can accomplish everything; what she wills is done. Liberty need but command, and forests are cleared, mountains are leveled, rich farms arise to provide havens for numberless generations. Whereas the proud city of Palmyra perished forgotten with the haughty woman who founded it, its ruins attesting that nothing endures save that which is free and remains free.

It seems that Kentucky will always have an advantage over the neighboring areas, for its territory is larger, its soil more fertile, its inhabitants more numerous, and it is situated on the Ohio, navigable in almost all seasons. This latter advantage is shared by two other settlements which I shall describe later.

The following toasts, given on the Fourth of July 1788 in Lexington, Kentucky, will give you an idea of the spirit of the settlers in this part of America:

"To the Western World—perpetual union based on the principle of equality, or else friendly separation."

"Free navigation on the Mississippi, at any price, except the price of liberty."

"Harmony with Spain and reciprocity of good offices."

"To our brothers in Muskingum—may their settlement prosper."

"May the Indians, enemies of America, be chastised by the force of arms!"

"May the Atlantic coast be just, the Western Territory be free, and both be happy!"

"A strong government based on federal principles."

"To the republic of Kentucky, the fourteenth star in the American constellation. . . ."

Fear of the Indians will undoubtedly keep many Europeans away from these parts for a long time, but it does not stop Americans, who merely build their houses closer together. As the settlements increase, new settlers push forward and force the Indians to withdraw.

I must here describe to you these American frontiersmen, who are undoubtedly destined to change the face of this part of the world. The frontiersman likes hunting and prefers it to farming. He raises only what he needs for his own use or to pay for his pleasures. Detesting work and any sort of ties and with no attachment to the place he inhabits, he loves adventure and is easily enticed by descriptions of better opportunities and finer country somewhere else. He enjoys fighting and is ready and willing to go off to war in Canada or Louisiana, but he will not enroll for more than a year, for he is also a husband and father and he likes some home life at least for a part of the year.

The frontiersman is courageous, daring, unafraid of death, and contemptuous of the Indians. He can sleep as soundly in the middle of a forest as he would surrounded by neighbors. When a sudden Indian raid alarms a settlement and a family is murdered, people within a range of two or three miles may worry, but no one else is concerned. The Indians almost never attack except in small parties, and as soon as the alarm is given all the Americans in the area get together and go off to hunt these unhappy savages, whom they are slowly decimating, for the Indians are miserably bad fighters and they are always defeated in the end.

The Indians most to be feared are those along the shores of Lake Erie, the Creeks, the Cherokees, the Chahtas [Choctaws] and the Chickasaws. They have recently been waging a cruel war against the inhabitants of Georgia and Cumberland.

If you wish a description of the Indians, read Penn's, which is still quite accurate:

Strong, well built, agile, their skins dark from the paint they put on themselves, they have small black eyes like the Jews. They rub grease on their bodies to protect themselves from the heat and cold. They eat venison, corn, beans, etc. Their language is lofty and concise. They love their children. They are generous, brave, honorable, and hospitable, but irascible and cruel when offended. They are accused of being cunning, shrewd, suspicious, thieving, gluttonous, and excessively vindictive. Their numbers are constantly diminishing because of wars, smallpox, liquor, abortions, and the hardships of their nomadic life.

It cannot be denied that the majority of their faults are the result of their contact with Europeans, who have taught them dishonesty. Never would the tomahawk have killed so cruelly had all the American frontiersmen been as peaceable and as honorable as the Quakers. The following story is but one example of the deceit practiced by Europeans. In one of the states an agreement was signed with the Indians according to which they would sell for a given sum of money as much land as a man could cover from sunrise to sunset. The English sent for a man reputed the fastest runner in America, who managed to cover three times as much ground as an ordinary man could have done. The Indians were furious at being tricked and immediately began a war.

The Indians' affection for the French is touching and indicative of their virtues and of the gratitude of which they are capable. A

Frenchman can travel among them from Canada to Illinois without weapons and in complete security. The Indians can tell by his appearance, by his skin, and by his speech to what nation he belongs, and they entertain him as a brother. But if they find him in the company of Americans, he suffers the same cruelty as the Americans, whom they detest.

This hatred, which seems almost ineradicable, permits no hope that a lasting harmony will ever prevail between the two peoples. Congress is taking, however, wise precautions to put an end to fighting and war. Henceforth no private individual and no state may buy land from the Indians. Laws have been passed severely punishing Americans who hunt on Indian territory. Various treaties have been signed with the largest and most respected Indian tribes, such as the Creeks, who are commanded by the famous [Alexander] McGillivray. Congress, under the leadership of Washington, has undertaken to pay them an annual subsidy of $1,500 for the land they have lost by the new treaty. You will also be pleased to hear that in order to encourage agriculture among the Indians Congress has promised to give them seeds, cattle, tools, and commissioners to instruct them.

These steps have been taken in the hope of slowly inducing the Indians to be peaceable but not with any expectation of leading them to adopt the ways of European civilization. Many examples discourage any such attempt. There have been cases of Indians who have been taken from their tribes in childhood, educated in schools, and raised among Europeans until they reached the age of twenty, who at their first visit to their own people took off their European dress and reverted to the independent Indian way of life, despite all efforts to stop them.

While making every effort to assure peace, Congress has not failed to take wise precautions to prevent Indian raids. Fort Franklin defends the frontiers of Pennsylvania and the Ohio is dotted with forts: Fort Harmar at the mouth of the Muskingum, Fort Steuben at the rapids of the Ohio, Post Vincennes on the Wabash, etc. All these posts contain well-trained troops, consisting of young volunteers who enlist for three years and who at the end of this time settle on lands in the area that are given to them, thus guaranteeing the security of the territory and at the same time contributing to its prosperity.

This change in policy by the American government will undoubtedly benefit the Indians, for the government is essentially peaceable by nature. It will, however, cause an upsurge in the Indian population, and then either the Indians will become civilized and be assimilated by the Americans or else a thousand causes will bring about their annihilation.

There is therefore no need to fear that the danger of the Indians will check the drive of the Americans in their mass progress toward the south. Everyone hopes that once navigation on the Mississippi becomes free, enormous markets will become available for the products which Americans produce in abundance and which are needed by the Spanish colonies. Will the Spaniards open this navigation willingly? Will the Americans have to force them to do so? This is the question. Negotiations are in progress, but they have been dragging on for four years. The suspicion exists that certain American states, fearing an emigration which would leave them stripped of population, are secretly backing the Spaniards. It is this covert support of the Spanish position which has given birth to the proposal that navigation on the Mississippi be closed for twenty-five years on condition that Americans have free trade with Spain. Virginia and Maryland, although they have the most to fear from western competition, have opposed this proposal on the ground that it is derogatory to the honor of the United States, and the majority of the other states have concurred.

The suspicions that Westerners have of the real intentions of the American government and of Congress are construed by some people as a sign that the Union will not last long and that there will be secession, particularly since the English of Canada are trying to persuade the Westerners to unite with them.

But I believe, for many reasons, that the Union will endure. The largest part of the land in the West belongs to men who live in the East; the continuous migrations from state to state keep the ties strong; and, finally, as it is in the interest of both Eastern and Western states to establish trade on a large scale with South America and to expand across the Mississippi, they must and will remain united in order to achieve these objectives. . . .

I sometimes imagine myself living a hundred years from now, and I see these wild forests replaced, not by cities, but by scattered farms stretching without interruption from New Hampshire to Quito. I see happiness and labor hand in hand. I see beauty adorning the daughters of nature, liberty and virtue rendering government and laws almost unnecessary, sweet tolerance replacing the cruel Inquisition. I see a festival in which Peruvians, Mexicans, Free Americans, and Frenchmen embrace one another as brothers, anathematizing tyranny and blessing the reign of liberty which brings all men into universal harmony. But what will become of the mines and the slaves? The mines will be shut. The slaves will be the brothers of their masters, and they will deserve to be their equals by sharing their knowledge and their way of life. But what will men do without gold, that cynosure of universal greed? It is not right for a free people to seek it if they must use the hands of slaves to wrest it from the earth. Will a free people ever be without some token by which they can exchange their goods? Gold has served despotism better than it has liberty, and freedom can always find a less dangerous medium of exchange. Our speculators are far from understanding that two revolutions are being prepared in the New World, revolutions which will change completely the commercial theories and practices of Europe. These will be the opening of a canal between the Atlantic and the Pacific and the abandonment of the mines of Peru.

Forgive me, my friend, if I do not dwell on all the many other changes which must be the inevitable consequences of American ideas, American enterprise, and the American character.

What is the American character? The following lines from *Tristram Shandy* define it rather well:

Nature, like a good mother, has shown the same kindness to them all. She has observed such an equal tenor in the distribution of her favors, as to bring nearly all the inhabitants to a level with each other; so that you will meet with few instances here of great genius, but you will find in all the inhabitants and in all classes good sense, understanding, and knowledge of all that concerns domestic happiness and the rights of man. Everybody has a share of this understanding, which is right. With us English, the case is quite different; we are all ups and downs. You are a great genius, or 'tis fifty to one you are a dunce. The extremes are more common than the mean.

General prosperity can be found only in this mean. There can be no slavery where all men are equally enlightened. It is difficult for despotism to creep in when all men's eyes are opened and watching, when *each man* is free and has his own principles. What has restored despotism almost everywhere? These very two "extremes" of which Sterne speaks—the men of power or genius who use the ignorant populace as a weapon with which to destroy the enlightened but aristocratic middle order. Here in America there are no men of great power, no men of genius, no aristocratic middle order, no populace.

AMERICA PERCEIVED

AMERICA PERCEIVED, a four-volume Series of primary sources, traces America's historical development through the eyes of foreign visitors, critics, and travelers. Each volume supplies actual accounts of foreign observers from the 17th through the 20th centuries.

These reporters hold their own particular point of view, neither right nor wrong, merely different from ours. They view America with perspectives shaped by different values, traditions, and institutions, perspectives that enrich our own understanding and appreciation of America.

Pendulum Press, Inc.

West Haven, Connecticut

PRINTED IN U.S.A.